Jesus
is
God,
Savior,
Lord and Master

as testified to by

God the Father,
Jesus Himself,
Angels,
The Apostles and Disciples,
and Others

as noted in

God's Written Word

compilation, summarization and comments

by

Douglas Keasling

Scripture references are direct quotations or adaptations from
the King James edition of the Holy Bible

ISBN: 0-7392-0254-5

Printed in the USA by

MP

MORRIS PUBLISHING

3212 East Highway 30 • Kearney, NE 68847 • 1-800-650-7888

❖❖❖ Contents ❖❖❖

Contents   5

Preface

This book was written primarily for myself, although I hope it will be helpful to many others. The thought behind it, the research and the doing of it have all added much to my understanding of the divinity, humanity and the accomplishments of our Lord and Savior Jesus Christ.

I am no expert in biblical languages, nor have I had formal training in Bible Colleges or Seminaries. I do not claim to have any special insights nor do I believe that my understanding is better than any other person's, so I have tried to keep my comments to a minimum, preferring to have the scripture speak for itself. I have compiled the information in this book, summarized it, edited it, ordered it, and made comments as I saw fit.

I tried to be consistent in the way I noted things. This was extremely difficult, because, it seemed, that each time I reread something I changed the way it was phrased or the symbols used. This would affect other entries, and ensuring that they were done the same way took much effort. I am certain that I did not catch all changes that should have been made, so you will find some inconsistencies. Please forgive, and interpret as best you can.

As you read the statements of Jesus about Himself and those of His apostles and others, I hope that the impact on you will be significant. It seems to me that a person would have to go to great lengths and be considerably self-deceived to deny that Jesus, His apostles and others said He is God. His credentials are impressive, and, if true, can only come from one who is God Himself.

This is intended to be a reference book, a reminder book and a book one can use for inspiration and worship. Use it when you need information about Jesus. Use it when you need to remind yourself about who Jesus is. Use it when you need to be convinced that the Jesus you worship is worthy of your worship, and use it to demonstrate to others what Jesus said of Himself, reports of what God said about Jesus and what many direct witnesses said about Him.

Thanks is given to those who reviewed this work early on and especially to my wife, Beth, who reviewed it more than once and always has supported me in my work and my various endeavors.

Introduction

The contents of this book are statements about Jesus as found in the New Testament. It is hoped that the impact of seeing these statements together will help us to better understand and appreciate Jesus and His mission. Doing so will tell us a lot about God as well, since in Jesus all the fullness of God dwells [Colossians 2:8-9] and He is God [Romans 9:5].

We can also know that God exists and know much about Him through His creation [Romans 1.18-21], but we cannot really know Him and why He acts as He does, if He does not reveal these Himself. He has done this primarily through His written word; written by men but revealed by God Himself. His word is not only revealing, it is consistent and makes sense, as no speculation can. We easily see how speculation and human desires can lead and have led us astray in our search for God and for meaning in life. Simplifying the process and listening directly to what God has to say, helps us to get at the reality of God as no speculation can. His word is extremely meaningful and completely sensible, needing very little comment or interpretation.

The Word of God speaks for itself and "is sharper than a twoedged sword" [Hebrews 4:12], so it really needs no amplification. God also tells us that His word, not my words, not your words, will accomplish what He wants it to [Isaiah 55:11]. Therefore, I have made my comments brief, expecting the width and depth of the statements made about Jesus by Himself, His disciples and others to speak for themselves.

The scripture statements I have used are often condensed and/or paraphrased for simplicity, although I have used word-for-word statements whenever possible, and they are from the King James version of the Bible. Please read the cited Scriptures directly to determine if they say what I claim they say.

I did change some of the King James words, such as, "thou" to "you", "unto" to "to", "art" to "are", etc. but left most of them unchanged. Sometimes I added words or a statement in parentheses in instances in which I felt there needed to be some clarity.

I have referred to some Old Testament statements or prophecies for background.

This book is divided into two sections: Statements Jesus Made About Himself and Statements Made By Jesus' Apostles and Others About Jesus. The categories and headings are essentially the same for the two sections. One or two categories have no statements under them because, although statements were made for that category by one group, there were not any made by the other. Also the statements in italics, my comments, are basically the same for consistency.

The statements about Jesus could be grouped differently. Many of them could fit into more than one of the categories (in some instances I have done so). But, even so, the impact of what the New Testament says about Jesus would be just as great.

When Jesus was speaking about Himself, I used "I" ("I am...", "I was...", etc.) to emphasize that He was speaking about Himself and I used "Jesus" ("Jesus is...", "Jesus was...", etc.) to emphasize that the apostles and others were speaking of Jesus. If Jesus is God then all statements about God apply to Jesus, but I have chosen not to use statements that seemed to me to apply to God the Father and are not also directly applied to Jesus as well, but there are many which seem to apply to both, or give each the character of the other. Pronouns used in scripture are not always clear about who they refer to. The authors and/or the translators of the New Testament use "He" (and others) in long sentences containing references to both God the Father and Jesus, and which One they refer to is sometimes difficult to determine.

The writers of the Epistles often use "in Christ", "through Christ", "of Christ", etc. These were difficult to translate into the "I" or "Jesus" format. I did do this with some, and others were not necessary to meet the purpose of this book.

I have used quotation marks (except for Jesus' own statements) for most of the spoken quotations or scripture references and cited the person or scripture quoted in parentheses or used the quotation followed by, 'said', 'asked', etc.

In those situations in which the verse cited used a pronoun or title for Jesus that seemed to refer to a previous verse, I used { } to note this. So, [Hebrews 2:{9}17] in the body or [{9}17] in the appendix means that the information is from chapter 2 verse 17, but the tie to Jesus is found in verse 9. If the referral is from a previous chapter, the reference will look like this, [Luke 9:{8:50}11] or [{8:50}11], noting that the information is from chapter 9 verse 11, but the tie is to chapter 8 verse 50. This was not necessary regarding Jesus' statements.

I combined actions or statements from different New Testament books that seemed to be referring to the same thing and separated them by one or more 📖.

I did not repeat 'I' or 'Jesus' before each statement in the Appendix, simply adding it at the beginning of each Bible book. You will need to provide them yourself, as you read the statements.

Use of the term 'God' alone is intended to mean God the Father.

One could easily add other statements to the categories, but I did not use statements that require much interpretation (according to my view), that require significant theological analysis or that are more about the process or the plan than directly about Jesus.

I chose the categories and their order (one hopes God was able to influence the choices). Some of them fell out very naturally and others did not. There are more groupings than I wanted, but combining some of them seemed to lessen both the impact and the understanding.

I chose the title:

**Jesus is
God,
Savior,
Lord and Master**

As testified to by

**God the Father,
Jesus Himself,
Angels,
the Apostles and Disciples
and Others**

As noted in

God's written Word,

which is rather lengthy, so it would be as descriptive as possible, fit the facts and follow traditional Christian belief. **Jesus is God** is evidenced by His credentials, His authority and His actions. **Jesus is Savior** is evidenced by His purpose, His life, His death and His resurrection. **Jesus is Lord and Master** is evidenced by His authority, His actions, His purpose and the fact that He is God and Savior. All of the information certainly places Jesus in a category far superior to man or any created being, one worthy to be worshiped and trusted.

Various names and titles used for Jesus—Jesus, Christ, Lord, God's Son—and their combinations presented some difficulty. As noted in the sections about Jesus as the Christ, Messiah or Anointed One, I made some choices about which to use and how to use them. Also, if Jesus was not used in connection with one of them, as Paul often did, using the term Christ alone, I used Jesus (Christ), with the Christ in parentheses to denote this, and did the same with other titles. Paul's use of "Christ" alone always points to Jesus. Anyway, one category cites Jesus as the Christ, the Messiah and the Anointed One.

I tried combining what Jesus said and what the others said under each category, but, although this was impressive and serves to refine the category, some of the impact of the statements was diluted. I suggest you do this for yourself to compare what Jesus said with what others said.

I am certain there are Scriptures I left out that could well have been included. I am also certain that some people will disagree with some of my use of Scriptures and the categorization. So be it. Any Scriptures left out or misinterpreted or flat out wrong are my responsibility. If I had any question about the application of a scripture to this work, I left it out.

Please enjoy this book. I hope it will have real meaning to you.

d. keasling, 3/99

Jesus

is

God,

Savior,

Lord and Master

as testified to by

God the Father,

Jesus Himself,

Angels,

the Apostles and Disciples,

and Others

as noted in

God's Written Word

Part 1: Statements Jesus Made About Himself

Jesus made many astounding claims about himself. The following are most of them. Some of the time he used the term "Son of Man", but then He claimed to be the Son of Man [see also Daniel 7:13-14]. I suspect His listeners knew exactly what He meant.

"But that you may know that the Son of Man has power on earth to forgive sins" (then He said to the sick of the palsy), "Arise, take up your bed, and go to your house." [Matthew 9:{4}6]

When Jesus came into the coasts of Caesarea Philippi, He asked His disciples, saying, "Whom do men say that I the Son of Man am?" [Matthew 16:13]

"But He held his peace and answered nothing. Again the high priest asked Him, and said to Him, 'Are You the Christ, the Son of the Blessed?' And Jesus said, 'I am: and you shall see the Son of Man sitting an the right hand of power, and coming in the clouds of heaven.'" [Mark 14.61-62]

"For as the Father has life in Himself; so He has given to the Son to have life in Himself; and has given Him authority to execute judgment also, because He is the Son of Man." [John 5:26-27]

"Then Jesus said to them, 'When you have lifted up the Son of Man, then shall you know that I am He, ...'" [John 8:28]

John the Baptist called Jesus the "Lamb of God" [John 1:29, 36], and the visions John had in Revelation included many references emphasizing that Jesus is the Lamb.

Jesus Himself said that people witness about themselves but that is meaningless, but He had the Father witness for Him [John 5:31-37] and that His purpose was to bear witness to the truth [John 18:37]. It is interesting to note that Jesus said that, even if people would not believe what He said about Himself, they should believe Him because of His works [John 5:36-39, 10:25 and 37-38]. John also said in 1 John [1 John 5:6-11] that God and the Spirit bear witness about who Jesus is and what He did.

I understand some group is voting about whether Jesus made comments that Scripture says He made. That seems audacious to me (and irrelevant to most of us), even for 'self-proclaimed' experts [Psalm 2:4].

Jesus seemed to be very clear about who He was and what He was doing. We question both of these because we do not want to believe, not because they are not believable. We cannot prove that what He or the others said are true, we must take them by faith. The proof is in the results— love, joy, peace, longsuffering, gentleness, goodness, faith, meekness, temperance [Galatians 5:22-23]—and, in the future, when that which was claimed will clearly be demonstrated.

I.   His Credentials

A. Jesus claimed to be God:

These statements are most astounding. They clearly say that Jesus, the Apostles and others said that Jesus is God. Our denial of this would be foolish. There is some differentiation between the Father and Jesus, because Jesus said that He and His Father are one [John 10:30], and yet Paul said that the kingdom will be returned to the Father, so the Father can be 'all in all' [1 Corinthians 15:23-28]. Paul also said that 'the head of Christ is God' [1 Corinthians 11:3]. Jesus also said that even He (the Son) did not know the day or the hour of His return [Mark 13:32] and that His Father 'is greater than I' [John 14:28]. The relationship between the Father, Jesus and the Holy Spirit has always been troublesome, but the comments that follow certainly show that Jesus is God. Besides, some things must be accepted by faith.

Jesus' statements to the devil are interesting, particularly His statement at the second temptation. After the devil challenged Him to throw Himself from the pinnacle of the temple to show that God would save Him, as scripture says, and to prove He was the Son of God, Jesus said, "It is written again, 'You shall not tempt the Lord your God'" [Matthew 4:5-7]. This could be interpreted three ways;

    1. do not tempt the Father (your Lord and God) to act to save Me and/or

*2. do not tempt Me (your Lord and God) to call on
     the angels to save Me and/or*
*3. do not tempt Me (your Lord and God) to tempt
     the Father to act to save Me.*
*In the last two of these cases Jesus would have been
claiming to be Lord and God. Both of these would be
appropriate, when compared with the other claims He
made.*

*Paul claims that God is King of kings and Lord of
lords [1 Timothy 6:13-16], and John's vision calls the
Lamb and the Man on a white horse KING OF KINGS
AND LORD OF LORDS [Revelation 17:14; 19:{11}16]. It
seems clear that John is talking about Jesus, making
Him equal with God.*

*Jesus and writers of the New Testament said that
Jesus is God and that He created and sustains all things.
His credentials certainly show that Jesus is God, Savior
and Lord and Master.*

Jesus said:

I say to you (the Jews), before Abraham was, I am, (Exodus
  3:14) [John 8:58]
I am Alpha and the Omega, the beginning and the ending
  [Revelation 1:8]
I am [Revelation 1:8]
I was [Revelation 1:8]
I am to come [Revelation 1:8]
I am the Almighty [Revelation 1:8]
I am Alpha and the Omega, the first and the last [Revelation
  1:11]
I am He who searches the reins (inward parts) and hearts
  [Revelation 2:23]
I am Alpha and Omega, the beginning and the end, the
  first and the last [Revelation 22:13]

B. Jesus claimed to be one with God:

*A created being cannot reasonably make or have
made for him the following claims. He even said, "...He
who has seen Me has seen the Father;..." [John 14:9].*

Jesus said:

I know My Father [John 8:54-55]

I and My Father are one [John 10:30]
I have the Father in Me [John 10:38]
I am in the Father [John 10:38]
I am in the Father [John 14:10]
I have the Father in Me [John 14:10]
I am in the Father [John 14:11]
I have the Father in Me [John 14:11]
I am in My Father [John 14:20]
I have all things that the Father has [John 16:15]
I had the glory with You, Father, before the world was [John 17:5]
I and You are one, Holy Father [John 17:11]
I have You, Father, in Me [John 17:21]
I am in You, Father [John 17:21]
I and You are one, Father [John 17:22]
I am in them (those You gave Me), Father [John 17:23]
I have You in Me, Father [John 17:23]
I have known You, righteous Father [John 17:25]

C. Jesus claimed He had God's qualities:

Jesus said:

I have the power on earth to forgive sins (proved by forgiving the sins of the man sick of the palsy and then
healing him) (Son of Man) [Matthew 9:1-6] 📖📖 I
have power on earth to forgive sins (proved by forgiving the sins of a man sick of the palsy and then healing him) (Son of Man) [Luke 5:23-24]
I send you prophets, and wise men, and scribes [Matthew
23:34]
I speak words that shall not pass away [Mark 13:31]
I am Lord also of the Sabbath (Son of Man) [Luke 6:5]
I cast out devils, and I do cures today and tomorrow [Luke
13:32]
I (the Son) quicken (give life to) whom I will [John 5:21]
I (the Son) have life in myself, as given by the Father, who
has life in Himself [John 5:26]
I will raise every one up at the last day, who sees Me, the
Son, and believes on Me, for this is the will of Him who
sent Me [John 6:40]
I am the light of the world [John 8:12]
I am He (the light of the world/from above/have true judg-
ment {in fact, God}) [John 8:12-24]

I have true judgment: for I am not alone, but I and the Father who sent Me [John 8:16]

I am the light of the world, as long as I am in the world [John 9:5]

I have power to lay down My life, and I have power to take it again: this commandment have I received of (from) My Father [John 10:18]

I give My sheep eternal life, and they shall never perish, neither shall any man pluck them out of My hand [John 10:27-28]

I am come a light into the world, that whoever believes on Me should (would) not abide in darkness [John 12:46]

I have all things that the Father has [John 16:15]

I am Alpha and Omega, the beginning and the ending [Revelation 1:8]

I am Alpha and Omega, the first and the last [Revelation 1:11]

I am the first and the last [Revelation 1:17]

I am He who is alive forevermore [Revelation 1:18]

I have the keys of hell and of death [Revelation 1:18]

I have the seven stars, the angels of the seven churches, in My right hand and am in the midst of the seven golden candlesticks, the seven churches [Revelation 1:12-20]

I am the first and the last [Revelation 2:8]

I am He that opens and no man shuts [Revelation 3:7]

I am He that shuts and no man opens [Revelation 3:7]

I am the Amen [Revelation 3:14]

I am Alpha and Omega, the beginning and the end, the first and the last [Revelation 22:13]

I have My reward with Me (when I come), to give to every man according as his work shall be (Isaiah 40:10) [Revelation 22:12]

I am the bright and morning star [Revelation 22:16]

D. Jesus said He is God's son:

I suppose we all could claim to be a 'son of God', particularly through adoption by Him [Galations 4:5], but none of us has been 'begotten' [John 1:14, 1 John 4:9; see also 1 Corinthians 4:15, 1 Peter 1:3, 1 John 5: 1] by God, so these statements seem to carry much more weight than that.

Jesus said:

I am, as you said, the Christ the Son of God (responding to the high priest) [Matthew 26:63-64] 📖📖 I am the Christ the Son of the Blessed (responding to the high priest) [Mark 14:61-62]

I, whom you have seen and who is talking with you, am the Son of God (response to the man born blind) [John 9:35-37]

I said, "I am the Son of God" (response to the Jews in the temple who said He blasphemed) [John 10:36]

I, the Son of God, have eyes like unto a flame of fire, and feet like fine brass [Revelation 2:18]

E. Jesus claimed He had a special relationship with the Holy Spirit:

Jesus said:

I send the Promise of My Father upon you (Acts 2:4) [Luke 24:49]

I will pray the Father, and He will give you another Comforter, that He may abide with you forever; even the Spirit of truth; whom the world cannot receive, because it sees Him not, neither knows Him [John 14:16-17]

I will send the Comforter, even the Spirit of truth, to you from the Father [John 15:26]

I shall be testified of by the Spirit of truth [John 15:26]

I tell you the truth; "It is expedient for you that I go away: for if I go not away, the Comforter will not come to you; but if I depart, I will send Him to you" [John 16:7]

I shall be glorified by the Spirit of truth, for He shall receive of Mine, and shall show it to you [John 16:13-14]

F. Jesus said He is the Christ, the Messiah, the Anointed One:

Christ (Greek) and Messiah (Hebrew) both mean God's anointed.

"Jesus" and "Lord" and "Christ" are used together at least 104 times (by my count) in the New Testament; "Jesus" and "Christ" together are used 154 times and "Christ" alone is used 270 times with 87 of them (by my interpretation) pointing directly to Jesus. There

are 9 that do not refer to Jesus at all (i.e. John the Baptist saying he was not the Christ). The other 174 indirectly refer to Jesus as the Christ.

Jesus said:

I am, as you said, the Christ the Son of God (response to the high priest) [Matthew 26:63-64] 🕮🕮 I am the Christ, the Son of the Blessed (response to the high priest) [Mark 14:61-62]

I, who speak to you, am the Messiah (response to the woman at the well) [John 4:25-26]

I told you (that I am the Christ), and you believed not [John 10:24-25]

G. Jesus said He was sent by God from heaven:

Jesus was with God (the Father), came from God, went back to God and will come again from God.
Jesus was in heaven, came from heaven, went back to heaven and will come again from heaven.

Jesus said:

I came down from heaven and am in heaven (Son of Man) [John 3:13]

I can of My own self do nothing: as I hear, I judge: and My judgment is just; because I seek not My own will, but the will of the Father who has sent Me [John 5:30]

I have greater witness than that of John: for the works which the Father has given Me to finish, the same works that I do, bear witness of Me, that the Father has sent Me [John 5:36]

I came down from heaven, not to do My own will, but the will of Him who sent Me [John 6:38]

I was sent by the living Father [John 6:57]

I have a doctrine that is not Mine, but His who sent Me [John 7:16]

I am not come of Myself [John 7:28]

I know Him: for I am from Him, and He has sent Me [John 7:29]

I am with you yet a little while, and then I go to Him who sent Me [John 7:33]

I have true judgment: for I am not alone, but I and the Father who sent Me [John 8:16]

I was sent by the Father who bears witness of Me [John 8:18]

I am from above [John 8:23]

I am not of this world [John 8:23]

I proceeded forth and came from God [John 8:42]

I came not of Myself [John 8:42]

I was sent by God [John 8:42]

I must work the works of Him who sent Me [John 9:4]

I have been sent into the world by the Father [John 10:36]

I said this, that they may believe that You sent Me, Father [John 11:41-42]

I did not say these things to you at the beginning, because I was with you, but now I go My way to Him who sent Me [John 16:4-5]

I came forth from the Father, and am come into the world [John 16:28]

I was sent by You, Father, the only true God [John 17:3]

I came out from You, Father [John 17:8]

I am not of the world [John 17:14 and 16]

I was sent by You, Holy Father, into the world [John 17:18]

I have been sent by You, Father [John 17:21]

I have been sent by You, Father [John 17:23]

I have been by You, righteous Father [John 17:25]

I have been sent by My Father, even so send I you [John 20:21]

H. Jesus claimed God's love and approval was on Him:

Although Jesus was loved by God, God did forsake Him on the cross (Psalm 22:1) [Matthew 27:46; Mark 15:34]. Whatever all that means, it certainly means that God would not save Him from death on the cross and probably could not even look on Him as He bore the sins of the world, but God did raise Him from the dead, which is certainly a great indication that Jesus was loved by God.

Jesus said:

I have been delivered all things of (by) My Father [Matthew 11:27] ⌸⌸ I have been delivered all things of (by) My Father [Luke 10:22]

I, the Son, am not known by any man, but the Father [Matthew 11:27] ⌸⌸ I, the Son, am not known by any man, but the Father [Luke 10:22]

I, the Son, am the only man who knows the Father, and
   he to whom the Son reveals Him [Matthew 11:27] 📖📖
   I, the Son, am the only one who knows who the Father
   is [Luke 10:22]
I "have the Spirit of the Lord upon Me" (Isaiah 61:1-2) [Luke
   4:17-21]
I (the Son) am loved by the Father, and He shows Me all
   things that He does [John 5:20]
I have greater witness than that of John: for the works
   which the Father has given Me to finish, the same works
   that I do, bear witness of Me, that the Father has sent
   Me [John 5:36]
I am come in My Father's name, and you receive Me not
   [John 5:43]
I know Him: for I am from Him, and He has sent Me [John
   7:29]
I was sent by the Father who bears witness of Me [John
   8:18]
I have not been left alone by the Father [John 8:29]
I do always those things that please the Father [John 8:
   29]
I am honored by My Father; of whom you say, that He is
   your God [John 8:54]
I am known by the Father, and I know the Father [John
   10:15]
I am loved by My Father, because I lay down My life, that I
   might take it again [John 10:17]
I have been sanctified by the Father [John 10:36]
I know that You hear always Me, Father [John 11:41-42]
I abide in My Father's love [John 15:10]
I say to you, "Whatever you ask the Father in My name,
   He will give it (to) you" [John 16:23]
I am not alone, because the Father is with Me [John 16:
   32]
I have You, Father, in Me [John 17:21]
I was given glory by You, Father [John 17:22]
I have been loved by You, Father [John 17:23]
I have been given glory by You, Father [John 17:24]
I was loved by You, Father, before the foundation of the
   world [John 17:24]

I. Jesus claimed the following qualities for Himself or made the following comparisons to Himself:

Is anyone foolish enough to make the following claims or allow such claims to be made for him, unless one could prove them? There are many of Jesus' qualities listed in other areas of this book.

Jesus said:

I am the Son of Man [Matthew 16:13]

I am the Son of Man (proved by forgiving the sins of a man sick of the palsy and then healing him) [Matthew 9:1-6] 📖📖 I am the Son of Man (proved by forgiving the sins of a man sick of the palsy and then healing him) [Luke 5:23-24]

I am One greater than the temple [Matthew 12:6]

I am greater than Jonah [Matthew 12:41] 📖📖 I am greater than Jonah [Luke 11:32]

I am greater than Solomon [Matthew 12:42] 📖📖 I am greater than Solomon [Luke 11:31]

I am the bread of life [John 6:35]

I am that bread of life [John 6:48]

I am the living bread which came down from heaven: if any man eat of this bread, he shall live forever: and the bread that I will give is My flesh, which I will give for the life of the world [John 6:51]

I am the resurrection [John 11:25]

I am the life [John 11:25]

I am the way [John 14:6]

I am the truth [John 14:6]

I am the life [John 14:6]

I am in you [John 14:20]

I am the true vine [John 15:1]

I am the vine [John 15:5]

I am the faithful and true witness [Revelation 3:14]

I am the beginning of the creation of God [Revelation 3:14]

I am the root and offspring of David [Revelation 22:16]

II. His Authority

The authority claimed by and for Jesus also empha-
sizes He was from God and is God. No one else could have
such authority.

A. Jesus claimed He spoke for God:

Jesus said:

I am come in My Father's name, and you receive Me not
[John 5:43]

I have a doctrine that is not Mine, but His who sent Me
[John 7:16]

I speak to the world those things which I have heard of
(from) Him who sent Me [John 8:26]

I do nothing of Myself; but as My Father has taught Me, I
speak these things [John 8:28]

I speak what I have seen with My Father [John 8:38]

I, a man who has told you the truth, which I have heard of
(from) God, you seek now to kill [John 8:40]

I have not spoken of Myself; but the Father who sent Me,
He gave Me a command, what I should say, and what I
should speak [John 12:49]

I speak, even as the Father said to Me [John 12:50]

I have given to them (the men You gave Me), Father, the
words You gave Me [John 17:8]

I have given them (those You gave Me) Your word, Holy Father
[John 17:14]

B. Jesus said He has all authority:

Jesus said:

I have been delivered all things of (by) My Father [Matthew
11:27]

I have been given all power in heaven and in earth [Matthew
28:18]

I have been delivered all things of (by) My Father [Luke
10:22]

I (the Son) have been committed all judgment by the
Father, who judges no man [John 5:22]
I (Your Son) was given by You, Father, power over all flesh,
that I should give eternal life to as many as You have
given Me [John 17:1-2]

C. Jesus said He has specific authority:

Jesus said:

I have the power on earth to forgive sins (proved by forgiving the sins of a man sick of the palsy and then
healing him) (Son of Man) [Matthew 9:1-6] 📖📖 I have
power on earth to forgive sins (proved by forgiving the
sins of a man sick of the palsy and then healing him)
(Son of Man) [Luke 5:23-24]

I am Lord even of the Sabbath (Son of Man) [Matthew 12:
8] 📖📖 I am Lord also of the Sabbath (Son of Man)
[Mark 2:28] 📖📖📖 I am Lord also of the Sabbath
(Son of Man) [Luke 6:5]

I also will ask you one thing, which if you tell me, I in like
wise will tell you by what authority I do these things;
"The baptism of John, was it from heaven, or of men?"
(to the chief priests and elders) [Matthew 21:23-25]
📖📖 I will also ask of you one question, and answer
Me, and I will tell you by what authority I do these
things; "The baptism of John, was it from heaven, or of
men?," answer Me (to the chief priests, and the
scribes, and the elders) [Mark 11:27-30] 📖📖📖 I will
also ask you one thing; and answer Me: "The baptism
of John, was it from heaven, or of men?" (to the chief
priests and the scribes and the elders) [Luke 20:1-4]

I will not tell you by what authority I do these things (because the chief priests and elders refused to answer
Jesus' question about John's baptism) [Matthew 21:
23-27] 📖📖 I will not tell you by what authority I do
these things (because the chief priests, scribes and
elders refused to answer Jesus' question about John's
baptism) [Mark 11:27-33] 📖📖📖 I will not tell you
by what authority I do these things (because the chief
priests and the scribes and the elders refused to an-

swer Jesus' question about John's baptism) [Luke 20:
1-8]

I have made the blind see, the lame walk, the lepers are
cleansed, the deaf hear, the dead are raised [Luke 7:
21-22]

I give you power to tread on serpents and scorpions, and
over all the power of the enemy (to the seventy) [Luke
10:19]

I (the Son) have been committed all judgment by the Father,
who judges no man [John 5:22]

I (the Son) have been given authority by the Father to execute judgment also, because I am the Son of Man [John
5:26-27]

I will raise every one up at the last day, who sees Me, the
Son, and believes on Me, for this is the will of Him who
sent Me [John 6:40]

I will raise him up at the last day whom the Father who
sent Me, draws to Me [John 6:44]

I have the power to lay down My life, and I have power to
take it again: this commandment have I received of (from)
My Father [John 10:18]

I give My sheep eternal life, and they shall never perish, neither shall any man pluck them out of My hand [John
10:27-28]

I am the only one a man goes through to get to the Father
[John 14:6]

I have the keys of hell and of death [Revelation 1:18]

I have the sharp sword with two edges [Revelation 2:12]

I have the seven stars [Revelation 3:1]

I have the seven Spirits of God [Revelation 3:1]

I have the key of David [Revelation 3:7]

I am He that opens, and no man shuts [Revelation 3:7]

I am He that shuts and no man opens [Revelation 3:7]

**D. Jesus said He has authority over mankind as Lord and
King and is our shepherd and High Priest:**

*Lord means "master" or "sovereign". The words
"Lord" and "Jesus" are used together in the New
Testament 38 times (by my count) as, 'Jesus our/the
Lord' or 'our/the Lord Jesus', etc. and another 104
times "Lord" and "Jesus" and "Christ" are used to-*

gether. I did not use those that seemed to be only titles, but the number (142) of them certainly enforces Jesus' importance as Lord.

Daniel said that one like the Son of Man came to the Ancient of Days and received a kingdom which would not be destroyed [Daniel 7:13-14]. Jesus came as Savior and will come as Savior and King.

Jesus said:

I will come in My kingdom (Son of Man) [Matthew 16:28]

I, the Lord, have need of them (an ass and a colt) [Matthew 21:2-3] ⬚⬚ I, the Lord, have need of it (a colt) [Mark 11:2-3]

I (the Shepherd) "will be smitten, and the sheep of the flock will be scattered, for it is written abroad" (Zechariah 13:7) [Matthew 26:31] ⬚⬚ I (the Shepherd) "will be smitten, and the sheep shall be scattered," for it is written (Zechariah 13:7) [Mark 14:27]

I am, as you say, a king (responding to Pilate): to this end I was born, and for this cause came I into the world, that I should bear witness to the truth [John 18:37]

I appoint to you a kingdom, as My Father appointed to Me [Luke 22:29]

I am the door of the sheep [John 10:7]

I am the door (of the sheep): by Me if any man enter in, he shall be saved, and shall go in and out, and find pasture [John 10:9]

I am come that they (the sheep) might have life, and that they might have it more abundantly [John 10:10]

I am the good shepherd: the good shepherd gives His life for the sheep [John 10:11]

I am the good shepherd [John 10:14]

I know My sheep [John 10:14]

I lay down My life for the sheep [John 10:15]

I have other sheep, which are not of this fold: them also I must bring [John 10:16]

I said to you (the Jews), "You believe not (even though My works bear witness of Me)", because you are not of My sheep [John 10:26]

I give My sheep eternal life, and they shall never perish, neither shall any man pluck them out of My hand [John 10:27-28]

I was given My sheep by My Father who is greater than all; no man is able to pluck them out of My Father's hand [John 10:27-29]

I am your Master [John 13:13]

I am your Lord [John 13:13]

I am your Lord [John 13:14]

I am your Master [John 13:14]

I have a kingdom but it is not of this world: if My kingdom were of this world, then would My servants fight, that I should not be delivered to the Jews [John 18: 36]

I say to you, Simon, son of Jonas, feed My lambs [John 21: 15]

I say to you, Simon, son of Jonas, feed My sheep [John 21: 16]

I say to you, Simon, son of Jonas, feed My sheep [John 21: 17]

I received of (from) My Father, power over the nations [Revelation 2:26-27]

III. His Purpose

Paul said that God accomplished in Christ Jesus His eternal purpose, which was to make known by the church to the principalities and powers in the heavenly places the manifold wisdom of God [Ephesians 3:10-11].

A. Jesus claimed He was the One to come as prophesied:

Jesus said:

I am not come to destroy the Law, or the prophets: I am come to fulfil [Matthew 5:17]

I go as it is written of Me (Son of Man) [Matthew 26:24] 📖📖 I go as it is written of Me (Son of Man) [Mark 14:21]

I (the Shepherd) "will be smitten, and the sheep of the flock will be scattered abroad," for it is written (Zechariah 13:7) [Matthew 26:31] 📖📖 I (the Shepherd) "will be smitten, and the sheep shall be scattered," for it is written (Zechariah 13:7) [Mark 14:27]

I, if I now pray to My Father, shall be given more than twelve legions of angels, but how then shall the Scriptures be fulfilled, that thus it must be [Matthew 26:53-54]

I sat daily with you teaching in the temple, and you laid no hold on Me, but all this was done that the Scriptures of the prophets might be fulfilled [Matthew 26:55-56] 📖📖 I was daily with you in the temple teaching, and you took Me not: but the Scriptures must be fulfilled [Mark 14:49]

I "was anointed by the Lord to preach the gospel to the poor" (Isaiah 61:1-2) [Luke 4:17-21]

I "was sent by the Lord to heal the brokenhearted, to preach deliverance to the captives, and recovering of sight to the blind, to set at liberty them that are bruised, to preach the acceptable year of the Lord" (Isaiah 61:1-2) [Luke 4:17-21]

I go up to Jerusalem, and all things that are written by the prophets concerning Me shall be accomplished (Son of Man) [Luke 18:31]

I spoke these words to you while I was yet with you, that all things must be fulfilled, which were written in the

Law of Moses, and in the Prophets, and the Psalms,
concerning Me [Luke 24:44]

I (the Christ) had to suffer, thus it is written [Luke 24:46]

I (the Christ) had to rise from the dead the third day, thus
it is written [Luke 24:46]

I am testified of (to) by the Scriptures [John 5:39]

I know whom I have chosen: but that the Scripture may
be fulfilled, "He who eats bread with Me has lifted up
his heel against Me" (Psalm 41:9) [John 13:18]

I, while I was with them in the world, kept them in Your
name, Holy Father: those You gave Me, and none of
them is lost, but the son of perdition; that the Scripture
might be fulfilled [John 17:12]

B. Jesus said He came to save us and give us life:

*Jesus' name means "savior". He saved us from our
sins, God's wrath, eternal death and sin's (Satan's) power
over us [Daniel 9:24; Acts 26:17-18; Hebrews 9:{24}26],
bringing us peace with God. Paul calls God the Savior
[1 Timothy 1:1 and 4:10], "...of God our Savior, and
the Lord Jesus Christ, who is our hope," and "...we trust
in the living God, who is the Savior of all men,...", again
both differentiating between God and Jesus and equating them. This act of saving includes the terms "forgiveness, redemption, justification and propitiation".*

Jesus said:

I have come to save that which was lost (Son of Man)
[Matthew 18:11]

I came to give My life a ransom for many (Son of Man)
[Matthew 20:28] 📖📖 I came to give My life a ransom for many (Son of Man) [Mark 10:45]

I am not come to destroy men's lives, but to save them
(Son of Man) [Luke 9:56]

I am come to seek and to save that which was lost (Son of
Man) [Luke 19:10]

I (God's only begotten Son) was given by God, that whoever believes in Me should not perish, but have everlasting life [John 3:16]

I (God's Son) was not sent into the world by Him (God) to
condemn the world; but that the world through Him
might be saved [John 3:17]

I would have given you living water [John 4:10]

I shall give him a well of water springing up into eternal
life, and he shall never thirst [John 4:14]

I (the Son) quicken (give life to) whom I will [John 5:21]

I (the Son of God) will be heard by the dead: and they that
hear shall live [John 5:25]

I will give you the meat which endures to everlasting life
(Son of Man) [John 6:27]

I will raise every one up at the last day, who sees Me, the
Son, and believes on Me, for this is the will of Him who
sent Me [John 6:40]

I will raise him up at the last day whom the Father who
sent Me, draws to Me [John 6:44]

I am the living bread which came down from heaven: if
any man eat of this bread, he shall live forever: and
the bread that I will give is My flesh, which I will give
for the life of the world [John 6:51]

I will raise up at the last day whoever eats My flesh and
drinks My blood, and he will have eternal life [John
6:54]

I speak to you the words that are spirit and that are life
[John 6:63]

I have come that they (the sheep) might have life, and that
they might have it more abundantly [John 10:10]

I give My sheep eternal life, and they shall never perish,
neither shall any man pluck them out of My hand [John
10:27-28]

I came not to judge the world, but to save the world [John
12:47]

I live, and because I live, you shall live also [19]

I (Your Son) was given by You, Father, power over all flesh,
that I should give eternal life to as many as You have
given Me [John 17:1-2]

C. Jesus said He came to bring strife and division:

*The implications of Jesus' teachings, life and
statements about Himself cause dissension between
and among people. His life and His statements are so*

strong that those who believe and those who do not
must be at odds. The absolute nature of statements,
such as; "I am the way, the truth, and the life: no man
comes to the Father, but by (through) Me" [John 14:6],
brings division. In fact, He said He came to bring a
sword, not peace, for His coming will "set a man at
variance against his father, and the daughter against
her mother" [Matthew 10:34-39].

Jesus said:

I send you forth as sheep in the midst of wolves...and you
   shall be hated by all men for My name's sake [Matthew
   10:16-22]
I am not come to send peace on earth, but a sword [Matthew
   10:34]
I am come to set a man at variance against his father, and the
   daughter against her mother, and the daughter in law
   against her mother in law, and a man's foes shall be
   those of his own household [Matthew 10:35-36]
I am come to send fire on the earth [Luke 12:49]
I am come to give peace on earth? I tell you, "No"; but rather
   division [Luke 12:51]
I was hated by the world before it hated you [John 15:18]
I have chosen you out of the world, therefore the world hates
   you [John 15:19]

D. Jesus said He came to serve:

The first time He came, Jesus came to serve. The
next time it will be to take over His kingdom as king.

Jesus said:

I came not to be ministered to, but to minister (Son of Man)
   [Matthew 20:28] ◫◫ I came not to be ministered to,
   but to minister (Son of Man) [Mark 10:45]
I "was sent by the Lord to heal the brokenhearted, to preach
   deliverance to the captives, and recovering of sight to
   the blind, to set at liberty them that are bruised, to
   preach the acceptable year of the Lord" (Isaiah 61:1-2)
   [Luke 4:17-21]

I have made the blind see, the lame walk, the lepers are cleansed, the deaf hear, the dead are raised [Luke 7: 21-22]

I cast out devils, and I do cures today and tomorrow [Luke 13:32]

I am among you as he who serves [Luke 22:27]

I have given you an example (washing the Disciples' feet), that you should do as I have done to you [John 13:15]

E. Jesus said His purpose was to do God's will:

The statements in IIA, "Jesus claimed He spoke for God", apply here, as well.

Jesus said:

I ask of You, O My Father, If it be possible, let this cup pass from Me: nevertheless not as I will, but as You will" [Matthew 26:39] 📖📖 I ask of You, Father, "Take away this cup from Me: nevertheless, not what I will, but what You will" [Mark 14:36] 📖📖📖 I ask of You, Father, "If You be willing, remove this cup from Me: nevertheless not My will, but Yours, be done" [Luke 22:42]

I ask of You, Father, "If this cup may not pass away from Me, except I drink it, Your will be done" [Matthew 26: 42]

I do the will of Him who sent Me [John 4:34]

I finish the work of Him who sent Me [John 4:34]

I (the Son) can do nothing of Myself, but what I see the Father do: for whatever He does, I also do likewise [John 5:19]

I can of My own self do nothing: as I hear, I judge: and My judgment is just; because I seek not My own will, but the will of the Father who has sent Me [John 5:30]

I came down from heaven, not to do My own will, but the will of Him who sent Me [John 6:38]

I do always those things that please the Father [John 8:29]

I keep My Father's word [John 8:54-55]

I must work the works of Him who sent Me [John 9:4]

I have power to lay down My life, and I have power to take it again: this commandment have I received of (from) My Father [John 10:18]

I do works in My Father's name; they bear witness of Me
[John 10:25]

I have shown you many good works from My Father, for
which of those works do you stone Me [John 10:32]

I know that His (the Father's) commandment is life everlasting [John 12:50]

I do not speak words to you of Myself: but the Father who
dwells in Me, He does the works [John 14:10]

I do as the Father gave Me commandment [John 14:31]

I have kept My Father's commandments [John 15:10]

I have made known to you all things that I have heard of
(from) My Father [John 15:15]

I have finished the work which You gave Me to do, Father
[John 17:4]

I shall drink the cup which My Father has given me [John
18:11]

F. Jesus claimed He would judge and reward:

*Although Jesus' purpose for coming into the world
was not to judge it but to save it, His second coming
will be as judge and king.*

Jesus said:

I will profess to those that work iniquity, "I never knew
you: depart from me" [Matthew 7:21-23]

I will confess before My Father who is in heaven whoever
confesses me before men [Matthew 10:32] 📖📖 I
shall confess before the angels of God whoever confesses Me before men (Son of Man) [Luke 12:8]

I will deny before My Father who is in heaven whoever denies
me before men [Matthew 10:33] 📖📖 I shall deny before the angels of God whoever denies Me before men
(Son of Man) [Luke 12:9]

I shall send forth My angels, and they shall gather out of
My kingdom all things that offend, and those which do
iniquity, and shall cast them into a furnace of fire:
there shall be wailing and gnashing of teeth (Son of
Man) [Matthew 13:41-42]

I shall come in the glory of My Father with His angels; and
then I shall reward every man according to his works
(Son of Man) [Matthew 16:27]

I shall separate them (the nations) one from another, as a
shepherd divides his sheep from the goats: I shall set
the sheep on My right hand, but the goats on the left;
then shall the King (Jesus Himself) say to them on His
right hand, "Come, blessed of My Father, inherit the
kingdom prepared for you from the foundation of the
world:" then shall He say also unto them on the left
hand, "Depart from Me, you cursed, into everlasting
fire," and these shall go into everlasting punishment:
but the righteous into life eternal (Son of Man) [Matthew
25:31-46]

I shall be ashamed of whomever is ashamed of Me and My
words in this adulterous and sinful generation, when I
come in the glory of My Father with the holy angels
(Son of Man) [Mark 8:38] ⧉⧉ I shall be ashamed of
him who is ashamed of Me and of My words when I
shall come in My own glory, and in My Father's, and of
the holy angels (Son of Man) [Luke 9:26]

I say to you (a lawyer), "It (the blood of Abel to the blood of
Zacharias) shall be required of this generation" [Luke
11:51]

I (the Son) have been committed all judgment by the Father,
who judges no man [John 5:22]

I (the Son) have been given authority by the Father to
execute judgment, because I am the Son of Man [John
5:26-27]

I can of My own self do nothing: as I hear, I judge: and My
judgment is just; because I seek not My own will, but
the will of the Father who has sent Me [John 5:30]

I will not accuse you to the Father: there is one that accuses you, even Moses, in whom you trust (to the
Jews) [John 5:45]

I will raise every one up at the last day, who sees Me, the
Son, and believes on Me, for this is the will of Him who
sent Me [John 6:40]

I judge no man [John 8:15]

I have true judgment: for I am not alone, but I and the
Father who sent Me [John 8:16]

I have many things to say and to judge of (about) you
[John 8:26]

I am come into this world for judgment (to judge) [John
    9:39]
I judge him not who hears my words, and believes not [John
    12:47]
I came not to judge the world, but to save the world [John
    12:47]
I have spoken the word which will judge, in the last day,
    he that rejects Me, and receives not My words [John
    12:48]
I will come to you (church of Ephesus) quickly, and will
    remove your candlestick out of his (its) place, except
    you repent [Revelation 2:5]
I will give to him who overcomes to eat from the tree of life,
    which is in the midst of the paradise of God [Revelation
    2:7]
I will give you (church in Smyrna) a crown of life, if you
    are faithful unto death [Revelation 2:10]
I will come to you (church in Pergamos) quickly, and will
    against fight them (Nicolaitanes) with the sword of My
    mouth, unless you repent [Revelation 2:16]
I will give to him who overcomes to eat of the hidden man-
    na [Revelation 2:17]
I will give to him who overcomes a white stone, and in the
    stone a new name written which no one knows save he
    who receives it [Revelation 2:17]
I will cast her (Jezebel) into a bed, and them who commit
    adultery with her into great tribulation, except they
    repent of their deeds [Revelation 2:22]
I will kill her children (Jezebel's) with death [Revelation 2:
    23]
I will give to every one of you (church in Thyatira) accord-
    ing to your works [Revelation 2:23]
I say to you, and to the rest in Thyatira, as many as have
    not this doctrine, and who have not known the depths
    of Satan, as they speak; "I will put upon you none
    other burden" [Revelation 2:24]
I will give him who overcomes, and keeps My works unto
    the end, power over the nations [Revelation 2:26]
I will give him who overcomes, and keeps My works until
    the end, the morning star [Revelation 2:26-28]
I will come upon you (church in Sardis) as a thief, if you
    shall not watch [Revelation 3:3]

I will not blot the name of him who overcomes out of the Book of Life [Revelation 3:5]

I will confess the name of him who overcomes before My Father, and before His angels [Revelation 3:5]

I will make them of the synagogue of Satan, who say they are Jews, and are not, but do lie, behold, I will make them to come and worship before your (church in Philadelphia) feet [Revelation 3:10]

I will make him who overcomes a pillar in the temple of My God, and He shall go no more out [Revelation 3:12]

I will write on him who overcomes the name of My God, and the name of the city of My God, which is new Jerusalem, which comes down out of heaven from My God [Revelation 3:12]

I will write on him who overcomes My new name [Revelation 3:12]

I rebuke and chasten as many as I love [Revelation 3:19]

I will grant to him who overcomes to sit with Me in My throne [Revelation 3:21]

I have My reward with Me (when I come), to give to every man according as his work shall be (Isaiah 40:10) [Revelation 22:12]

G. Jesus claimed He gave God glory:

Of course, all that Jesus did gave God glory. He even said, "He who has seen Me has seen the Father" [John 14:9], and Paul said that in Christ dwells all the fullness of the Godhead bodily [Colossians 2:9].

Jesus said:

I honor My Father, and you do dishonor Me [John 8:49]

I do seek not My own glory [John 8:50]

I want You to glorify Your name, Father [John 12:28]

I am glorified, and God is glorified in Me (Son of Man) [John 13:31]

I will do whatever you ask in My name, that the Father may be glorified in the Son [John 14:13]

I ask You, Father, now that the hour is come; to glorify Your Son, that Your Son also may glorify You [John 17:1]

I have glorified You on earth, Father [John 17:4]

H. Jesus claimed He came for other reasons:

Jesus said:

I am not come to call the righteous, but sinners to
repentance [Matthew 9:13] ▢▢ I came not to call
the righteous, but sinners to repentance [Mark 2:17]
▢▢▢ I came not to call the righteous, but sinners,
to repentance [Luke 5:32]

I am not sent but to the lost sheep of the house of Israel
[Matthew 15:24]

I came forth to preach [Mark 1:38]

I must preach the kingdom of God to the other cities also:
for therefore am I sent [Luke 4:43]

I shall become a sign to this generation (Son of Man) [Luke
11:30]

I came to this hour for this cause (to be a sacrifice), so
shall I say, "Father, save Me from this hour?" [John
12:27]

I am, as you say, a king (responding to Pilate): to this end
I was born, and for this cause came I into the world,
that I should bear witness to the truth [John 18:37]

IV. His Actions

Jesus did many things [John 21:25] while here on earth. Those below are included to testify to their importance in explaining who Jesus is and what He did. He preached, taught (many called Him teacher but these references were not included), prayed, performed miracles, did (and does) good things for us, intercedes for us and rewards us.

A. Jesus claimed He performed miracles:

Jesus said:

I will; "be clean" (healing a leper) [Matthew 8:3] 📖📖 I will; "be clean" (healing a leper) [Mark 1:41] 📖📖📖 I will, "be clean" (healing a leper) [Luke 5:13]

I say to you, "Arise, take up your bed, and go to your house," (healing a man sick of the palsy) [Matthew 9:6] 📖📖 I say to you, "Arise, and take up your couch, and go into your house" (healing a man sick of the palsy) [Luke 5:24]

I cast out devils by the Spirit of God, not by Beelzebub [Matthew 12:25-28] 📖📖 I cast out devils with the finger of God, not, as you say, by Beelzebub [Luke 11:17-20]

I say to you, Damsel, "Arise" (raising Jairus' daughter from the dead) [Mark 5:41] 📖📖 I say to you, maid, "Arise" (raising Jairus' daughter from the dead) [Luke 8:54]

I charge you, deaf and dumb spirit, come out of him and enter no more into him [Mark 9:25]

I say to you, young man, "Arise" (raising a widow's son) [Luke 7:14]

I have made the blind see, the lame walk, the lepers are cleansed, the deaf hear, the dead are raised [Luke 7:21-22]

I perceive that virtue (power) is gone out of me (after being touched by a woman with an issue of blood) [Luke 8:46]

I cast out devils, and I do cures today and tomorrow [Luke 13:32]

I say to you, "Rise, take up your bed, and walk" (healing a
    man with an infirmity) [John 5:8]
I have done one work, and you all marvel [John 7:21]
I have made a man every whit whole on the Sabbath day
    [John 7:23]
I say to you, go, wash in the pool of Siloam (healing a man
    born blind) [John 9:7]
I go, that I may awake him (Lazarus) out of sleep (raise him
    from the dead) [John 11:11-14]
I did among them the works which no other man did [John
    15:24]

B. Jesus claimed He does and has done many other things, including teaching, preaching and praying.

There are other actions Jesus did or will do that are located in other portions of this book.

Jesus said:

I will make you fishers of men, if you follow Me (to Simon
    and Andrew) [Matthew 4:19] 📖📖 I will make you to
    become fishers of men, if you come after Me (to Simon
    and Andrew) [Mark 1:17]
I thank You, Father, Lord of heaven and earth, because
    You have hidden these things from the wise and pru-
    dent and have revealed them to babes [Matthew 11:25]
    📖📖 I thank You, O Father, Lord of heaven and
    earth, that You have hid these things from the wise
    and prudent, and have revealed them to babes [Luke
    10:21]
I, the Son, and he to whomsoever the Son will reveal the
    Father, are the only ones who know the Father [Matthew
    11:27] 📖📖 I, the Son, and he to whom the Son will
    reveal the Father, are the only ones who know who the
    Father is [Luke 10:22]
I will give the heavy laden rest [Matthew 11:28]
I speak to them in parables: because they seeing see not;
    and hearing they hear not, neither do they under-
    stand [Matthew 13:13]
I sow the good seed (Son of Man) [Matthew 13:37]

I also say to you that you are Peter, and upon this rock I will build My church [Matthew 16:18]

I will give to you the keys of the kingdom of heaven: and whatever you shall bind on earth shall be bound in heaven: and whatever you shall loose on earth shall be loosed in heaven (to Peter) [Matthew 16:19]

I am there in the midst of two or three who are gathered together in My name [Matthew 18:20]

I have told you before they (false Christs and false prophets) shall arise [Matthew 24:23-25]

I, the Master, will keep the passover at your (a man's) house with My disciples, for My time is at hand [Matthew 26:18] 📖📖 I, the Master, say (to the good man of the house), "Where is the guestchamber, where I shall eat the passover with My disciples?" [Mark 14:14] 📖📖📖 I, the Master, say to you (the master of the house), "Where is the guestchamber, where I shall eat the passover with My disciples?" [Luke 22:11]

I say to you (His disciples), "I will not drink henceforth of this fruit of the vine, until that day when I drink it new with you in My Father's kingdom" [Matthew 26:29] 📖📖 I say to you (the twelve apostles), "I will drink no more of the fruit of the vine, until that day that I drink it new in the kingdom of God" [Mark 14:25] 📖📖📖 I say to you (the twelve apostles), "I will not drink of the fruit of the vine, until the kingdom of God shall come" [Luke 22:18]

I will go and pray yonder [Matthew 26:36]

I sat daily with you, teaching in the temple, and you laid no hold on Me, but all this was done that the Scriptures of the prophets might be fulfilled [Matthew 26:55-56] 📖📖 I was daily with you in the temple teaching, and you took Me not: but the Scriptures must be fulfilled [Mark 14:49] 📖📖📖 I was with you daily in the temple, you stretched forth no hands against Me: but this is your hour, and the power of darkness [Luke 22:53]

I am with you alway, even to the end of the world [Matthew 28:20]

I have foretold you all (end time) things, so take heed [Mark 13:23]

I have preached the gospel to the poor [Luke 7:21-22]

I will give you (those who are persecuted) a mouth and wisdom, which all your adversaries shall not be able to gainsay (oppose) nor resist [Luke 21:15]

I appoint to you a kingdom, as My Father appointed to Me [Luke 22:29]

I have prayed for you, Simon, that your faith fail not: and when you are converted, strengthen your brethren [Luke 22:31-32]

I say to you, "We speak that (what) we do know, and testify that (what) we have seen; and you receive not our witness" (to Nicodemus) [John 3:11]

I would have given you living water [John 4:10]

I sent you (His disciples) to reap whereon you bestowed no labor [John 4:38]

I dwell in him, and he in Me, who eats My flesh and drinks My blood [John 6:56]

I, the Son, if I make you free, you shall be free indeed [John 8:36]

I thank You, Father, that you have heard Me [John 11:41]

I go to prepare a place for you, and if I go and prepare a place for you, I will come again [John 14:2-3]

I will receive you to Myself; that where I am, there you may be also [John 14:3]

I do works [John 14:12]

I will do anything you ask in My name [John 14:14]

I will not leave you comfortless: I will come to you [John 14:18]

I will manifest Myself to him who keeps My commandments [John 14:21]

I and My Father will love him, and we will come to Him, and make Our abode with him who loves Me and keeps My words [John 14:23]

I have spoken these things to you, being yet present with you [John 14:25]

I leave My peace with you, My peace I give to you: not as the world gives, give I to you, so let not your heart be troubled, neither let it be afraid [John 14:27]

I have spoken to you the word that has made you clean [John 15:3]

I have spoken these things to you, that My joy may remain in you, and that your joy might be full [John 15:11]

I henceforth call you not servants; for the servant knows not know what his lord does: but I have called you friends; (His disciples) [John 15:15]

I have chosen you and ordained you, that you should go and bring forth fruit [John 15:16]

I command you that you love one another [John 15:17]

I have spoken to them, so they now have no cloke (excuse) for their sin (those who are of the world) [John 15:18-22]

I said to you, "The servant is not greater than his lord" [John 15:20]

I have spoken these things to you, that you should not be offended [John 16:1]

I have told you these things, that when the time shall come, you may remember that I told you of them [John 16:4]

I have said these things to you, so sorrow has filled your heart [John 16:6]

I have yet many things to say to you, but you cannot bear them now [John 16:12]

I have spoken these things to you in proverbs: but the time comes, when I shall no more speak to you in proverbs, but I shall show you plainly of the Father [John 16:25]

I say not to you, that I will pray the Father for you at that day: for the Father Himself loves you, because you have loved Me, and have believed that I came out from God [John 16:26-27]

I have spoken these things to you, that in Me you might have peace [John 16:33]

I have overcome the world, so be of good cheer [John 16:33]

I have finished the work which You gave Me to do, Father [John 17:4]

I have manifested Your name, Father, to the men You gave Me out of the world [John 17:6]

I pray for them, Father: I pray not for the world, but for them You have given Me; for they are Yours, and all Mine are yours, and Yours are Mine [John 17:9-10]

I, while I was with them in the world, kept them in Your name, Holy Father: those You gave Me, and none of them is lost, but the son of perdition; that the Scripture might be fulfilled [John 17:12]

I speak these things in the world, Holy Father, that they (those You gave Me) might have My joy fulfilled in themselves [John 17:13]

I pray not, Holy Father, that You should take them (those You gave Me) out of the world, but that You should keep them from the evil [John 17:15]

I have sent them (those You gave Me), Holy Father, into the world [John 17:18]

I sanctify Myself [John 17:19]

I do not pray for these alone (those You gave Me), but for them also who shall believe on Me through their word [John 17:20]

I have given them (those You gave Me) the glory which You gave Me, Father [John 17:22]

I have declared to them (those You gave Me) Your name, righteous Father, and will declare it: that the love wherewith You have loved Me may be in them, and I in them [John 17:26]

I spoke openly to the world [John 18:20]

I ever (always) taught in the synagogues, whither the Jews always resort [John 18:20]

I ever (always) taught in the temple, whither the Jews always resort [John 18:20]

I have said nothing in secret [John 18:20]

I have been sent by My Father, even so send I you [John 20:21]

I stand at the door and knock [Revelation 3:20]

I will, if any man hear My voice and open the door, come in to him and sup (eat) with him [Revelation 3:20]

I, Jesus, have sent My angel to testify to you these things in the churches [Revelation 22:16]

V. His Suffering

Jesus' suffering is well described by Isaiah (Isaiah 53) long before the fact. This passage says that His suffering was all part of God's plan to bring redemption to the world.

I suspect that Jesus is still suffering at our hands because so many reject Him, and, because those of us who do not are not as committed as we should be. He is still hated (and always will be) by the world, because He reveals its evil works [John 7:7] and refuses to be a part of it. His followers will suffer for the same reasons, and because they refuse to give allegiance to governments or ideologies, reserving final allegiance for Him.

Jesus said:

I shall also suffer of them (Son of Man) [Matthew 17:12] 📖📖 I must suffer many things and be set at nought (given no value) (Son of Man) [Mark 9:12]

I shall be betrayed into the hands of men (Son of Man) [Matthew 17:22] 📖📖 I am delivered into the hands of men, and they shall kill Me (Son of Man) [Mark 9:31] 📖📖📖 I shall be delivered into the hands of men (Son of Man) [Luke 9:44]

I shall be betrayed to the chief priests and to the scribes, and they shall condemn Me to death (Son of Man) [Matthew 20:18] 📖📖 I shall be delivered to the chief priests, and to the scribes; and they shall condemn Me to death (Son of Man) [Mark 10:33]

I shall be delivered to the Gentiles by the chief priests and the scribes to be mocked and scourged (beaten) and crucified (Son of Man) [Matthew 20:18-19] 📖📖 I shall be delivered by the chief priests and scribes to the Gentiles: they shall mock Me, and shall scourge (beat) Me, and shall spit on Me, and shall kill Me (Son of Man) [Mark 10:33-34] 📖📖📖 I shall be delivered to the Gentiles, and shall be mocked, and spitefully entreated, and spit on, and they shall scourge (beat) Me, and put Me to death (Son of Man) [Luke 18:32-33]

I say to you, "One of you shall betray Me" [Matthew 26:21] 📖📖 I say to you, "One of you who eats with Me shall betray Me" [Mark 14:18] 📖📖📖 I have a betrayer whose hand is with Me on the table [Luke 22:21] 📖📖📖📖 I say to you, that one of you shall betray Me [John 13:21]

I shall be betrayed by him who dips his hand with Me in the
   dish [Matthew 26:23] 📖📖 I shall be betrayed by one of
   the twelve, who dips with Me in the dish [Mark 14:18-20]
   📖📖📖 I shall be betrayed by him to whom I shall give a
   sop (piece of bread), when I have dipped it [John 13:21-
   26]

I (the Shepherd) "will be smitten, and the sheep of the flock
   will be scattered abroad," for it is written (Zechariah 13:
   7) [Matthew 26:31] 📖📖 I (the Shepherd) "will be smitten, and the sheep shall be scattered," for it is written
   (Zechariah 13:7) [Mark 14:27]

I say to you, Peter, that this night, before the cock crow, you
   will deny Me thrice [Matthew 26:34] 📖📖 I say to you,
   Peter, that this day, even in this night, before the cock
   crow twice, you shall deny Me thrice [Mark 14:30] 📖📖📖
   I tell you, Peter, "The cock shall not crow this day, before
   you shall thrice deny that you know Me" [Luke 22:34]
   📖📖📖📖 I say to you, Peter, "The cock shall not crow
   till you have denied Me thrice" [John 13:37-38]

I am exceedingly sorrowful, even unto death [Matthew 26:
   38] 📖📖 I am exceedingly sorrowful unto death [Mark
   14:34]

I ask of You, O My Father, "If it be possible, let this cup pass
   from Me: nevertheless not as I will, but as You will"
   [Matthew 26:39] 📖📖 I ask of You, Father, "Take away
   this cup from Me: nevertheless, not what I will, but what
   You will" [Mark 14:36] 📖📖📖 I ask of You, Father, "If
   You be willing, remove this cup from Me: nevertheless not
   My will, but Yours, be done" [Luke 22:42]

I ask of You, Father, "If this cup may not pass away from Me,
   except I drink it, Your will be done" [Matthew 26:42]

I am being betrayed into the hands of sinners, behold the
   hour is at hand (Son of Man) [Matthew 26:45] 📖📖 I
   am betrayed into the hands of sinners, the hour is come
   (Son of Man) [Mark 14:41]

I am forsaken by My God (Psalm 22:1) [Matthew 27:46] 📖📖
   I am forsaken by My God (Psalm 22:1) [Mark 15: 34]

I must suffer many things and be rejected by the elders and
   chief priests and scribes (Son of Man) [Luke 9:22]

I have a baptism to be baptized with; and how am I strait-
   ened till it (anxious for it to) be accomplished [Luke 12:
   50]

I must first suffer many things (Son of Man) [Luke 17:24-25]

I must first be rejected of (by) this generation (Son of Man)
   [Luke 17:24-25]

I have desired to eat this passover with you before I suffer [Luke 22:15]

I have temptations (trials) [Luke 22:28]

I say to you (the twelve apostles), "What is written must yet be accomplished in me, 'And He was reckoned among the transgressors': for the things concerning Me have an end" (Isaiah 53:12) [Luke 22:37]

I am being betrayed by your kiss? (to Judas) (Son of Man) [Luke 22:48]

I "must be delivered into the hands of sinful men, and be crucified" (two men at the tomb reporting what Jesus had said to the women who had come with Him from Galilee and certain other women) (Son of Man) [Luke 24:7]

I (the Christ) ought to have suffered (must suffer) these things, and to enter into My glory [Luke 24:26]

I said to you, that you have seen Me, and believe not [John 6:36]

I am hated by the world, because I testify of it, that the works thereof are evil [John 7:7]

I do not have a devil (as you say) [John 8:48-49]

I honor My Father, and you do dishonor Me [John 8:49]

I now have a troubled soul [John 12:27]

I know whom I have chosen: but that the Scripture may be fulfilled, "He who eats bread with Me has lifted up his heel against Me" (Psalm 41:9) [John 13:18]

I will not talk much with you hereafter: for the prince of this world comes, and (he) has nothing in Me [John 14:30]

I was hated by the world before it hated you [John 15:18]

I am hated without cause (by those who are of the world) (Psalm 69:4) [John 15:18-25]

VI. His Death

Jesus had to die because without the shedding of blood there is no forgiveness [Leviticus 17:11; Hebrews 9:22]. This is God's plan, not yours or mine and was His plan from the foundation of the world [Revelation 13:8]. For some reason, God believes His thoughts are higher than ours [Isaiah 55:8-9]. I guess this means that His plans are better than ours—sorry.

A. Jesus said He would be and was killed:

Jesus said:

I shall be killed by them (the hands of men) (Son of Man) [Matthew 17:23] 📖📖 I am delivered into the hands of men, and they shall kill Me (Son of Man) [Mark 9:31]

I shall be betrayed to the chief priests and to the scribes, and they shall condemn Me to death (Son of Man) [Matthew 20:18]

I shall be delivered to the Gentiles by the chief priests and the scribes to be mocked and scourged (beaten) and crucified (Son of Man) [Matthew 20:18-19] 📖📖 I shall be delivered by the chief priests and scribes to the Gentiles: they shall mock Me, and shall scourge (beat) Me, and shall spit on Me, and shall kill Me (Son of Man) [Mark 10:33-34] 📖📖📖 I shall be delivered to the Gentiles, and shall be mocked, and spitefully entreated, and spit on, and they shall scourge (beat) Me, and put Me to death (Son of Man) [Luke 18:32-33]

I drink the cup (His suffering and death) [Mark 10:38]

I am to be baptized (His suffering and death) [Matthew 20:23] 📖📖 I am baptized (His suffering and death) [Mark 10:38]

I came to give My life a ransom for many (Son of Man) [Matthew 20:28] 📖📖 I came to give My life a ransom for many (Son of Man) [Mark 10:45]

I want you to drink all of it (this cup), for this is (represents) My blood of the new testament (covenant), which is shed for many for the remission of sins [Matthew 26:

27-28] 📖📖 I shed My blood for many; this is (represents) my blood of the new testament (covenant) [Mark 14:23-24] 📖📖📖 I shed My blood for you: this cup is (represents) the new testament (covenant) in My blood [Luke 22:20]

I must be slain (Son of Man) [Luke 9:22]

I must walk today, and tomorrow, and the day following: for it cannot be that a prophet perish out of Jerusalem [Luke 13:33]

I commend My spirit into Your hands, Father [Luke 23:46]

I know that you are Abraham's seed (descendant); but you seek to kill Me, because My word has no place in you [John 8:37]

I, a man who has told you the truth, which I have heard of (from) God, you seek now to kill [John 8:40]

I am the good shepherd: the good shepherd gives His life for the sheep [John 10:11]

I am loved by My Father, because I lay down My life, that I might take it again [John 10:17]

I lay down My life of myself: no man takes it from Me [John 10:18]

I came to this hour for this cause (to be a sacrifice), so shall I say, "Father, save Me from this hour?" [John 12:27]

I am He who was dead [Revelation 1:18]

I was dead [Revelation 2:8]

B. Jesus said He would be killed by crucifixion:

Crucifixion was not only a horrible way to die, but such death was also pronounced a curse by God Himself [Deuteronomy 21:22-23; Galations 3:13].

Jesus said:

I shall be delivered to the Gentiles by the chief priests and the scribes to be mocked and scourged (beaten) and crucified (Son of Man) [Matthew 20:18-19]

I will be betrayed to be crucified in two days (Son of Man) [Matthew 26:2]

I "must be delivered into the hands of sinful men, and be crucified" (two men at the tomb reporting what Jesus

had said to women who had come with Him from Galilee
and certain other women) (Son of Man) [Luke 24:7]
I must be lifted up (Son of Man) [John 3:14]
I, if I be lifted up from the earth, will draw all men to Me
[John 12:32]

C. Jesus said His death would be for remission of sins:

*Remission means to "forgive, pardon or not exact
a penalty for". Jesus' death then means that those
who accept His death have been forgiven and will not
receive the penalty for being sinners and for sinning,
eternal death.*

*This is also closely related to IIIB, "Jesus said He
came to save us and give us life".*

Jesus said:

I came to give My life a ransom for many (Son of Man)
[Matthew 20:28] 📖📖 I came to give My life a ransom for many (Son of Man) [Mark 10:45]

VII. His Burial

Jesus said:

I will be three days and three nights in the heart of the earth
(Son of Man) [Matthew 12:40]

I was done a good work by this woman, for in pouring this
fragrant oil on My body, she did it for My burial [Matthew
26:10-12] 📖📖 I was done a good work by this woman,
for she is come aforehand to anoint My body to the burying [Mark 14:6-8]

VIII.   His Resurrection

If Jesus was not raised from the dead, preaching is vain, faith is vain and there is no resurrection for any [1 Corinthians 15:14-20]. Can there be any doubt that Jesus rose from the dead?
I suspect that the number of those who saw Jesus alive after His resurrection are more than those who witness many historical events that we easily accept. Paul says that He was seen alive by over 500 at once [1 Corinthians 15:6] and by Paul himself and the apostles.

Jesus said:

I want you to tell this vision (the Transfiguration) to no man, until I am risen from the dead (Son of Man) [Matthew 17: 9]

I shall be raised again the third day (Son of Man) [Matthew 17:23]

I shall rise again the third day (Son of Man) [Matthew 20:19] 📖📖 I shall rise again the third day (Son of Man) [Mark 10:34] 📖📖📖 I shall rise again the third day (Son of Man) [Luke 18:33]

I, after I am risen again, will go before you into Galilee [Matthew 26:32] 📖📖 I, after I am risen, will go before you into Galilee [Mark 14:28]

I "will rise again after three days" (chief priests and Pharisees testifying about what Jesus had said) [Matthew 27:62-63]

I shall be seen in Galilee by My brethren [Matthew 28:10]

I will rise the third day, after I am killed (Son of Man) [Mark 9:31]

I must be raised the third day (Son of Man) [Luke 9:22]

I shall be perfected the third day [Luke 13:32]

I "must rise again the third day" (two men at the tomb reporting what Jesus had said to women who had come with Him from Galilee and certain other women) (Son of Man) [Luke 24:7]

I will raise this temple (His body) up in three days, after it is destroyed [John 2:19-21]

I am loved by My Father, because I lay down My life, that I might take it again [John 10:17]

I have power to lay down My life, and I have power to take it
again: this commandment I have received of (from) My Father
[John 10:18]

I live, and because I live, you shall live also [John 14:19]

I will see you again, and your heart shall rejoice [John 16:
22]

I am He who lives [Revelation 1:18]

I am alive [Revelation 2:8]

IX. His Return

There are many Scriptures that speak of the day of Jehovah, in that day, the last day or the day of the Lord. Some Scriptures [1 Corinthians 5:5; 2 Corinthians 1:14; Philippians 1:10, 2:16] state that Jesus has a "day". Are these the same? No doubt.

The second time Jesus comes to earth it will be as KING OF KINGS AND LORD OF LORDS [Revelation 19:11-16]. He will take vengeance on those who have rejected Him. This will be a truly awe inspiring sight, but to many it will be a time of great fear [Revelation 6:14-17].

Jesus said:

I shall come in the glory of My Father with His angels; and then I shall reward every man according to his works (Son of Man) [Matthew 16:27]

I will come in My kingdom (Son of Man) [Matthew 16:28]

I shall come as the lightning comes out of the east and shines even to the west (Son of Man) [Matthew 24:27]

I shall come in the clouds of heaven with power and great glory, and all the tribes of the earth shall see me (Son of Man) [Matthew 24:30] ▥▥ I shall come in the clouds with great power and glory (Son of Man) [Mark 13:26] ▥▥▥ I shall come in a cloud with power and great glory (Son of Man) [Luke 21:27]

I shall send My angels (as He returns) with a great sound of a trumpet, and they shall gather together My elect from the four winds, from one end of heaven to the other (Son of Man) [Matthew 24:30-31] ▥▥ I shall send My angels (as He returns), and shall gather together My elect from the four winds, from the uttermost part of earth to the uttermost part of heaven (Son of Man) [Mark 13:26-27]

I shall come as the days of Noah were, before the flood, they were eating and drinking, marrying and giving in marriage (Son of Man) [Matthew 24:37-39] ▥▥ I will be revealed in the day when people eat, drink, marry wives, are given in marriage, buy, sell, plant, and build (Son of Man) [Luke 17:27-30]

I am coming at an hour when you think not (do not expect) (Son of Man) [Matthew 24:44] ▥▥ I am coming at an hour when you think not (do not expect) (Son of Man) [Luke 12:40]

I shall come in the clouds of heaven (Son of Man) [Matthew 26:64] 〔〕〔〕 I shall come in the clouds of heaven (Son of Man) [Mark 14:62]

I shall be ashamed of whomever is ashamed of Me and My words in this adulterous and sinful generation, when I come in the glory of My Father with the holy angels (Son of Man) [Mark 8:38] 〔〕〔〕 I shall be ashamed of him who is ashamed of Me and of My words, when I shall come in My own glory, and in My Father's, and of the holy angels (Son of Man) [Luke 9:26]

I (the Son) do not know that day and that hour (coming of the Son of Man) [Mark 13:26-32]

I, say to you, I say to all, "Watch" (for His return) [Mark 13:37]

I say to you (Pharisees), "You shall not see Me, until the time comes when you shall say, 'Blessed is He who comes in the name of the Lord'" [Luke 13:35]

I shall be in My day as the lightning, that lightens out of the one part under heaven, shines to the other part under heaven (Son of Man) [Luke 17:24]

I wonder if I shall find faith on the earth when I come (Son of Man) [Luke 18:8]

I go to prepare a place for you, and if I go and prepare a place for you, I will come again [John 14:2-3]

I go away and come again to you [John 14:28]

I am to come [Revelation 1:8]

I will come [Revelation 2:25]

I come quickly [Revelation 3:11]

I come as a thief (without further notice) [Revelation 16:15]

I come quickly [Revelation 22:7]

I come quickly [Revelation 22:12]

I surely come quickly [Revelation 22:20]

X. His Character.

The character of Jesus is an example of the character He wants in His followers: humility, compassion, completion of assignments, a servant attitude, sinlessness, truth in judgment and love. This character is attested to by most of the statements in this book.

Jesus said:

I want to fulfill all righteousness [Matthew 3:15]

I am meek and lowly in heart [Matthew 11:29]

I have compassion on the multitude, because they continue with Me now three days, and have nothing to eat: and I will not send them away fasting, lest they faint in the way [Matthew 15:32] 📖📖 I have compassion on the multitude, because they have now been with Me three days and have nothing to eat: and if I send them away fasting to their own houses, they will faint by the way: for divers (some or many) of them have come from far [Mark 8:2]

I do not want you to forbid the little children to come to me; for of such is the kingdom of heaven [Matthew 19:14] 📖📖 I want you to let the little children to come to Me, and forbid them not: for of such is the kingdom of God [Mark 10:14] 📖📖📖 I want you to let the little children to come to Me, and forbid them not: for of such is the kingdom of God [Luke 18:16]

I often would have gathered your children together, O Jerusalem, even as a hen gathers her chickens under her wings, and you would not! [Matthew 23:37] 📖📖 I often would have gathered your children together, O Jerusalem, as a hen gathers her brood under her wings, and you would not! [Luke 13:34]

I must be about My Father's business (when Jesus was 12 years old) [Luke 2:49]

I go, as it was determined (Son of Man) [Luke 22:22]

I am among you as he who serves [Luke 22:27]

I ask you to forgive them (those who crucified Him→us?), Father; for they know not what they do [Luke 23:34]

I work, and My Father works [John 5:17]

I will in no wise cast out him who comes to Me [John 6:37]

I should lose nothing of all the Father who sent Me has given Me, but should raise it up again at the last day, for this is His will [John 6:39]

I do not condemn you: go, and sin no more (to a woman caught in adultery) [John 8:11]

I know whence I came, and whither I go [John 8:14]

I have true judgment: for I am not alone, but I and the Father who sent Me [John 8:16]

I am One who bears witness of Myself [John 8:18]

I do nothing of Myself; but as My Father has taught Me, I speak these things [John 8:28]

I tell you the truth, you believe Me not [John 8:45]

I lay down My life of Myself: no man takes it from Me [John 10:18]

I give to you a new commandment, that you love one another; as I have loved you [John 13:34]

I would have told you if My Father's house did not have many mansions [John 14:2]

I love him who keeps My commandments [John 14:21]

I love the Father [John 14:31]

I have loved you [John 15:9]

I have loved you [John 15:12]

I henceforth call you not servants; for the servant knows not what his lord does: but I have called you friends (His disciples) [John 15:15]

I will that they also, whom You have given Me, Father, be with Me where I am [John 17:24]

I "have lost none of them whom You gave Me" (saying of Jesus) [John 18:9]

I shall drink the cup which My Father has given Me [John 18:11]

I have finished it (His sacrifice) [John 19:30]

I also hate the deeds of the Nicolaitanes (some kind of false doctrine) [Revelation 2:6 and 15]

I gave her (Jezebel) space to repent of her fornication; and she repented not [Revelation 2:21]

I am holy [Revelation 3:7]

I am true [Revelation 3:7]

XI. His Glory

A. Jesus said He was returning to His Father in heaven to sit at His right hand:

Jesus is not only in heaven at God's right hand, he is also there advocating and interceding for us [Romans 8:34; Hebrews 7:25; 1 John 2:1]!

Jesus said:

I shall sit on the throne of My glory [Matthew 19:28]

I shall sit on the throne of My glory when I come in My glory, and all the holy angels (come) with Me (Son of Man) [Matthew 25:31]

I shall sit at the right hand of power (Son of Man) [Matthew 26:64] I shall sit at the right hand of the Power (Son of Man) [Mark 14:62] I shall sit on the right hand of the Power of God (Son of Man) [Luke 22:69]

I am with you yet a little while, and then I go to Him who sent Me [John 7:33]

I will be where you cannot come [John 7:34]

I go My way, and you shall seek me, and shall die in your sins: whither I go, you cannot come [John 8:21]

I now say to you, little children, "Yet a little while I am with you; you shall seek Me: and as I said to the Jews, where I go, you cannot come" [John 13:33]

I go to My Father [John 14:12]

I am going to the Father [John 14:28]

I have told you before it come to pass, that, when it is come to pass, you might believe (His return to the Father) [John 14:29]

I did not say these things to you at the beginning, because I was with you, but now I go My way to Him who sent Me [John 16:4-5]

I go to My Father, and you see Me no more [John 16:10]

I go to the Father, so a little while, and you shall not see Me: and again, a little while, and you shall see Me [John 16:16]

I leave the world, and go to the Father [John 16:28]

I am no more in the world [John 17:11]

I come to You, Holy Father [John 17:11]

I come to You, Holy Father [John 17:13]

I am not yet ascended to My Father, so touch Me not: but
go to My brethren, and say to them, "I ascend to My
Father, and your Father; and to My God and your God"
(to Mary Magdalene) [John 20:17]

I overcame, and am set down with My Father in His throne
[Revelation 3:22]

B. Jesus said He has been and will be glorified:

Jesus said:

I shall come in the glory of My Father with His angels; and
then I shall reward every man according to his works
(Son of Man) [Matthew 16:27]

I shall be ashamed of whomever is ashamed of Me and My
words in this adulterous and sinful generation, when I
come in the glory of My Father with the holy angels
(Son of Man) [Mark 8:38] 🕮🕮 I shall be ashamed of
him who is ashamed of Me and of My words, when I
shall come in My own glory, and in My Father's, and of
the holy angels (Son of Man) [Luke 9:26]

I (the Christ) ought to have suffered (must suffer) these
things, and to enter into My glory [Luke 24:26]

I receive not honor from men [John 5:41]

I, the Son of God, will be glorified thereby (raising of Lazarus)
[John 11:4]

I should (shall) be glorified: the hour is come (Son of Man)
[John 12:23]

I am glorified, and God is glorified in Me (Son of God) [John
13:31]

I shall be glorified by the Spirit of truth, for He shall receive of Mine, and shall show it to you [John 16:13-14]

I had the glory with You, Father, before the world was [John
17:5]

I am glorified in them (the men You gave Me), Father [John
17:9-10]

I was given glory by You, Father [John 17:22]

I have given them (those You gave Me) the glory which You
gave Me, Father [John 17:22]

I have been given glory by You, Father [John 17:24]

XII. Other

A. Jesus claimed he was human and of Jewish lineage and was in the line of the promises and the kings:

His suffering and death also attest to His humanity.

Jesus said:

I have nowhere to lay My head (Son of Man) [Matthew 8:
20] 📖📖 I have not where to lay My head (Son of Man)
[Luke 9:58]

I came eating and drinking (Son of Man) [Matthew 11:19]
📖📖 I have come eating and drinking (Son of Man)
[Luke 7:34]

I was done a good work by this woman, for in pouring this
fragrant oil on My body, she did it for My burial
[Matthew 26:10-12] 📖📖 I was done a good work by
this woman, for she is come aforehand to anoint My
body to the burying [Mark 14:6-8]

I have flesh and bones, as you (the eleven) see Me have
(after His resurrection from the dead) [Luke 24:39]

I thirst (during His crucifixion) [John 19:28]

B. Jesus made other statements about Himself:

Jesus said:

I want you to take My yoke upon you, and learn of Me, for
My yoke is easy and My burden is light [Matthew 11:
29-30]

I want you to take heed that no man deceive you, for
many shall come in My name, saying, "I am Christ,"
and shall deceive many [Matthew 24:4-5] 📖📖 I want
you to take heed lest any man deceive you: for many
shall come in My name, saying, "I am Christ;" and
shall deceive many [Mark 13:5-6] 📖📖📖 I want you
to take heed that you be not deceived: for many shall
come in My name , saying, "I am Christ;" and, "The time
draws near:" therefore go not after them [Luke 21:8]

I want you to take, eat (the bread); this is (represents) My
body [Matthew 26:26] ⏏⏏ I want you to take, eat
(this bread): this is (represents) My body [Mark 14:22]
⏏⏏⏏ I want you to do this (eat the bread) in remembrance of Me: this is (represents) My body which is giv-
en for you [Luke 22:19]

I beheld Satan as lightning fall from heaven (after the seventy returned) [Luke 10:18]

I say to you (one of the malefactors crucified with Jesus),
"Today you shall be with Me in paradise" [Luke 23:43]

I have meat to eat that you know not of [John 4:32]

I live by the Father [John 6:57]

I go not up yet to this feast (Feast of Tabernacles); for My
time is not yet full come [John 7:8]

I will not always be here with you [John 12:8]

I count you as My friends, if you do whatever I command
you [John 15:14]

I say to you, that you shall weep and lament, but the world
shall rejoice: and you shall be sorrowful, but your sorrow (at His death) shall be turned into joy (at His
resurrection) [John 16:20]

I am He (Jesus of Nazareth) [John 18:5]

I have told you that I am He (Jesus of Nazareth) [John 18:
7-8]

I shall be witnessed to by you (the apostles) in Jerusalem,
and in all Judea, and in Samaria, and to the uttermost
part of the earth [Acts 1:8]

I know your works (church of Ephesus), and your labor,
and your patience, and how you cannot bear them who
are evil [Revelation 2:2]

I have somewhat against you (church of Ephesus), because you have left your first love [Revelation 2:4]

I know your works (church in Smyrna), and tribulation,
and poverty [Revelation 2:9]

I know the blasphemy of them who say they are Jews and
are not, but are the synagogue of Satan [Revelation 2:
9]

I know your works (church in Pergamos), and where you
dwell, even where Satan's seat is [Revelation 2:13]

I have a few things against you (church in Pergamos),
because you have there them who hold the doctrine of
Balaam, who taught Balac to cast a stumbling block

before the children of Israel, to eat things sacrificed to idols, and to commit fornication [Revelation 2:14]

I know your works (church in Thyatira), and charity, and service, and faith, and your patience [Revelation 2:19]

I have a few things against you (church in Thyatira), because you suffer that woman Jezebel, who calls herself a prophetess, to teach and to seduce My servants to commit fornication, and to eat things sacrificed to idols [Revelation 2:20]

I know your works (church in Sardis), that you have a name that you are alive, and (but) are dead [Revelation 3:1]

I have not found your works (church in Sardis) perfect before God [Revelation 3:2]

I know your works (church in Philadelphia): for you have little strength, and have kept My word, and have not denied My name [Revelation 3:8]

I have set before you an open door (church in Philadelphia), and no man can shut it [Revelation 3:8]

I will make them of the synagogue of Satan, who say they are Jews, and are not, but do lie, behold, I will make them to come and worship before your (church in Philadelphia) feet [Revelation 3:9]

I have loved you (church in Philadelphia) [Revelation 3:9]

I know your works (church of the Laodiceans), that they are neither cold nor hot [Revelation 3:15]

I would that you (church of the Laodiceans) were cold or hot; so then because you are lukewarm, and neither cold nor hot, I will spew you out of my mouth [Revelation 3:15-16]

I counsel you (church of the Laodiceans) to buy of (from) Me gold tried in the fire, that you may be rich; and white garments that you may be clothed [Revelation 3:18]

Part 2: Statements Made By Jesus' Apostles and Others About Jesus.

The testimony of different Scripture writers in different contexts is interesting, as is the consistency of that testimony, even though they may be emphasizing different things.

I.   His Credentials

A. The apostles and others claimed that Jesus is God:

These statements are most astounding. They clearly say that Jesus, the apostles and others said that Jesus is God. Our denial of this would be foolish. There is some differentiation between the Father and Jesus, because Jesus said that He and His Father are one [John 10:30] and, yet Paul said that the kingdom will be returned to the Father, so the Father can be 'all in all' [1 Corinthians 15:23-28]. Paul also said that 'the head of Christ is God' [1 Corinthians 11:3]. Jesus also said that even He (the Son) did not know the day or the hour of His return [Mark 13:32] and that His Father 'is greater than I' [John 14:28]. The relationship between the Father, Jesus and the Holy Spirit has always been troublesome, but the comments that follow certainly show that Jesus is God. Besides, some things must be accepted by faith.

Jesus' statements to the devil are interesting, particularly His statement at the second temptation. After the devil challenged Him to throw Himself from the pinnacle of the temple to show that God would save Him as scripture says and to prove He was the Son of God, Jesus said, "It is written again, 'You shall not tempt the Lord your God'" [Matthew 4:5-7]. This could be interpreted three ways;

1. *do not tempt the Father (your Lord and God) to act to save Me and/or*
2. *do not tempt Me (your Lord and God) to call on the angels to save Me and/or*

   3. *do not tempt Me (your Lord and God) to tempt the Father to act to save Me.*

In the last two of these cases Jesus would have been claiming to be Lord and God. Both of these would be appropriate, when compared with the other claims He made.

Paul claims that God is King of kings and Lord of lords [1 Timothy 6:13-16], and John's vision calls the Lamb and the Man on a white horse KING OF KINGS AND LORD OF LORDS [Revelation 17:14; 19:{11}16]. It seems clear that John is talking about Jesus, making Him equal with God.

Jesus and writers of the New Testament said that Jesus is God and that He created and sustains all things. His credentials certainly show that Jesus is God, Savior and Lord and Master.

The Apostles and others said:

Jesus "shall be called Immanuel, which being interpreted is, God with us," said an angel to Joseph (Isaiah 7:14) [Matthew 1:21-23]

Jesus (the Word) was God [John 1:1, 14]

Jesus, "You are my God," said Thomas (after he had touched Jesus' hands and side) [John 20:26-28]

Jesus (Christ) is God blessed for ever [Romans 9:5]

Jesus Christ is our great God [Titus 2:13]

Jesus (the Son) is God [Hebrews 1:8]

Jesus Christ is our God [2 Peter 1:1]

Jesus Christ is the true God [1 John 5:20]

B. The apostles and others claimed that Jesus is one with God:

A created being cannot reasonably make or have made for him the following claims. He even said, "...He who has seen Me has seen the Father;..." [John 14:9].

The apostles and others said:

Jesus (the Word) was in the beginning with God [John 1:1-2]

Jesus Christ is in the Bosom of the Father [John 1:17-18]

Jesus "(the Son) has been given all things into His hand by the Father," answered John the Baptist [John 3:35]

Jesus was sought by the Jews the more to kill Him, because He not only had broken the Sabbath, but said also that God was His Father, making Himself equal with God [John 5:{16}17-18]

Jesus (Christ) is God's [1 Corinthians 3:23]

Jesus (Christ) is the image of God [2 Corinthians 4:4]

Jesus (Christ) is the One through whom God created all things [Ephesians 3:9]

Jesus Christ had the form of God [Philippians 2:5-6]

Jesus Christ was equal with God [Philippians 2:5-6]

Jesus (God's Son) is the image of the invisible God [Colossians 1:{13}15]

Jesus (God's Son) has all the fullness dwelling in Him [Colossians 1:{13}19]

Jesus (Christ) and His Father have all the treasures of wisdom hidden in them [Colossians 2:2-3]

Jesus (Christ) and His Father have all the treasures of knowledge hidden in them [Colossians 2:2-3]

Jesus (Christ) has dwelling in Him all the fullness of the Godhead bodily [Colossians 2:8-9]

Jesus (God's Son) is the brightness of God's glory [Hebrews 1:{2}3]

Jesus (God's Son) is the express image of God's Person [Hebrews 1:{2}3]

Jesus (the Lamb) and the Lord God Almighty are the temple of it (the New Jerusalem) [Revelation 21:22]

Jesus (the Lamb) is its (the New Jerusalem) light [Revelation 21:23]

Jesus' (the Lamb) and God's throne has a pure river of water of life, clear as crystal, proceeding from it [Revelation 22:1]

Jesus' (the Lamb) and God's throne shall be in it (the New Jerusalem) [Revelation 22:3]

C. The apostles and others claimed that Jesus has God's qualities:

The apostles and others said:

Jesus called His twelve disciples to Him and gave them power against unclean spirits, to cast them out, and to heal all manner of sickness and all manner of disease [Matthew 10:{9:35}1]

Jesus astonished those of His own country with His wisdom and mighty works [Matthew 13:{51}54]

Jesus (the Word) made all things [John 1:1-3]

Jesus (the Word) has life in Him [John 1:1-4]

Jesus (the true Light) was in the world, and the world was made by Him, and the world knew Him not [John 1:6-10]

Jesus (the Word) was full of grace [John 1:14]

Jesus (the Word) was full of truth [John 1:14]

Jesus "(Lord), to whom shall we go? You have the words of eternal life," was Peter's answer to Jesus' question, "Will you also go away?" [John 6:67-68]

Jesus, "God's Son, is the Holy One" (Peter's response to the people at the temple) [Acts 3:13-14]

Jesus, "God's son, is the Just" (Peter's response to the people at the temple) [Acts 3:13-14]

Jesus, "God's Son, is the Prince of Life" (Peter's response to the people at the temple) [Acts 3:13-15]

Jesus "(the Just One) you have been now the betrayers and murderers of," Stephen said to the council [Acts 7:52]

Jesus Christ is the one Lord by whom are all things [1 Corinthians 8:6]

Jesus (Christ) knew no sin [2 Corinthians 5:20-21]

Jesus (Christ) is far above all principality, and power, and might, and dominion, and every name that is named [Ephesians 1:20-21]

Jesus Christ was equal with God [Philippians 2:5-6]

Jesus Christ the Lord is able even to subdue all things to Himself [Philippians 3:20-21]

Jesus (God's Son) is the image of the invisible God [Colossians 1:{13}15]

Jesus (God's Son) created all things [Colossians 1:{13}16]

Jesus (God's Son) is before all things [Colossians 1:{13}17]

Jesus (God's Son) is the One in whom all things consist [Colossians 1:{13}17}

Jesus (God's Son) is the beginning [Colossians 1:{13}18]

Jesus (God's Son) has all the fullness dwelling in Him [Colossians 1:{13}19]

Jesus (Christ) and His Father have all the treasures of wisdom hidden in them [Colossians 2:2-3]

Jesus (Christ) and His Father have all the treasures of knowledge hidden in them [Colossians 2:2-3]

Jesus (Christ) has dwelling in Him all the fullness of the Godhead bodily [Colossians 2:8-9]

Jesus (Christ) has forgiven you all trespasses [Colossians 2:{11}13]

Jesus (God's Son) is the One through whom God made the worlds [Hebrews 1:1-2]

Jesus (God's Son) is the express image of God's Person [Hebrews 1:{2}3]

Jesus (God's Son) upholds all things by the word of His power [Hebrews 1:{2}3]

Jesus (God's Son) "is to be worshiped by all the angels of God" [Hebrews 1:{2}6]

Jesus (the Son), "the heavens are the works of Your hands" (Psalm 102:25) [Hebrews 1:{8}10]

Jesus (the Son), "You, Lord, in the beginning have laid the foundation of the earth" (Psalm 102:25) [Hebrews 1:{8} 10]

Jesus continues ever [Hebrews 7:{22}24]

Jesus is holy [Hebrews 7:{22}26]

Jesus is harmless [Hebrews 7:{22}26]

Jesus is undefiled [Hebrews 7:{22}26]

Jesus Christ is the same yesterday [Hebrews 13:8]

Jesus Christ is the same today [Hebrews 13:8]

Jesus Christ is the same forever [Hebrews 13:8]

Jesus Christ our Lord is the Lord of glory [James 2:1]

Jesus Christ is the righteous [1 John 2:1]

Jesus (God's Son) has eternal life in Him [1 John 5:11]

Jesus Christ is eternal life [1 John 5:20]

D. The apostles and others claimed that Jesus is God's son:

I suppose we all could claim to be a 'son of God', particularly through adoption by Him [Galations 4:5], but none of us has been 'begotten' (John 1:14, 1 John 4:9; see also 1 Corinthians 4:15, 1 Peter 1:3, 1 John 5: 1) by God, so these statements seem to carry much more weight than that.

The apostles and others said:

Jesus (the young Child) was taken to Egypt with His mother by night by Joseph: and was there until the death of Herod: that it might be fulfilled which was spoken of (about) the Lord by the prophet, saying, "Out of Egypt have I called My son" (Hosea 11:1) [Matthew 2:14-15]

Jesus "is My beloved Son" (voice from heaven at Jesus' baptism) [Matthew 3:16-17] 📖📖 Jesus, "You are My beloved Son" (voice from heaven at Jesus' baptism) [Mark 1:9-11] 📖📖📖 Jesus, "You are My beloved Son" (voice from heaven at Jesus' baptism) [Luke 3:21-22]

Jesus, "what have we to do with You, Son of God? Are You come hither to torment us before the time?," cried out two devil possessed men [Matthew 8:28-29] 📖📖 Jesus, "what have I to do with You, Son of the most high God? I adjure You by God, that You torment me not," cried out a man with an unclean spirit [Mark 5:7] 📖📖📖 Jesus, "what have I to do with You, Son of God Most High? I beseech You, torment me not," said with a loud voice by a man with devils [Luke 8:26-28]

Jesus, "of a truth You are the Son of God," said those in the boat after Jesus had walked on the water [Matthew 14:{31}33]

Jesus, "You are the Son of the living God," said Peter when Jesus asked His disciples, "Whom do men say that I the Son of Man am?" [Matthew 16:13-16]

Jesus "is My beloved Son" (voice out of the cloud at Jesus' Transfiguration) [Matthew 17:{1}5] 📖📖 Jesus "is My beloved Son" (voice out of the cloud at Jesus' Transfiguration) [Mark 9:{5}7] 📖📖📖 Jesus "is My beloved Son" (voice out of the cloud at Jesus' Transfiguration) [Luke 9:35-36]

Jesus "truly was the Son of God," said the centurion, and they that were with him, fearing greatly, as they watched Jesus, and when they saw the earthquake and those things that were done [Matthew 27:54] ▢▢ Jesus "truly was the Son of God," said the centurion, who stood over against Him, when he saw that Jesus cried out and gave up the ghost (died) [Mark 15:{37}39]

Jesus Christ is the Son of God [Mark 1:1]

Jesus, "You are the Son of God," cried out unclean spirits, when they saw Him, and they fell down before Him [Mark 3:{7}11]

Jesus "shall be called the Son of the Highest," an angel said to Mary [Luke 1:31-32]

Jesus "shall be called the Son of God, because the Holy Ghost shall come upon you, and the power of the Highest shall overshadow you" an angel said to Mary after she said to the angel, "How shall this be, seeing I know not a man?" (Isaiah 7:14) [Luke 1:{31}35]

Jesus, "You are Christ the Son of God," cried out devils, as they came out of many [Luke 4:{35}41]

Jesus (the Word) had glory as of the only begotten of the Father [John 1:14]

Jesus Christ is the only begotten Son (of the Father) [John 1:17-18]

Jesus "is the Son of God," said John the Baptist, baring record of what he saw [John 1:{29}34]

Jesus, "Rabbi, You are the Son of God," Nathanael said [John 1:48-49]

Jesus was sought by the Jews the more to kill Him, because He had not only broken the Sabbath, but said also that God was His Father, making Himself equal with God [John 5:{16}17-18]

Jesus, "we believe and are sure that You are that Christ, the Son of the living God," Peter answered Him [John 6:67-69]

Jesus, "Lord, I believe (You are the Son of God)," he (the man blind from birth) said, and he worshiped Him [John 9:35-38]

Jesus, "Lord, I believe that You are the Christ, the Son of God, who should (would) come into the world," said Martha, Lazarus' sister [John 11:25-27]

Jesus "by our law, ought to die, because He made Himself the Son of God," the Jews answered Pilate [John 19:5-7]

Jesus is the Christ, the Son of God [John 20:31]

Jesus "is God's Son (Peter's response to the people at the temple) [Acts 3:13]

Jesus "is God's Son (Peter's response to the people at the temple) [Acts 3:26]

Jesus "Christ is the Son of God," Philip was answered by a man of Ethiopia [Acts 8:37]

Jesus (Christ) was straightway preached that He is the Son of God by Saul in the synagogues [Acts 9:20]

Jesus "was raised up by God again, as it is also written in the second Psalm, 'You are My Son, this day have I begotten You'" (Psalm 2:7) (Paul speaking in the Antioch synagogue) [Acts 13:33]

Jesus Christ our Lord is God's son [Romans 1:1-3]

Jesus Christ our Lord was declared to be the Son of God with power, according to the spirit of holiness, by the resurrection from the dead [Romans 1:3-4]

Jesus Christ, God's own Son, was sent by God in the likeness of sinful flesh, for (because of) sin [Romans 8:2-3]

Jesus (God's own Son) was not spared by God but delivered up by Him for us all [Romans 8:32]

Jesus Christ our Lord's Father is God [Romans 15:6]

Jesus Christ our Lord is God's son [1 Corinthians 1:9]

Jesus Christ our Lord's Father is God [2 Corinthians 1:3]

Jesus Christ, the Son of God, was preached among you by us [2 Corinthians 1:19]

Jesus Christ our Lord's Father is God [2 Corinthians 11:31]

Jesus "(Christ) is the Son of God," said Paul to Peter and the others [Galatians 2:20]

Jesus Christ our Lord's Father is God [Ephesians 1:3]

Jesus is God's Son [1 Thessalonians 1:9-10]

Jesus (God's Son), "You are My Son" (Psalms 2:7) [Hebrews 1:{2}5]

Jesus (God's Son), "This day have I begotten You" (Psalm 2:7) [Hebrews 1:{2}5]

Jesus (God's Son) "will be to Me a Son" [Hebrews 1:{2}5]

Jesus is the Son of God [Hebrews 4:14]

Jesus (Christ), "You are My Son" [Hebrews 5:5]

Jesus (Christ), "Today I have begotten You" (Psalm 2:7) [Hebrews 5:5]

Jesus (Christ) was a Son [Hebrews 5:{5}8]

Jesus Christ our Lord's Father is God [1 Peter 1:3]

Jesus Christ "is My beloved Son, in whom I am well pleased" (voice from the Excellent Glory) [2 Peter 1:16-17]

Jesus Christ is the Father's Son [1 John 1:3]

Jesus Christ is God's son [1 John 1:7]

Jesus Christ is God's son [1 John 3:21-23]

Jesus (God's only begotten Son) was sent by God into the world, manifesting His love toward us, that we might live through Him (Jesus) [1 John 4:9]

Jesus is the Son of God (whoever shall confess this has God abiding in him, and he in God) [1 John 4:15]

Jesus is begotten of God [1 John 5:1]

Jesus is the Son of God (he who believes this overcomes the world) [1 John 5:5]

Jesus Christ is God's Son [1 John 5:20]

Jesus Christ the Lord is the Son of God the Father [2 John 3]

E. The apostles and others claimed that Jesus had a special relationship with the Holy Spirit:

The apostles and others said:

Jesus Christ was a child of the Holy Ghost [Matthew 1:18]

Jesus Christ "is of the Holy Ghost," said an angel to Joseph [Matthew 1:{18}20]

Jesus saw the Spirit of God descending like a dove and lighting upon Him (at His baptism) [Matthew 3:16] 📖📖 Jesus, coming up out of the water, saw the heavens opened and the Spirit like a dove descending upon Him (at His baptism) [Mark 1:9-10] 📖📖📖 Jesus had the Holy Ghost descend in bodily shape like a dove upon Him (at His baptism) [Luke 3:21-22] 📖📖📖📖 Jesus "had the Spirit descend from heaven like a dove, and it abode Him," said John the Baptist, baring record of Jesus' baptism [John 1:{29}32]

Jesus was led up of (by) the Spirit into the wilderness to be tempted of (by) the devil [Matthew 4:1-11] 📖📖 Jesus was driven into the wilderness by the Spirit, and

He was there in the wilderness forty days, tempted of
(by) Satan [Mark 1:{9}12-13] ⊞⊞⊞ Jesus, being full
of the Holy Ghost returned from Jordan, and was led
by the Spirit into the wilderness, being forty days tempted of (by) the devil [Luke 4:1-2]

Jesus "Christ will baptize you with the Holy Ghost," preached John the Baptist [Mark 1:{1}8] ⊞⊞ Jesus "is He
who baptizes with the Holy Ghost," said John the Baptist,
baring record of Jesus' baptism [John 1:{29}32-33]

Jesus returned in the power of the Spirit to Galilee [Luke
4:14]

Jesus spake concerning the Spirit, whom those who believe on Him should receive: for the Holy Ghost was not
yet given, because Jesus was not yet glorified [John 7:
39]

Jesus breathed on them (to receive the Holy Spirit) [John
20:{21}22]

Jesus had given commandments through the Holy Ghost
to the apostles whom He had chosen [Acts 1:1-2]

Jesus, being assembled together with them (the apostles
whom He had chosen), commanded them that they should
not depart from Jerusalem, but wait for the promise of
the Father (the Holy Spirit), which, said He, "You have
heard of (from) me" [Acts 1:{1}4]

Jesus, "having received of (from) the Father the promise of
the Holy Ghost, shed forth this, which you now see
and hear" (Peter's explanation at Pentecost) [Acts 2:32-
33]

Jesus "of Nazareth was anointed by God with the Holy Ghost"
(Peter speaking to Cornelius' household) [Acts 10:38]

Jesus (Christ), through the eternal Spirit, offered Himself
without spot to God [Hebrews 9:14]

**F. The apostles and others claimed that Jesus is the
Christ, the Messiah, the Anointed One:**

*Christ (Greek) and Messiah (Hebrew) both mean God's
anointed.*

*"Jesus" and "Lord" and "Christ" are used together
at least 104 times (by my count) in the New Testament;
"Jesus" and "Christ" together are used 154 times and
"Christ" alone is used 270 times with 87 of them (by*

*my interpretation) pointing directly to Jesus.   There
are 9 that do not refer to Jesus at all (i.e. John the Baptist
saying he was not the Christ).   The other 174 indirectly refer to Jesus as the Christ.*

The apostles and others said:

Jesus is called Christ [Matthew 1:16]

Jesus, "You are the Christ," said Peter when Jesus asked
His disciples, "Whom do men say that I the Son of Man
am?" [Matthew 16:13-16]   📖📖 Jesus, "You are the
Christ," said Peter when Jesus asked His disciples, "Whom
do men say that I am?" [Mark 8:27-29] 📖📖📖 Jesus,
"You are the Christ of God," said Peter when Jesus
asked His disciples, "But whom say you that I am?" [Luke
9:{8:50}20]

Jesus charged His disciples that they should tell no man
that He was Jesus the Christ [Matthew 16:20]   📖📖
Jesus charged them (His disciples) that they should
tell no one about Him (that He was the Christ) [Mark
8:{27}29-30] 📖📖📖 Jesus straitly charged them (His
disciples), and commanded them to tell no man that
thing (that He was the Christ) [Luke 9:{8:50}21]

Jesus, "who is called Christ," Pilate said to the multitude
[Matthew 27:17]

Jesus, "is called Christ," Pilate said to the multitude [Matthew
27:22]

Jesus "(a Savior) is Christ the Lord, born to you this day in
the city of David," said an angel to the shepherds [Luke
2:11]

Jesus is the Lord's Christ was revealed to Simeon by the
Holy Ghost [Luke 2:25-32]

Jesus, "You are Christ, the Son of God," cried out devils,
as they came out of many [Luke 4:{35}41]

Jesus rebuked the devils, suffering them not to speak: for
they knew that He was Christ [Luke 4:{35}41]

Jesus was led to Pilate by the whole multitude, and they
began to accuse Him, saying, "We found this fellow perverting the nation and forbidding to give tribute to
Caesar, saying that He Himself is Christ a king" [Luke
23:{22:63}1-2]

Jesus "is the Messias, which is, being interpreted, the Christ,"
said Andrew to his brother, Simon [John 1:{38}41]

Jesus "is indeed the Christ" (the people of Samaria) [John 4:{34}42]

Jesus, "we believe and are sure that You are that Christ, the Son of the living God," Peter answered Him [John 6:67-69]

Jesus brought division among the people, many of them saying, "Of a truth this is the Prophet," and others saying, "This is the Christ," but some were saying, "shall Christ come out of Galilee? Has not the Scripture said, that Christ comes of the seed of David, and out of the town of Bethlehem, where David was?" [John 7:{39} 41]

Jesus, "Lord, I believe that You are the Christ, the Son of God, who should (would) come into the world," said Martha, Lazarus' sister [John 11:25-27]

Jesus is the Christ, the Son of God [John 20:31]

Jesus "was made both Lord and Christ by God" (Peter at Pentecost) [Acts 5:36]

Jesus Christ was taught and preached by the apostles [Acts 5:40-42]

Jesus is very Christ was proved by Saul to the Jews who dwelt at Damascus, and this confounded them [Acts 9:22]

Jesus, "whom I preach to you, is the Christ" (as opened and alleged out of the scriptures by Paul to the Jews in the synagogue at Thessalonica) [Acts 17:3]

Jesus was Christ (Paul's testimony to the Jews in Corinth) [Acts 18:5]

Jesus was Christ (Apollos showed this by the Scriptures, mightily convincing the Jews in Achaia of this, and that publicly) [Acts 18:28]

Jesus is the Christ (denial of this makes one a liar and antichrist) [1 John 2:22]

Jesus is the Christ (whoever believes this is born of God) [1 John 5:1]

Jesus "(our Lord's Christ), the kingdoms of this world are become the kingdoms of our Lord and of You, His Christ" (great voices in heaven) [Revelation 11:15]

Jesus "(our Lord's Christ) shall reign forever and ever" (great voices in heaven) [Revelation 11:15]

G. The apostles and others claimed that Jesus was sent by God from heaven:

Jesus was with God (the Father), came from God, went back to God and will come again from God.
Jesus was in heaven, came from heaven, went back to heaven and will come again from heaven.

The apostles and others said:

Jesus "of Nazareth, let us alone; what have we to do with You? Are You come to destroy us? I know You who You are, the Holy One of God," a man with an unclean spirit cried out [Mark 1:23-24] 🕮🕮 Jesus "of Nazareth, let us alone; what have we to do with You? Are You come to destroy us? I know You, who You are; the Holy One of God," a man with a spirit of an unclean devil cried out with a loud voice [Luke 4:33-34]

Jesus (the Word) was in the beginning with God [John 1:1-2]

Jesus "is the son of Joseph, whose father and mother we know. How is it then that He says, 'I came down from heaven'?" (the Jews) [John 6:42]

Jesus "has opened my eyes, yet you know not from whence (where) He is, herein is a marvelous thing. Now we know that God hears not sinners: but if any man be a worshipper of God, and does His will, him He hears. Since the world began was it not heard that any man opened the eyes of one that was born blind. If this man were not of (from) God, He could do nothing," said the man who was blind from his birth to the Jews [John 9:{14}30-33]

Jesus knew that he was come from God [John 13:3]

Jesus, "now are we sure that you know all things, and need not that any man should ask you: by this we believe that you came forth from God," His disciples said to Him [John 16:{19}30]

Jesus, "God's Son, was sent by God to bless you" (Peter's response to the people at the temple) [Acts 3:26]

Jesus Christ, God's own Son, was sent by God in the likeness of sinful flesh, for (because of) sin [Romans 8:2-3]

Jesus (God's Son), when the fullness of time had come, was sent forth by God [Galatians 4:4]

Jesus (God's only begotten Son) was sent by God into the world, manifesting His love toward us, that we might live through Him (Jesus) [1 John 4:9]

Jesus (God's Son) was sent by God to be the propitiation (make amends/atone) for our sins [1 John 4:10]

Jesus (the Son) was sent by the Father to be the Savior of the world [1 John 4:14]

H. The apostles and others claimed that God's love and approval was on Jesus:

Although Jesus was loved by God, God did forsake Him on the cross (Psalm 22:1) [Matthew 27:46; Mark 15:34]. Whatever all that means, it certainly means that God would not save Him from death on the cross and probably could not even look on Him as He bore the sins of the world, but God did raise Him from the dead, which is certainly a great indication that Jesus was loved by God.

The apostles and others said:

Jesus "is My beloved Son" (voice from heaven at Jesus' baptism) [Matthew 3:16-17] 📖📖 Jesus, "You are My beloved Son" (voice from heaven at Jesus' baptism) [Mark 1:9-11] 📖📖📖 Jesus, "You are My beloved Son" (voice from heaven at Jesus' baptism) [Luke 3:21-22]

Jesus, "in You I am well pleased" (voice from heaven at Jesus' baptism) [Matthew 3:16-17] 📖📖 Jesus, "in You I am well pleased" (voice from heaven at Jesus' baptism) [Mark 1:9-11] 📖📖📖 Jesus, "in You I am well pleased" (voice from heaven at Jesus' baptism) [Luke 3:21-22]

Jesus "is My beloved Son" (voice out of the cloud at Jesus' Transfiguration) [Matthew 17:{1}5] 📖📖 Jesus "is My beloved Son" (voice out of the cloud at Jesus' Transfiguration) [Mark 9:{5}7] 📖📖📖 Jesus "is My beloved Son" (voice out of the cloud at Jesus' Transfiguration) [Luke 9:35-36]

Jesus "(the Son) is loved by the Father," answered John the Baptist [John 3:35]

Jesus "(the Son) has been given all things into His hand by the Father," answered John the Baptist [John 3: 35]

Jesus "of Nazareth, a Man approved of (by) God among you by miracles and wonders and signs, which God did by Him in the midst of you, as you yourselves also know" (Peter's explanation at Pentecost) [Acts 2:22]

Jesus "was made both Lord and Christ by God" (Peter's explanation at Pentecost) [Acts 2:36]

Jesus "is Your holy child who was anointed by You" (prayer of Peter and John and their companions) [Acts 4:27]

Jesus "of Nazareth was anointed by God with the Holy Ghost" (Peter speaking to Cornelius' household) [Acts 10:38]

Jesus "of Nazareth was anointed by God with power" (Peter speaking to Cornelius' household) [Acts 10:38]

Jesus "of Nazareth had God with Him" (Peter speaking to Cornelius' household) [Acts 10:38]

Jesus (Christ), since He lives, He lives to God [Romans 6: 9-10]

Jesus' (Christ) head is God [1 Corinthians 11:3]

Jesus (God's Son) is dear to God [Colossians 1:13]

Jesus (God's Son) was appointed heir of all things by God [Hebrews 1:1-2]

Jesus (the Son), "God, even Your God, has anointed You with the oil of gladness above Your fellows" [Hebrews 1:{8}9]

Jesus (Christ) in the days of His flesh, when He had offered up prayers and supplications with strong crying and tears to Him who was able to save Him from death, and was heard in that (because) He feared [Hebrews 5:{5}7]

Jesus Christ "is My beloved Son, in whom I am well pleased" (voice from the Excellent Glory) [2 Peter 1:16-17]

I. **The apostles and others claimed the following qualities for Jesus or made the following comparisons to Jesus.**

Is anyone foolish enough to make the following claims or allow such claims to be made for him, unless one could prove them? There are many of Jesus' qualities listed in other areas of this book.

The apostles and others said:

Jesus "of Nazareth was a prophet," said Cleopas and another man to Jesus [Luke 24:13-19]

Jesus "of Nazareth was mighty in deed," said Cleopas and another man to Jesus [Luke 24:13-19]

Jesus "of Nazareth was mighty in word," said Cleopas and another man to Jesus [Luke 24:13-19]

Jesus was the Word [John 1:1, 14]

Jesus' (the Word) life was the light of men [John 1:1-4]

Jesus (the true Light) lights every man who comes into the world [John 1:1-9]

Jesus "is the Lamb of God," said John the Baptist [John 1: 29]

Jesus "is He of whom I said, 'After me comes a man who is preferred before me: for He was before me,'" said John the Baptist [John 1:29-30]

Jesus "is the Lamb of God," John the Baptist said, looking on Jesus as He walked [John 1:36]

Jesus, "God's Son, is the Holy One" (Peter's response to the people at the temple) [Acts 3:13-14]

Jesus, "God's Son, is the Just" (Peter's response to the people at the temple) [Acts 3:13-14]

Jesus, "God's Son, is the Prince of Life" (Peter's response to the people at the temple) [Acts 3:13-15]

Jesus "Christ of Nazareth, who was set a nought (deemed to be of no value) of (by) you builders, is become the head of the corner (cornerstone)" (Peter speaking to the rulers of the people and elders of Israel) (Psalm 118: 22) [Acts 4:10-11]

Jesus "(the Just One) you have been now the betrayers and murderers of," Stephen said to the council [Acts 7:52]

Jesus (Christ) is the power of God [1 Corinthians 1:24]

Jesus (Christ) is the wisdom of God [1 Corinthians 1:24]

Jesus Christ is made to us wisdom from God [1 Corinthians 1:30]

Jesus Christ is made to us righteousness from God (Jeremiah 23:6) [1 Corinthians 1:30]

Jesus is made to us sanctification from God [1 Corinthians 1: 30]

Jesus Christ is made to us redemption from God [1 Corinthians 1:30]

Jesus Christ is the foundation which is laid; (any) other foundation can no man lay [1 Corinthians 3:11]

Jesus (Christ) is our Passover [1 Corinthians 5:7]

Jesus (Christ) was the spiritual Rock that followed them (Israel during the Exodus) [1 Corinthians 10:4]

Jesus (Christ) "is the seed of Abraham" [Galatians 3:16]

Jesus Christ Himself is our peace [Ephesians 2:13-14]

Jesus Christ Himself is the chief cornerstone [Ephesians 2:20]

Jesus (Christ) is the head of the body [Ephesians 4:15-16]

Jesus (Christ) is head of the church [Ephesians 5:23]

Jesus (Christ) is savior of the body [Ephesians 5:23]

Jesus Christ our Lord is our hope [1 Timothy 1:1]

Jesus Christ has in Himself the promise of life [2 Timothy 1:1]

Jesus (God's Son) was made so much better than the angels [Hebrews 1:{2}4]

Jesus (God's Son) has by inheritance obtained a more excellent name than they (the angels) [Hebrews 1:{2}4]

Jesus Christ, this Man was counted worthy of more glory than Moses, inasmuch as He who has built the house has more honor than the house [Hebrews 3:{1}3]

Jesus was made higher than the heavens [Hebrews 7:{22} 26]

Jesus is the author of our faith [Hebrews 12:2]

Jesus is the finisher of our faith [Hebrews 12:2]

Jesus is the Mediator of the new covenant [Hebrews 12:24]

Jesus Christ our Lord is the Lord of glory [James 2:1]

Jesus Christ is the righteous [1 John 2:1]

Jesus Christ is the faithful witness [Revelation 1:5]

Jesus (the Lamb) "is the Lion of the tribe of Judah," an elder said to John [Revelation 5:5-9]

Jesus (the Lamb) "is the Root of David," an elder said to John [Revelation 5:5-9]

Jesus (one like the Son of Man, sitting on a cloud) had on His head a golden crown, and in His hand a sharp sickle [Revelation 14:14]

Jesus "(the Lamb) is Lord of lords and King of kings," an angel said to John [Revelation 17:14]

Jesus' (the king on a white horse) name is called The Word of God [Revelation 19:11-16]

Jesus (the king on a white horse) has on His vesture (garment) and on His thigh a name written: KING OF KINGS AND LORD OF LORDS [Revelation 19:11-16]

II. His Authority

The authority claimed by and for Jesus also emphasizes He was from God and is God. No one else could have such authority.

A. The apostles and others claimed that Jesus speaks for God:

The apostles and others said:

Jesus (God's Son) is God's spokesman in these last days [Hebrews 1:1-2]

B. The apostles and others claimed that Jesus has all authority:

The apostles and others said:

Jesus "(the Son) has been given all things into His hand by the Father," answered John the Baptist [John 3:35]

Jesus knew that the Father had given all things into His hands [John 13:3]

Jesus "Christ is Lord of all" (Peter speaking to Cornelius' household) [Acts 10:36]

Jesus "of Nazareth was anointed by God with power" (Peter speaking to Cornelius' household) [Acts 10:38]

Jesus (Christ) is over all [Romans 9:5]

Jesus Christ our Lord has power [1 Corinthians 5:4]

Jesus (Christ) is far above all principality, and power, and might, and dominion, and every name that is named [Ephesians 1:20-21]

Jesus (Christ) has all things put under His feet by God [Ephesians 1:20-22]

Jesus Christ the Lord is able even to subdue all things to Himself [Philippians 3:20-21]

Jesus (God's Son) is before all things [Colossians 1:{13}17]

Jesus (God's Son) has the preeminence in all things [Colossians 1:{13}18]

Jesus (God's Son) was appointed heir of all things by God [Hebrews 1:1-2]

Jesus (God's Son) upholds all things by the word of His power [Hebrews 1:{2}3]

Jesus (the Son), "I will make Your enemies Your footstool" (Psalm 110:1) [Hebrews 1:{8}13]

Jesus Christ has angels and authorities and powers made subject to Him [1 Peter 3:21-22]

Jesus has divine power [2 Peter 1:2-3]

Jesus Christ our Lord has power [2 Peter 1:16]

Jesus' "(God's Christ) power has come" (a loud voice in heaven) [Revelation 12:10]

C. The apostles and others claimed that Jesus has specific authority:

The apostles and others said:

Jesus called His twelve disciples to Him and gave them power against unclean spirits, to cast them out and to heal all manner of sickness and all manner of disease [Matthew 10:{9:35}1]

Jesus "Christ will baptize you with the Holy Ghost," preached John the Baptist [Mark 1:{1}8]

Jesus Christ is the one Mediator between God and men [1 Timothy 2:5]

Jesus Christ abolished death [2 Timothy 1:10]

Jesus destroyed him who had the power of death, that is, the devil [Hebrews 2:{9}14]

Jesus is the Mediator of the new covenant [Hebrews 12:24]

Jesus (the Son of God) gives us whatever we ask, if we ask anything according to His will [1 John 5:13-15]

Jesus Christ has made us kings and priests to God and His Father [Revelation 1:5-6]

D. The apostles and others claimed that Jesus has authority over mankind as Lord and King and is our shepherd and High Priest:

Lord means "master" or "sovereign". The words "Lord" and "Jesus" are used together in the New Testament 38 times (by my count) as, 'Jesus our/the Lord' or 'our/the Lord Jesus', etc. and another 104

times "Lord" and "Jesus" and "Christ" are used to-
gether. I did not use those that seemed to be only
titles, but the number (142) of them certainly enforces
Jesus' importance as Lord.

Daniel said that one like the Son of Man came to
the Ancient of Days and received a kingdom which
would not be destroyed [Daniel 7:13-14]. Jesus came
as Savior and will come as Savior and King.

The apostles and others said:

Jesus "was born King of the Jews, for we have seen His
star in the East, and are come to worship Him," said
wise men from the East [Matthew 2:1-2]

Jesus' doctrine astonished them, for He taught as one having authority (sermon on the mountain) [Matthew 7:
28-29]

Jesus, "grant that these my two sons may sit, the one on
Your right hand, and the other on the left, in Your
kingdom," said the mother of Zebedee's sons [Matthew
20:{17}21]

Jesus, "are You the King of the Jews?," the governor (Pilate)
asked Him [Matthew 27:11] 📖📖 Jesus, "are You the
King of the Jews?," Pilate asked Him [Mark 15:2] 📖📖📖
Jesus "are You the King of the Jews?," Pilate asked
Him [Luke 23:{22:63}3] 📖📖📖📖 Jesus, "are You the
King of the Jews?," Pilate said to Him [John 18:33]

Jesus had set up over His head (on the cross) His accusation written, "THIS IS JESUS THE KING OF THE
JEWS" [Matthew 27:37] 📖📖 Jesus had the superscription of His accusation written over (on the cross),
"THE KING OF THE JEWS" [Mark 15:{15}26] 📖📖📖
Jesus had a supercription written over Him (on the
cross) in letters of Greek, and Latin, and Hebrew: THIS
IS THE KING OF THE JEWS" [Luke 23:{34}38] 📖📖📖📖
JESUS "OF NAZARETH THE KING OF THE JEWS" was
written as a title, and put on the cross by Pilate [John
19:18-19]

Jesus astonished them at His doctrine: for He taught as
one that had authority (in the synagogue at Capernaum)
[Mark 1:{17}22]

Jesus "shall be given the throne of His Father David by
the Lord God," an angel said to Mary [Luke 1:31-32]

Jesus "shall reign over the house of Jacob forever," an angel said to Mary [Luke 1:31-33]

Jesus "shall have a kingdom with no end," an angel said to Mary [Luke 1:31-33]

Jesus "(a Savior) is Christ the Lord, born to you this day in the city of David," said an angel to the shepherds [Luke 2:11]

Jesus was led to Pilate by the whole multitude, and they began to accuse Him, saying, "We found this fellow perverting the nation, and forbidding to give tribute to Caesar, saying, that He Himself is Christ a king" [Luke 23:{22:63}1-2]

Jesus "has done nothing amiss," said the other malefactor, who then said to Jesus, "Lord, remember me when you come into Your kingdom" [Luke 23:39-42]

Jesus, "Rabbi, You are the King of Israel," Nathanael said [John 1:48-49]

Jesus, "You are my Lord," said Thomas (after he had touched Jesus' hands and side) [John 20:26-28]

Jesus "Christ is Lord of all" (Peter speaking to Cornelius' household) [Acts 10:36]

Jesus "is another king, said Jason and some brethren," cried the Jews to the rulers of Thessalonica [Acts 17:6-7]

Jesus Christ our Lord is God's son [Romans 1:3]

Jesus (Christ) is Lord of the dead [Romans 14:9]

Jesus (Christ) is Lord of the living [Romans 14:9]

Jesus Christ is our Lord [1 Corinthians 1:2]

Jesus Christ is our Lord [1 Corinthians 1:9]

Jesus (Christ) is the head of every man [1 Corinthians 11:3]

Jesus (Christ) will deliver the kingdom to God, even the Father (at the end) [1 Corinthians 15:23-24]

Jesus (Christ) will put down all rule and all authority and power [1 Corinthians 15:23-24]

Jesus (Christ) must reign, till He has put all enemies under His feet [1 Corinthians 15:{23}25]

Jesus Christ shall have every tongue confess that He is Lord (Isaiah 45:23) [Philippians 2:11]

Jesus (God's Son) has a kingdom [Colossians 1:13]

Jesus Christ is our Lord [1 Timothy 1:2]

Jesus Christ is our Lord [1 Timothy 1:12]

Jesus Christ is the one mediator between God and men [1 Timothy 2:5]

Jesus Christ will judge the quick (living) and the dead at His appearing and His kingdom [2 Timothy 4:1]

Jesus (the Son) "Your throne, O God, is forever and ever" (Psalm 45:6) [Hebrews 1:8]

Jesus (God's Son) "has a scepter of righteousness as the scepter of His kingdom" (Psalm 45:6) [Hebrews 1:8]

Jesus (the Son), "I will make Your enemies Your footstool" (Psalm 110:1) [Hebrews 1:{8}13]

Jesus is a merciful and faithful High Priest in things pertaining to God [Hebrews 2:{9}17]

Jesus Christ is the Apostle and High Priest of our confession [Hebrews 3:1]

Jesus the Son of God is our great High Priest [Hebrews 4: 14]

Jesus (Christ) glorified not himself to be made an High Priest [Hebrews 5:5]

Jesus (Christ), "You are a priest forever after the order of Melchisedec" (Psalm 110:4) [Hebrews 5:5-6]

Jesus (Christ) "was called by God a High Priest after the order of Melchisedec" (Psalm 110:4) [Hebrews 5:{5}10]

Jesus was made high priest forever ever after the order of Melchisedec [Hebrews 6:20]

Jesus has an unchangeable priesthood [Hebrews 7:{22}24]

Jesus is a High Priest [Hebrews 7:{22}26]

Jesus needs not daily, as those high priests, to offer up sacrifice, first for His own sins, and then for the people's, for this He did once, when he offered up Himself [Hebrews 7:{22}27]

Jesus (Christ) has (be)come an High Priest of the good things to come, by a greater and more perfect tabernacle, not made with hands, that is to say, not of this building [Hebrews 9:11]

Jesus (Christ) by (with) His own blood entered in once into the Holy Place, having obtained eternal redemption for us [Hebrews 9:11-12]

Jesus Christ's enemies will be made His footstool [Hebrews 10:{10}13]

Jesus is the Mediator of the new covenant [Hebrews 12:24]

Jesus our Lord is that great Shepherd of the sheep, through the blood of the everlasting covenant [Hebrews 13:20]

Jesus Christ glorifies God [1 Peter 4:11]

Jesus is our Lord [2 Peter 1:2]

Jesus Christ is our Lord [2 Peter 1:11]

Jesus Christ has an everlasting kingdom [2 Peter 1:11]

Jesus Christ is our Lord [2 Peter 1:16]

Jesus Christ is our Lord [2 Peter 2:20]

Jesus Christ is our Lord [2 Peter 3:18]

Jesus Christ is the prince of the kings of the earth [Revelation 1:5]

Jesus "(the Lamb) shall feed them and lead them to living fountains of waters," an elder said to John [Revelation 7:17]

Jesus "(our Lord's Christ), the kingdoms of this world are become the kingdoms of our Lord and of You, His Christ" (great voices in heaven) [Revelation 11:15]

Jesus "(our Lord's Christ) shall reign forever and ever" (great voices in heaven) [Revelation 11:15]

Jesus "(the Lamb) is Lord of lords and King of kings," an angel said to John [Revelation 17:14]

Jesus (the king on a white horse) has many crowns on His head [Revelation 19:11-16]

Jesus (the king on a white horse) has a sharp sword that goes out of His mouth, that with it He should smite the nations [Revelation 19:11-16]

Jesus (the king on a white horse) shall rule the nations with a rod of iron [Revelation 19:11-16]

Jesus (the king on a white horse) has on His vesture (garment) and on His thigh a name written: KING OF KINGS AND LORD OF LORDS (Revelation 19:11-16]

Jesus (Christ) will reign for a thousand years [Revelation 20:4]

Jesus (Christ) will reign for a thousand years [Revelation 20:6]

III. His Purpose

Paul said that God accomplished in Christ Jesus His eternal purpose, which was to make known by the church to the principalities and powers in the heavenly places the manifold wisdom of God [Ephesians 3:10-11].

A. **The apostles and others claimed that Jesus was the One to come as prophesied:**

The apostles and others said:

Jesus "shall save His people from their sins," said an angel to Joseph [Matthew 1:21]

Jesus "(Christ) was to be born in Bethlehem of Judea, for so it is written by the prophet," the chief priests and scribes responded to Herod (Micah 5:2) [Matthew 2:4-5]

Jesus (the young Child) was taken to Egypt with His mother by night by Joseph: and was there until the death of Herod: that it might be fulfilled which was spoken of (about) the Lord by the prophet, saying, "Out of Egypt have I called My son" (Hosea 11:1) [Matthew 2:14-15]

Jesus (the young Child) came into the land of Israel and dwelt in a city called Nazareth: that it might be fulfilled which was spoken by the prophets, "He shall be called a Nazarene" [Matthew 2:21-23]

Jesus fulfilled that which was spoken by Isaiah the prophet, saying, "Himself took our infirmities and bare our sicknesses" [Matthew 8:{14}16-17]

Jesus rode into Jerusalem on an ass, that it might be fulfilled which was spoken by the prophet, saying, "Tell the daughter of Sion, 'Behold, your King comes to you, meek, and sitting on an ass, a colt the foal of an ass'" (Zechariah 9:9) (the Triumphal Entry) [Matthew 21:1-9] 📖📖 Jesus, when He had found a young ass, sat thereon; as it is written, "Fear not, daughter of Sion: behold, your King comes, sitting on an ass's colt" (the Triumphal Entry) (Zechariah 9:9) [John 12:14-15]

Jesus' garments were parted (divided) by them, casting lots: that it might be fulfilled which was spoken by the prophet, "They parted (divided) My garments among them, and on (for) My vesture (clothing) they cast lots" (Psalm

22:18) [Matthew 27:{27}35] 📖📖 Jesus' garments were given to each of four soldiers, and they cast lots for His coat that the Scripture might be fulfilled, which says, "They parted My raiment among them, and for My vesture (clothing) they did cast lots" (Psalm 22:18) [John 19:23-24]

Jesus' body was given by Pilate to a rich man from Arimathea, named Joseph, who also himself was Jesus' disciple: and he wrapped it in a clean linen cloth, and laid it in his own new tomb, which he had hewn out in the rock: and he rolled a great stone to the door of the sepulchre (Isaiah 53:9) [Matthew 27:57-60]

Jesus was crucified with two thieves, and so the Scripture was fulfilled which says, "And He was numbered with the transgressors" (Isaiah 53:12) [Mark 15:{15} 27-28]

Jesus "shall be great," an angel said to Mary [Luke 1:31-32]

Jesus was brought to Jerusalem to be presented to the Lord, when the days of her (Mary's) purification according to the law of Moses were accomplished (as it is written in the law of the Lord, "Every male who opens the womb shall be called holy to the Lord") [Luke 2:{21}22-23]

Jesus (after His resurrection) beginning at Moses and all the prophets, expounded to them (Cleopas and another man) in all the Scriptures the things concerning Himself [Luke 24:{15}27]

Jesus "of Nazareth, the son of Joseph, is Him of whom Moses in the law, and the prophets did write," said Philip to Nathanael [John 1:45]

Jesus spake, and departed, and did hide Himself from them, but though He had done so many miracles before them, yet they believed not on Him: that the saying of Esaias the prophet might be fulfilled, which he spake, "Lord, who has believed our report? And to whom has the arm of the Lord been revealed?" (Isaiah 53:1) [John 12:36-38]

Jesus, knowing that all things were now accomplished, that the Scripture might be fulfilled, said, "I thirst" [John 19:28]

Jesus' legs were not broken. This was done that the Scripture should be fulfilled, "A bone of Him shall not be broken" (Psalm 34:20) [John 19:33-36]

Jesus' side was pierced with a spear, and forthwith came there out blood and water. This was done that again another Scripture should be fulfilled which says, "They shall look on Him whom they pierced" (Zechariah 12:10) [John 19:34-37]

Jesus "of Nazareth's flesh did not see corruption" (Peter's explanation at Pentecost) (Psalm 16:10) [Acts 2:{22}27-31]

Jesus "has fulfilled those things which God had shewed by the mouth of all His prophets, that the Christ should (would) suffer" (Peter's response to the people at the temple) [Acts 3:{13}18]

Jesus "was raised up by God again, as it is also written in the second Psalm, 'You are My Son, this day have I begotten You'" (Psalm 2:7) (Paul speaking in the Antioch synagogue) [Acts 13:33]

Jesus Christ must needs have risen again from the dead, as reasoned out of the Scriptures by Paul to the Jews in the synagogue at Thessalonica [Acts 17:1-3]

Jesus "(Christ) should (would) suffer," Paul answered King Agrippa, citing Moses and the prophets [Acts 26:{15}23]

Jesus "(Christ) should (would) be the first that should (would) rise from the dead," Paul answered King Agrippa, citing Moses and the prophets [Acts 26:{15}23]

Jesus "(Christ) should (would) show light to the people and to the Gentiles," Paul answered King Agrippa, citing Moses and the prophets [Acts 26:{15}23]

Jesus (Christ) died for our sins according to the Scriptures (Isaiah 53:12) [1 Corinthians 15:3]

Jesus (Christ) rose again the third day according to the Scriptures [1 Corinthians 15:3-4]

Jesus (Christ) was made a curse for us: for it is written, "Cursed is everyone who hangs on a tree" (Deuteronomy 21:23) [Galatians 3:13]

Jesus (Christ) was foreordained before the foundation of the world [1 Peter 1:19-20]

B. The apostles and others claimed that Jesus came to save us and give us life:

Jesus' name means "savior". He saved us from our sins, God's wrath, eternal death and sin's (Satan's) power over us [Daniel 9:24; Acts 26:17-18; Hebrews 9:{24}26], bringing us peace with God. Paul calls God the Savior [1 Timothy 1:1 and 4:10], "...of God our Savior, and the Lord Jesus Christ, who is our hope," and "...we trust in the living God, who is the Savior of all men,....", again both differentiating between God and Jesus and equating them. This act of saving includes the terms "forgiveness, redemption, justification and propitiation".

The apostles and others said:

Jesus "shall save His people from their sins," said an angel to Joseph [Matthew 1:21]

Jesus "(a Savior) is Christ the Lord, born to you this day in the city of David," said an angel to the shepherds [Luke 2:11]

Jesus "is indeed the Savior of the world" (the people of Samaria) [John 4:{34}42]

Jesus "Christ of Nazareth is the only one with salvation, for there is none other name under heaven given among men, whereby we must (can) be saved" (Peter speaking to the rulers of the people and elders of Israel) [Acts 4: 10-12]

Jesus "has been exalted by God to be a Savior" (the words of Peter and the other apostles to the council) [Acts 5:30-31]

Jesus "gives repentance to Israel" (the words of Peter and the other apostles to the council) [Acts 5:30-31]

Jesus "gives forgiveness of sins" (the words of Peter and the other apostles to the council) [Acts 5:30-31]

Jesus "is a Savior to Israel raised by God according to His promise" (Paul speaking in the Antioch synagogue) [Acts 13:23]

Jesus "justifies all who believe from all things, from which you could not be justified by the law of Moses" (Paul speaking in the Antioch synagogue) [Acts 13:{33}39]

Jesus "Christ the Lord, if believed on, shall save you and your house," said Paul and Silas to the keeper of the prison [Acts 16:25-31]

Jesus (Christ's) gospel is the power of God to salvation to everyone who believes; to the Jew first and also to the Greek [Romans 1:16]

Jesus Christ has redemption [Romans 3:24]

Jesus Christ has been set forth by God to be a propitiation (make amends/atone), through faith in His blood [Romans 3:24-25]

Jesus our Lord was raised again for our justification [Romans 4:24-25]

Jesus Christ our Lord brings us peace with God [Romans 5:1]

Jesus (Christ) justified us by His blood [Romans 5:8-9]

Jesus (Christ) saves us from wrath [Romans 5:8-9]

Jesus (Christ), God's Son, by His death reconciled us to God [Romans 5:8-10]

Jesus (Christ), God's Son, saves us by His life [Romans 5:8-10]

Jesus Christ our Lord gives us the atonement (reconciliation with God) [Romans 5:9-11]

Jesus Christ's free gift (reconciliation with God) abounded to many [Romans 5:9-15]

Jesus Christ's free gift (reconciliation with God) is of (from) many offenses to justification [Romans 5:15-16]

Jesus Christ the One Man shall make many righteous by His obedience [Romans 5:17-19]

Jesus Christ is made to us redemption from God [1 Corinthians 1:30]

Jesus (Christ) is sacrificed for us [1 Corinthians 5:7]

Jesus Christ is the one Lord by whom we are [1 Corinthians 8:6]

Jesus (Christ) shall make all alive [1 Corinthians 15:22]

Jesus Christ, with God, reconciles us to God [2 Corinthians 5:18-19]

Jesus (Christ) was made to be sin for us; that we might be made the righteousness of God in Jesus [2 Corinthians 5:20-21]

Jesus (Christ) has redeemed us from the curse of the law [Galatians 3:13]

Jesus Christ, the Beloved, brings us redemption through His blood [Ephesians 1:5-7]

Jesus Christ, the Beloved, brings us forgiveness of sins [Ephesians 1:5-7]

Jesus (Christ) is the Savior of the body [Ephesians 5:23]

Jesus Christ the Lord is the Savior [Philippians 3:20]

Jesus (God's Son) brings us redemption through His blood [Colossians 1:13-14]

Jesus (God's Son) brings us forgiveness of sins [Colossians 1:13-14]

Jesus (God's Son) made peace through the blood of the cross [Colossians 1:{13}20]

Jesus (God's Son) reconciles all things to Himself [Colossians 1:{13}20-21]

Jesus (God's Son) in the body of His flesh through death, presents us holy and unblameable and unreproveable in His sight [Colossians 1:{13}22]

Jesus delivers us from the wrath to come [1 Thessalonians 1:10]

Jesus Christ our Lord obtains salvation for us [1 Thessalonians 5:9]

Jesus Christ came into the world to save sinners [1 Timothy 1:15]

Jesus Christ gave Himself a ransom for all, to be testified in due time [1 Timothy 2:5-6]

Jesus Christ is our Savior [2 Timothy 1:10]

Jesus Christ has in Himself salvation [2 Timothy 2:10]

Jesus Christ the Lord is our Savior [Titus 1:4]

Jesus Christ is our Savior [Titus 2:13]

Jesus Christ gave Himself for us [Titus 2:13-14]

Jesus Christ redeems us from every lawless deed [Titus 2:13-14]

Jesus Christ is our Savior [Titus 3:6]

Jesus (God's Son) by Himself purged our sins [Hebrews 1:{2}3]

Jesus is the captain of their (our) salvation [Hebrews 2:{9} 10]

Jesus delivered those who through the fear of death were all their lifetime subject to bondage [Hebrews 2:{9}15]

Jesus made reconciliation (with God) for the sins of the people [Hebrews 2:{9}17]

Jesus (Christ) became the author of eternal salvation to all those who obey Him [Hebrews 5:{5}9]

Jesus is also able to save those to the uttermost who come to God by (through) Him [Hebrews 7:{22}25]

Jesus (Christ) by (with) His own blood entered in once into the Holy Place, having obtained eternal redemption for us [Hebrews 9:11-12]

Jesus (Christ) shall appear the second time without sin unto salvation, to those who look for Him [Hebrews 9:28]

Jesus Christ, this Man, offered one sacrifice for sins forever [Hebrews 10:{10}12]

Jesus Christ by one offering has perfected forever those who are sanctified [Hebrews 10:{10}14]

Jesus' (Christ) precious blood redeems us [1 Peter 1:18-19]

Jesus Christ is our Savior [2 Peter 1:1]

Jesus Christ is our Savior [2 Peter 1:11]

Jesus Christ is our Savior [2 Peter 2:20]

Jesus Christ is our Savior [2 Peter 3:18]

Jesus Christ's blood cleanses us from all sin [1 John 1:7]

Jesus Christ is the propitiation (make amends/atone) for our sins: and not for ours only, but also for the sins of the whole world [1 John 2:1-2]

Jesus (the Son) has promised us, even eternal life [1 John 2:24-25]

Jesus (God's Son) was sent by God to be the propitiation (make amends/atone) for our sins [1 John 4:10]

Jesus (the Son) was sent by the Father to be the Savior of the world [1 John 4:14]

Jesus Christ is eternal life [1 John 5:20]

Jesus washed us from our sins in His own blood [Revelation 1:5]

Jesus (the Lamb), "You have redeemed us to God by Your blood out of every kindred, and tongue, and people, and nation," sung by four beasts and four and twenty elders who fell down before the Lamb [Revelation 5:8-9]

C. The apostles and others said that Jesus brought strife and division:

The implications of Jesus' teachings, life and statements about Himself cause dissension between and among people. His life and His statements are so strong that those who believe and those who do not must be at odds. The absolute nature of statements; such as, "I am the way, the truth, and the life: no man comes to the Father, but by (through) Me" [John 14:6], brings division. In fact, He said He came to bring a sword, not peace, for His coming will "set a man at variance against his father, and the daughter against her mother" [Matthew 10:34-39].

The apostles and others said:

Jesus "is set for the fall and rising again of many in Israel," said Simeon to Mary, Jesus' mother [Luke 2:{27}34]

Jesus "is set for a sign which shall be spoken against that the thoughts of many hearts may be revealed," said Simeon to Mary, Jesus' mother [Luke 2:{27}34-35]

Jesus "is a good man," some said: others said, "No, but He deceives the people" [John 7:{6}12]

Jesus brought division among the people, many of them saying, "Of a truth this is the Prophet," and others saying, "This is the Christ," but some were saying, "shall Christ come out of Galilee? Has not the scripture said, that Christ comes of the seed of David, and out of the town of Bethlehem, where David was?" [John 7:{39}40-43]

Jesus "is not from God, because He keeps not the Sabbath day," some of the Pharisees said, and others said, "How can a man who is a sinner do such miracles?," and there was a division among them [John 9:{14}16]

Jesus' sayings caused a division again among the Jews. Many of them said, "He has a devil, and is mad: why hear you Him?," and others said, "These are not the words of Him who has a devil. Can a devil open the eyes of the blind?" [John 10:{7}19-21]

D. The apostles and others said that Jesus came to serve:

The first time He came, Jesus came to serve. The next time it will be to take over His kingdom as king.

The apostles and others said:

Jesus Christ was a minister of (to) the circumcision for the truth of God, to confirm the promises made to the fathers [Romans 15:8]

Jesus Christ took the form of a servant [Philippians 2:5-7]

E. The apostles and others said that Jesus' purpose was to do God's will.

The apostles and others said:

Jesus (Christ), since He lives, He lives to God [Romans 6:9-10]

Jesus (Christ) pleased not Himself [Romans 15:3]
Jesus' (Christ) head is God [1 Corinthians 11:3]
Jesus Christ was faithful to Him who appointed Him [Hebrews 3:1-2]

F. The apostles and others claimed that Jesus would judge and reward:

Although Jesus' purpose for coming into the world was not to judge it but to save it, His second coming will be as judge and king.

The apostles and others said:

Jesus "of Nazareth commanded us to preach to the people, and to testify that it is He who was ordained by God to be the Judge of (the) quick (those alive) and (the) dead" (Peter to Cornelius' household) [Acts 10:{38}42]

Jesus "(that Man), whom God has ordained, will judge the world in righteousness," said Paul on Mar's Hill [Acts 17:31]

Jesus Christ shall be the one by whom God will judge the secrets of men [Romans 2:16]

Jesus (Christ) has the judgment seat [Romans 14:10]

Jesus Christ our Lord has a day in which we may be blameless [1 Corinthians 1:8]

Jesus the Lord has a day [2 Corinthians 1:14]

Jesus (Christ) has the judgment seat [2 Corinthians 5:10]

Jesus (Christ) has a day until which we are to be sincere and without offense [Philippians 1:10]

Jesus (Christ) has a day that I (Paul) want to be able to rejoice in, having not run in vain, neither labored in vain, because you shine as lights in the world; holding forth the word of life [Philippians 2:15-16]

Jesus' (the Lord) day so comes as a thief in the night [1 Thessalonians 5:2]

Jesus the Lord shall be revealed in flaming fire taking vengeance on those who know not God [2 Thessalonians 1:7-8]

Jesus the Lord shall be revealed in flaming fire taking vengeance on those who obey not the gospel of our Lord Jesus Christ [2 Thessalonians 1:7-8]

Jesus Christ will judge the quick (living) and the dead at His appearing and His kingdom [2 Timothy 4:1]

Jesus (the Son), "I will make Your enemies Your footstool" (Psalm 110:1) [Hebrews 1:{8}13]

Jesus Christ's enemies will be made His footstool [Hebrews 10:{10}13]

Jesus (One like the Son of Man, sitting on a cloud) thrust in His sickle on the earth; and the earth was reaped [Revelation 14:14-16]

Jesus (the king on a white horse) in righteousness judges and makes war [Revelation 19:11-16]

Jesus (the king on a white horse) has a sharp sword that goes out of His mouth, that with it He should smite the nations [Revelation 19:11-16]

Jesus (the king on a white horse) treads the winepress of the fierceness and wrath of Almighty God [Revelation 19:11-16]

G. The Apostles and others claimed that Jesus gave God glory:

Of course, all that Jesus did gave God glory. He even said, "He who has seen Me has seen the Father" [John 14:9], and Paul said that in Christ dwells all the fullness of the Godhead bodily [Colossians 2:9].

The apostles and others said:

Jesus (Christ), through the eternal Spirit, offered Himself without spot to God [Hebrews 9:14]

H. The Apostles and others claimed that Jesus came for other reasons:

The apostles and others said:

(There are none)

IV. His Actions

Jesus did many things [John 21:25] while here on earth. Those below are included to testify to their importance in explaining who Jesus is and what He did. He preached, taught (many called Him teacher but these references were not included), prayed, performed miracles, did (and does) good things for us, intercedes for us and rewards us.

A. **The apostles and others claimed that Jesus performed miracles:**

The apostles and others said:

Jesus went about all Galilee, healing all manner of sickness and all manner of disease among the people [Matthew 4:23]

Jesus was brought all sick people who were taken with divers diseases and torments, and those who were possessed with devils, and those who were lunatick, and those who had the palsy; and He healed them [Matthew 4:23-24]

Jesus cleansed a leper [Matthew 8:1-3] 📖📖 Jesus cleansed a leper [Mark 1:40-45] 📖📖📖 Jesus cleansed a man full of leprosy [Luke 5:12-14]

Jesus healed a centurion's paralyzed servant, who lay at home sick of the palsy, grievously tormented [Matthew 8:5-13] 📖📖 Jesus healed a centurion's sick, ready to die servant [Luke 7:1-10]

Jesus touched Peter's wife's mother's hand, and the fever left her [Matthew 8:14-15] 📖📖 Jesus took Simon's wife's mother's hand, and lifted her up: and immediately the fever left her [Mark 1:{25}29-31] 📖📖📖 Jesus rebuked the fever in Simon's wife's mother, and it left her [Luke 4:{35}38-39]

Jesus was brought many who were possessed with devils: and He cast out the spirits with His word [Matthew 8:{14}16] 📖📖 Jesus cast out many devils [Mark 1:{25}34] 📖📖📖 Jesus made devils come out of many [Luke 4:{35}41]

Jesus healed all who were sick [Matthew 8:{14}16] ⊞⊞ Jesus
healed many who were sick of (with) divers (various) diseases
[Mark 1:{25}34] ⊞⊞⊞ Jesus laid His hands on every one
of the sick, and healed them [Luke 4:{35}40]

Jesus rebuked the winds and the sea: and there was a great
calm [Matthew 8:{18}23-27] ⊞⊞ Jesus rebuked the
wind and the sea, and the wind ceased, and there was a
great calm [Mark 4:{3:7}34-41] ⊞⊞⊞ Jesus rebuked
the wind and the raging of the water: and they ceased,
and there was a calm [Luke 8:{7:40} 22-25]

Jesus "is even obeyed by the winds and the sea. What man-
ner of man is this?," said the men (Jesus' disciples)
[Matthew 8:{18}27] ⊞⊞ Jesus "is even obeyed by the
wind and the sea. What manner of man is this?," they
(Jesus' disciples) said to one another [Mark 4:{3:7}34-41]
⊞⊞⊞ Jesus "commands even the winds and water,
and they obey Him. What manner of man is this!," they
(Jesus' disciples) said to one another [Luke 8:{7:40}25]

Jesus cast devils out of two who were possessed by them
[Matthew 8:28-33] ⊞⊞ Jesus cast (an) unclean spir-
it(s) out of a man [Mark 5:1-20] ⊞⊞⊞ Jesus cast devils out of a man [Luke 8:26-39]

Jesus gave permission to the devils to go into the herd of
swine, and when they were come out, they went into
the herd of swine: and, behold, the whole herd of swine
ran violently down a steep place into the sea, and perished in the waters [Matthew 8:{29}31-32] ⊞⊞ Jesus
gave the unclean spirit(s) leave to enter the swine, and
the unclean spirit(s) went out, and entered into the
swine: and the herd ran violently down a steep place
into the sea (there were about 2,000), and were choked
in the sea [Mark 5:12-13] ⊞⊞⊞ Jesus suffered (allowed) the unclean spirits to enter the swine, then went
the devils out of the man, and entered into the swine:
and the herd ran violently down a steep place into the
lake, and were choked [Luke 8:{30}31-33]

Jesus healed a man sick of the palsy [Matthew 9:1-8] ⊞⊞
Jesus healed a man sick of the palsy [Mark 2:3-12] ⊞⊞⊞
Jesus healed a man sick of the palsy [Luke 5:18-26]

Jesus raised from the dead the daughter of a certain ruler
[Matthew 9:18-26] ⊞⊞ Jesus raised from the dead the
daughter of one of the rulers of the synagogue, Jairus by

name [Mark 5:21-43] 📖📖📖 Jesus raised from the dead the only daughter of a man named Jairus, a ruler of the synagogue [Luke 8:41-56]

Jesus healed a woman who was diseased with an issue of blood twelve years, when she touched the hem of His garment [Matthew 9:19-22] 📖📖 Jesus healed a woman who had an issue of blood twelve years, when she touched His garment [Mark 5:25-34] 📖📖📖 Jesus healed a woman having an issue of blood twelve years, when she touched the border of His garment [Luke 8:43-48]

Jesus healed two blind men [Matthew 9:27-31]

Jesus cast a devil out of a dumb man possessed with a devil [Matthew 9:{30}32-34]

Jesus went about all the cities and villages, healing every sickness and every disease among the people [Matthew 9:35]

Jesus restored whole the withered hand of a man on a Sabbath day [Matthew 12:{1}9-13] 📖📖 Jesus restored whole the withered hand of a man on a Sabbath day [Mark 3:{2:19}1-5] 📖📖📖 Jesus restored the withered right hand of a man on a Sabbath [Luke 6:6-11]

Jesus healed all those in the multitude [Matthew 12:15] 📖📖 Jesus healed the people who had need of healing [Luke 9:{8:50}11]

Jesus healed one possessed with a devil, blind, and dumb (mute) [Matthew 12:{15}22] 📖📖 Jesus was casting a devil out of a dumb (mute) man [Luke 11:{10:41}14]

Jesus did not many mighty works there (His own country) because of their unbelief [Matthew 13:{57}58] 📖📖 Jesus could there do no mighty work (His own country), save that He laid His hands on a few sick folk and healed them, and He marvelled because of their unbelief [Mark 6:{4}5-6]

Jesus fed about 5,000 men, beside women and children with five loaves and two fish [Matthew 14:13-21] 📖📖 Jesus fed about 5,000 men with five loaves of bread and two fish [Mark 6:32-44] 📖📖📖 Jesus fed about 5,000 men with five loaves and two fish [Luke 9:{8:50} 12-17] 📖📖📖📖 Jesus fed about 5,000 men with five loaves and two fish [John 6:1-14]

Jesus healed the sick in the multitude [Matthew 14:14]

Jesus went to them (His disciples), walking on the sea [Matthew 14:22-33] ⊞⊞ Jesus came to them (His disciples), walking on the sea [Mark 6:{34}45-52] ⊞⊞⊞ Jesus walked on the sea [John 6:15-21]

Jesus made the diseased who touched the hem of His garment perfectly whole [Matthew 14:{31}35-36] ⊞⊞ Jesus healed the sick who touched Him (border of His garment?) [Mark 6:{34}56]

Jesus made whole the daughter of a woman of Canaan who was grievously vexed with a devil [Matthew 15:21-28] ⊞⊞ Jesus cast forth (out) a devil from the young daughter of a Syro-Phoenician woman [Mark 7:24-30]

Jesus healed the lame, blind, mute, maimed and many others [Matthew 15:29-30]

Jesus made the multitude wonder, when they saw the dumb to speak, the maimed to be whole, the lame to walk, and the blind to see [Matthew 15:29-31]

Jesus fed 4,000 men, beside women and children, with seven loaves and a few fish [Matthew 15:32-39] ⊞⊞ Jesus fed 4,000 with seven loaves and a few fish [Mark 8:1-10]

Jesus rebuked the devil, and he departed out of him (a child) [Matthew 17:14-21] ⊞⊞ Jesus rebuked a foul (deaf and dumb) spirit in a child, and it came out of him [Mark 9:14-29] ⊞⊞⊞ Jesus rebuked an unclean spirit, healing a child who was thrown down and torn by the devil [Luke 9:37-42]

Jesus was followed by great multitudes: and He healed them [Matthew 19:2]

Jesus gave sight to two blind men [Matthew 20:29-34]

Jesus healed the blind and the lame who came to Him in the temple [Matthew 21:{12}14]

Jesus did wonderful things, as seen by the chief priests and scribes [Matthew 21:{12}15]

Jesus caused a fig tree to wither away [Matthew 21:18-22] ⊞⊞ Jesus caused a fig tree to wither away [Mark 11:12-22]

Jesus rebuked an unclean spirit, and it cried out with a loud voice and came out of him (the man with an unclean spirit) [Mark 1:23-28] ⊞⊞ Jesus rebuked an unclean devil and it came out of him (the man with a spirit of an unclean devil) [Luke 4:33-37]

Jesus amazed them all, insomuch that they questioned among themselves, saying, "What thing is this? What new doctrine is this? For with authority, commands He even the unclean spirits, and they do obey Him" (those in the synagogue at Capernaum who saw Jesus cast an unclean spirit out of a man) [Mark 1:25-27] 📖📖 Jesus amazed all, and they spake among themselves, saying, "What a word is this! For with authority and power He commands the unclean spirits, and they come out" (people in Capernaum who saw Jesus cast an unclean devil out of a man) [Luke 4:35-36]

Jesus cast out devils [Mark 1:{25}39]

Jesus had healed many; insomuch that they pressed upon Him for to touch Him, as many as had plagues [Mark 3:{7}10]

Jesus healed a deaf man with an impediment in his speech [Mark 7:{27}31-37]

Jesus astonished them beyond measure, so they were saying, "He has done all things well: He makes both the deaf to hear and the dumb (mute) to speak" [Mark 7:{27}37]

Jesus gave sight to a blind man [Mark 8:{17}22-26]

Jesus gave sight to blind Bartimaeus [Mark 10:46-52] 📖📖 Jesus gave sight to a certain blind man [Luke 18:35-43]

Jesus (the Lord) worked with them (the eleven), confirming the word with signs following (after He was received up into heaven) [Mark 16:20]

Jesus "depart from me; for I am a sinful man, O Lord," Simon Peter said in astonishment after catching many fish at Jesus' command [Luke 5:{4:35}4-9]

Jesus healed those with diseases and those who were vexed with unclean spirits [Luke 6:{11}17-19]

Jesus' power healed those who sought to touch Him [Luke 6:{11}19]

Jesus (the Lord) raised the widow's son from the dead [Luke 7:11-16]

Jesus, in that same hour, cured many of their infirmities and plagues, and of evil spirits; and to many who were blind He gave sight [Luke 7:{19}21]

Jesus healed Mary called Magdalene, out of whom went seven devils, Joanna the wife of Chusa Herod's steward, Susanna and many others who had been healed of evil spirits and infirmities [Luke 8:{7:40}2-3]

Jesus healed, on the Sabbath, a (Satan-bound) woman who
had a spirit of infirmity eighteen years, and was bowed
together, and could in no wise lift up herself [Luke 13:
10-17]

Jesus healed a man with dropsy on the Sabbath day [Luke
14:1-6]

Jesus cleansed ten lepers [Luke 17:11-19]

Jesus healed the cut-off ear of the servant of the high priest
[Luke 22:47-51]

Jesus changed water to wine at a wedding in Cana [John
2:1-10]

Jesus was in Jerusalem at the Passover, and in the feast
day, many believed in His name when they saw the
miracles which He did [John 2:{13}23]

Jesus healed a nobleman's child who had a fever [John 4:
46-54]

Jesus healed a man at the pool of Bethesda on the Sabbath,
who had an infirmity thirty and eight years [John 5:1-
16]

Jesus was followed by a great multitude, because they
saw His miracles which He did on those who were diseased [John 6:1-2]

Jesus "is of a truth the Prophet who should (would) come
into the world," said those men (His disciples), when
they had seen the miracle (feeding the 5,000) that Jesus
did [John 6:14]

Jesus was believed on by many of the people who said,
"When Christ comes, will He do more miracles than these
which this Man has done?" [John 7:{28}31]

Jesus healed on a Sabbath a man who was blind from
birth [John 9:1-41]

Jesus "made clay, and anointed mine eyes, and said to
me, 'Go to the pool of Siloam, and wash:' and I went
and washed, and I received sight," said the man blind
from birth to the neighbors and those who before had
seen that he was blind [John 9:11-15]

Jesus raised Lazarus from the dead [John 11:1-44]

Jesus truly did many other signs in the presence of His
disciples, which are not written in this book [John 20:
30]

Jesus "of Nazareth, a Man approved of (by) God among you
by miracles and wonders and signs, which God did by

Him in the midst of you, as you yourselves also know"
(Peter's explanation at Pentecost) [Acts 2:22]
Jesus "Christ makes you whole: arise and make your bed,"
said Peter to Aeneas [Acts 9:34]
Jesus "of Nazareth healed all who were oppressed of (by) the
devil" (Peter speaking to Cornelius' household) [Acts 10:
38]

**B. The apostles and others claimed that Jesus does and
has done many other things, including teaching, preaching and praying:**

*There are other actions Jesus did or will do that
are located in other portions of this book.*

The apostles and others said:

Jesus was baptized by John in the Jordan [Matthew 3:13-
16] 𝄢𝄢 Jesus was baptized of (by) John in Jordan
[Mark 1:9] 𝄢𝄢𝄢 Jesus was baptized [Luke 3:21]
Jesus dwelt in Capernaum [Matthew 4:13]
Jesus began to preach [Matthew 4:17]
Jesus asked Simon called Peter, and Andrew his brother,
James the son of Zebedee, and John his brother to follow Him [Matthew 4:18-22] 𝄢𝄢 Jesus called Simon
and Andrew his brother, James the son of Zebedee, and
John his brother, and they went after Him [Mark 1:16-
20]
Jesus went about all Galilee, teaching in their synagogues
[Matthew 4:23]
Jesus went about all Galilee, preaching the gospel of the
kingdom [Matthew 4:23]
Jesus taught them (the multitudes on a mountain) [Matthew
5:{4:23}1-2]
Jesus' doctrine astonished them, for He taught as one having authority (sermon on the mountain) [Matthew 7:28-
29]
Jesus told him (the leper) to tell no one (about his cleansing) [Matthew 8:4] 𝄢𝄢 Jesus straitly charged him
(the leper) to say nothing to any man (about his
cleansing) [Mark 1:{41}43-44] 𝄢𝄢𝄢 Jesus charged

him (the man full of leprosy) to tell no one (about his cleansing) [Luke 5:12-14]

Jesus made the men (His disciples) marvel (by calming the winds and the sea) [Matthew 8:{18}27] ⬛⬛ Jesus made them (His disciples) fear exceedingly (by calming the wind and the sea) [Mark 4:{3:7}39-41] ⬛⬛⬛ Jesus made them (His disciples) afraid and wonder (by calming the wind and the sea) [Luke 8:{7:40}25]

Jesus went about all the cities and villages, teaching in their synagogues [Matthew 9:35]

Jesus went about all the cities and villages, preaching the gospel of the kingdom [Matthew 9:35]

Jesus called His twelve disciples to Him and gave them power against unclean spirits, to cast them out, and to heal all manner of sickness and all manner of disease [Matthew 10:{9:35}1] ⬛⬛ Jesus called the twelve to Him, and began to send them forth two by two; and gave them power over unclean spirits [Mark 6:{4}7] ⬛⬛⬛ Jesus called His twelve disciples together, and gave them power and authority over all devils, and to cure diseases, and He sent them to preach the kingdom of God, and to heal the sick [Luke 9:{8:50}1-2]

Jesus' twelve apostles are these; The first, Simon, who is called Peter, and Andrew his brother; James the son of Zebedee, and John his brother; Philip and Bartholomew; Thomas and Matthew the publican; James the son of Alphaeus, and Lebbaeus, whose surname was Thaddaeus; Simon the Canaanite, and Judas Iscariot, who also betrayed Him [Matthew 10:{9:35}1-3] ⬛⬛ Jesus called to Him whom He would, and He ordained twelve, that they should be with Him, and that He might send them forth to preach, and to have power to heal sicknesses, and to cast out devils: and Simon He surnamed Peter; and James the son of Zebedee, and John the brother of James; and He surnamed them Boanerges, which is, The sons of thunder: and Andrew, and Philip, and Bartholomew, and Matthew, and Thomas, and James the son of Alphaeus, and Thaddaeus, Simon the Canaanite; and Judas Iscariot [Mark 3:{7}13-19] ⬛⬛⬛ Jesus called to Him His disciples: and of (from) them He chose twelve, whom also He named apostles; Simon, (whom He also named Peter), and Andrew his brother, James and John, Philip and

Bartholomew, Matthew and Thomas, James the son of Alphaeus, and Simon called the Zelotes, Judas, the brother of James, and Judas Iscariot, who also was the traitor [Luke 6:{11}13-17]

Jesus departed thence to teach and to preach in their cities [Matthew 11:1]

Jesus did works [Matthew 11:2]

Jesus charged the multitudes that they should not make Him known [Matthew 12:15-16]

Jesus amazed all the people [Matthew 12:{15}22-23]

Jesus spoke (put forth, etc.) many things to them in parables [Matthew 13:1-3 and 10 and 24 and 31 and 33 and 34 and 53]

Jesus, when He had come to His own country, taught them in their synagogue [Matthew 13:{51}54]

Jesus astonished those of His own country with His wisdom and mighty works [Matthew 13:{51}54]

Jesus offended them (the people of His own country) [Matthew 13:57]

Jesus took the five loaves, and the two fish, and looking up to heaven, He blessed, and brake (them), and gave the loaves to His disciples [Matthew 14:{16}19] ▯▯ Jesus, when He had taken the five loaves and the two fish, looked up to heaven, and blessed, and brake the loaves, and gave them to His disciples to set before them; and the two fish divided He among them all [Mark 6:{34}41] ▯▯▯ Jesus took the five loaves and the two fish, and looking up to heaven, He blessed them, and brake (them), and gave (them) to the disciples to set before the multitude [Luke 9:{8:50}16] ▯▯▯▯ Jesus took the loaves, and when He had given thanks, He distributed them to the disciples: and likewise of the fish [John 6:11]

Jesus, when He had sent the multitudes away, went up into a mountain apart to pray [Matthew 14:22-23]

Jesus stretched forth His hand, and caught him (Peter), as he was beginning to sink [Matthew 14:30-31]

Jesus offended the Pharisees (because He said that it is what came out of the mouth that defiles a man not what goes into it) [Matthew 15:{1}12]

Jesus commanded the multitude to sit down on the ground, and He took the seven loaves and the fish, and gave thanks, brake them and gave (them) to His disciples [Matthew 15:{34}35-36] ⬜⬜ Jesus commanded the people to sit down on the ground: and He took the seven loaves, and gave thanks, and brake (the loaves), and gave (them) to His disciples to set before them (the people); and He blessed a few small fish, and commanded them (His disciples) to set them also before them (the people) [Mark 8:{1}6-7]

Jesus told them (His disciples) to beware of the doctrine of the Pharisees and Sadducees [Matthew 16:{8}12]

Jesus talked with Moses and Elias (at the Transfiguration) [Matthew 17:{1}3] ⬜⬜ Jesus talked with Moses and Elias (at the Transfiguration) [Mark 9:4] ⬜⬜⬜ Jesus talked with two men, Moses and Elias (at the Transfiguration) [Luke 9:{8:50}28-31]

Jesus charged them (Peter, James and John), that they should tell the vision to no man, until the Son of Man (Jesus Himself) be risen again from the dead [Matthew 17:9] ⬜⬜ Jesus charged them (Peter, James and John) that they should tell no man what things they had seen (the Transfiguration), till the Son of Man (Jesus Himself) were risen from the dead [Mark 9:{8}9]

Jesus laid His hands on the little children [Matthew 19:13-15] ⬜⬜ Jesus took the young children up in His arms, put His hands on them, and blessed them [Mark 10:13-16] ⬜⬜⬜ Jesus was brought also infants, that He would touch them [Luke 18:15-17]

Jesus was set on an ass and a very great multitude spread their garments in the way; others cut down branches from the trees, and strawed (spread) them in the way, and the multitude that went before, and that followed cried, saying: "Hosanna to the son of David: blessed is He who comes in the name of the Lord; Hosanna in the Highest" (the Triumphal Entry) [Matthew 21:6-9] ⬜⬜ Jesus sat on the colt and many spread their garments in the way: and others cut down branches off the trees, and strawed (spread) them in the way, and they that went before, and they that followed cried, saying: "Hosanna; blessed is He who comes in the name of the Lord: blessed be the kingdom of our father David, that comes in the name of the Lord: Hosanna in the Highest" (the Triumphal Entry) [Mark

11:6-11] □□□□ Jesus was set on the colt, and as He went, they spread their clothes in the way, and when He was come nigh, even now at the descent of the Mount of Olives, the whole multitude of the disciples began to rejoice and praise God with a loud voice for all the mighty works that they had seen; saying: "Blessed be the King who comes in the name of the Lord: peace in heaven, and glory in the highest" (the Triumphal Entry) [Luke 19:35-38] □□□□□ Jesus was met by much people that were come to the feast, when they heard that He was coming to Jerusalem, and they took branches of palm trees, and cried, "Hosanna: blessed is The King of Israel who comes in the name of the Lord" (the Triumphal Entry) [John 12:12-13]

Jesus went into the temple of God and cast out all them who sold and bought in the temple [Matthew 21:12] □□ Jesus went into the temple, and began to cast out them who sold and bought in the temple, and overthrew the tables of the moneychangers, and the seats of them who sold doves; and would not suffer (let) that any man should carry any vessel through the temple [Mark 11:15] □□□ Jesus went into the temple, and began to cast out those who sold therein, and those who bought [Luke 19:{35}45]

Jesus made the chief priests and scribes sore displeased (by the wonderful things He did, and by the children crying out in the temple and saying, "Hosanna to the Son of David") [Matthew 21:{12}15]

Jesus was teaching in the temple [Matthew 21:23-24]

Jesus spoke to them again by parables [Matthew 22:1]

Jesus made them (Pharisees) marvel (because of His response about the payment of taxes) [Matthew 22:{18} 21-22]

Jesus astonished the multitudes at His doctrine [Matthew 22:23-33]

Jesus had silenced the Sadducees [Matthew 22:{29}34]

Jesus was not answered a word by any man, neither durst (did) any man from that day forth ask Him any more questions [Matthew [22:{41}46]

Jesus, as they were eating (the Passover meal), took bread, and blessed it, and brake it, and gave it to the disciples [Matthew 26:26] □□ Jesus, as they did eat (the Passover

meal), took bread, and blessed and brake it, and gave to
them (the twelve) [Mark 14:22] ▨▨▨ Jesus took bread
(at the Passover meal), and gave thanks, and brake it, and
gave it to them (the twelve apostles) [Luke 22:{20:34}19]

Jesus took the cup (at the Passover meal), and gave thanks,
and gave it to them (His disciples) [Matthew 26:{26}27]
▨▨ Jesus took the cup (at the Passover meal), and
when He had given thanks, He gave it to them (the
twelve) [Mark 14:{22}23] ▨▨▨ Jesus likewise also
took the cup after supper (at the Passover meal) [Luke
22:{20:34}20]

Jesus held His peace (kept silent) before the high priest
(Isaiah 53:7) [Matthew 26:63]

Jesus, when He was accused of (by) the chief priests and
elders, and when Pilate said to Him, "Hear You not
how many things they testify against You?," answered
never a word [Matthew 27:11-14] ▨▨ Jesus, while
being accused of many things by the chief priests, and
when Pilate asked Him again, saying, "Answer You
nothing?   Behold how many things they witness
against You," answered nothing (Isaiah 53:7) [Mark
15:3-5]

Jesus "goes before you (His disciples) into Galilee," an angel said to Mary Magdalene and the other Mary [Matthew
28:5-7] ▨▨ Jesus "is going before you into Galilee:
there shall you see Him, as He said to you," a young
man in a long white garment said to Mary Magdalene,
Mary the mother of James, and Salome [Mark 16:{6}7]

Jesus went into Capernaum, and straightway on the Sabbath
day He entered the synagogue, and taught [Mark 1:{17}
21]

Jesus astonished them at His doctrine: for He taught them as
one that had authority (in the synagogue at Capernaum)
[Mark 1:{17}22]

Jesus suffered not (did not allow) the devils to speak, because
they knew Him [Mark 1:{25}34]

Jesus departed into a solitary place, and there prayed [Mark
1:{25}35]

Jesus preached in their synagogues throughout all Galilee
[Mark 1:{25}39]

Jesus preached the word to them [Mark 2:{1:45}2]

Jesus taught the multitude [Mark 2:{8}13]

Jesus straitly charged the unclean spirits that they should not make Him known [Mark 3:{7}11-12]

Jesus began to teach by the sea side, and He taught them many things by parables [Mark 4:{3:7}2]

Jesus, with many such parables, spake the word to them, as they were able to hear it, but without a parable spake He not to them [Mark 4:{3:7}33-34]

Jesus, when they were alone, expounded (explained) all things (that He had said in parables) to His disciples, [Mark 4:{3:7} 34]

Jesus made all men of Decapolis marvel (because He cast unclean spirits out of a man) [Mark 5:20]

Jesus charged them (Peter, James, John, the father and mother of the child) straitly that no man should know it (raising Jairus' daughter from the dead) [Mark 5: {36}43] ⬙⬙ Jesus charged Jairus' daughter's parents that they should tell no man what was done (His raising her from the dead) [Luke 8:{50}56]

Jesus began to teach in the synagogue on the Sabbath [Mark 6:{5:36}2]

Jesus astonished many (of His own country), so they said, "From whence has this Man these things? And what wisdom is this which is given to him, that even such mighty works are wrought by His hands" [Mark 6: {5:36}2]

Jesus offended them (the people of His own country) [Mark 6:{5:36}3]

Jesus went roundabout the villages, teaching [Mark 6:{4}6]

Jesus began to teach them (much people in the desert) many things [Mark 6:34]

Jesus charged them that they should tell no one (about the healing of a deaf man with an impediment in his speech) [Mark 7:{27}36]

Jesus rebuked Peter, because Peter began to rebuke Him for saying that He must suffer and be killed [Mark 8: {27}31-33]

Jesus, as He was wont (accustomed), taught them again [Mark 10:{9:39}1]

Jesus took aside the twelve, and began to tell them what things should (would) happen to Him [Mark 10:32]

Jesus entered into Jerusalem, and into the temple: and when He had looked round about on all things, and now the eventide was come, He went out to Bethany with the twelve [Mark 11:11]

Jesus began to speak to them by (with) parables [Mark 12: {11:33}1]

Jesus taught in the temple [Mark 12:35]

Jesus appeared first to Mary Magdalene (after He rose from the dead), out of whom He had cast seven devils [Mark 16:9]

Jesus, after that, appeared in another form to two of them, as they walked [Mark 16:{9}12]

Jesus, afterward, appeared to the eleven as they sat at meat [Mark 16:{9}14]

Jesus upbraided the eleven with (for) their unbelief and hardness of heart, because they believed not those who had seen Him after He was risen [Mark 16:{9}14]

Jesus, when He was 12 years old, was found sitting in the midst of doctors in the temple, both listening to them and asking them questions, and all who heard Him were astonished at His understanding and answers [Luke 2: 42-47]

Jesus taught in their synagogues [Luke 4:14-15]

Jesus went into the synagogue at Nazareth on the Sabbath day, and stood up to read [Luke 4:{14}16]

Jesus made them (those in the synagogue at Nazareth) wonder at the gracious words which proceeded out of His mouth [Luke 4:{14}22]

Jesus filled them (those in the synagogue at Nazareth) with wrath, when they heard these things, and they rose up and thrust Him out of the city, and they led Him to the brow of the hill whereon their city was built, that they might cast Him down headlong, but He passing through the midst of them went on His way [Luke 4:{14}28-30]

Jesus came down to Capernaum, a city of Galilee, and was teaching them on the Sabbath days [Luke 4:{14}31]

Jesus astonished them (in Capernaum) at His doctrine: for His word was with power [Luke 4:{14}32]

Jesus preached in the synagogues of Galilee [Luke 4:{35}44]

Jesus taught the people out of the ship [Luke 5:{4:35}3]

Jesus was teaching [Luke 5:{12}17]

Jesus amazed them all (by healing the man sick of the palsy) [Luke 5:{22}26]

Jesus spake a parable to them [Luke 5:{31}36]

Jesus taught in the synagogue on another Sabbath [Luke 6:{3}6]

Jesus filled them (the scribes and Pharisees) with madness (because He healed the man with a withered hand on the Sabbath) [Luke 6:9-11]

Jesus went out into a mountain to pray, and continued all night in prayer to God [Luke 6:{11}12]

Jesus spake a parable to them [Luke 6:{11}39]

Jesus "forgives sins also," they who sat at meat with Him began to say within themselves [Luke 7:{40}49]

Jesus went throughout every city and village, preaching and showing the glad tidings of the kingdom of God [Luke 8:{7:40}1]

Jesus spake to much people by (with) a parable [Luke 8:{7:40}4]

Jesus received the people, and spake to them of (about) the kingdom of God [Luke 9:{8:50}11]

Jesus was alone praying [Luke 9:{8:50}18]

Jesus' made everyone wonder at all the things He did [Luke 9:43]

Jesus (the Lord) appointed other seventy also, and sent them two and two before His face into every city and place, where He himself would come [Luke 10:1]

Jesus rejoiced in spirit [Luke 10:21]

Jesus was praying [Luke 11:{10:41}1]

Jesus made the people wonder (by casting a devil out of a dumb (mute) man) [Luke 11:{10:41}14]

Jesus spake a parable to them [Luke 12:{10:41}16]

Jesus (Lord) "speak You this parable to us, or even to all?," Peter said to Him [Luke 12:{10:41}41]

Jesus spake also this parable [Luke 13:{2}6]

Jesus was teaching in one of the synagogues on the Sabbath [Luke 13:{2}10]

Jesus' adversaries were ashamed (after His answer to the ruler of the synagogue about healing the Satan bound woman on the Sabbath) [Luke 13:{12}17]

Jesus went through the cities and villages, teaching, and journeying toward Jerusalem [Luke 13:{12}22]

Jesus put forth a parable to those who were bidden, when He marked how they chose out the chief rooms (to honor themselves) [Luke 14:{3}7]

Jesus spake this parable to them [Luke 15:{14:3}3]

Jesus spake a parable to them to this end, that men ought always to pray, and not to faint [Luke 18:{17:17}1]

Jesus spake this parable to certain (people) who trusted in themselves that they were righteous, and despised others [Luke 18{17:17}9]

Jesus added and spake a parable, because He was nigh to Jerusalem, and because they thought that the kingdom of God should appear immediately [Luke 19:{9}11]

Jesus taught daily in the temple, but the chief priests and the scribes and the chief of the people sought to destroy Him, and could not find what they might do: for all the people were very attentive to hear Him [Luke 19:{35}47-48]

Jesus taught the people in the temple [Luke 20:{19:35}1]

Jesus preached the gospel in the temple [Luke 20:{19:35} 1]

Jesus began to speak this parable [Luke 20:8-9]

Jesus was teaching in the temple [Luke 21:{20:34}37-38]

Jesus took the cup (at the Passover meal), and gave thanks [Luke 22:{20:34}14-17]

Jesus (after His resurrection) beginning at Moses and all the prophets, expounded to them (Cleopas and another man) in all the Scriptures the things concerning Himself [Luke 24:{15}27]

Jesus took bread, and blessed it, and brake (it), and gave (it) to them, and their eyes were opened, and they knew Him [Luke 24:{15}30-31]

Jesus vanished out of their sight [Luke 24:{15}31]

Jesus "talked with us by the way, and opened to us the Scriptures, and our heart burned within us," Cleopas and another man said to one another [Luke 24:{15}32]

Jesus Himself stood in the midst of them (the eleven and them who were with them), but they were terrified and affrighted, and supposed they had seen a spirit (after His resurrection) [Luke 24:36-37] 𝄆𝄇 Jesus came and stood in the (their) midst that same day at evening, being the first day of the week, when the doors were shut where the disciples were assembled for fear of the Jews [John 20:19]

Jesus showed them (the eleven and those who were with them) His hands and feet, and while they yet believed not for joy, and wondered, He took a piece of boiled

fish, and of an honeycomb, and did eat before them
(after His resurrection) [Luke 24:{36}40-43] 🕮🕮 Jesus
shewed them His hands and His side (after His resurrection). Then were the disciples glad, when they saw
the Lord [John 20:{19} 20]

Jesus opened their (the eleven and them who were with
them) understanding, that they might understand the
Scriptures [Luke 24:{36}45]

Jesus led them out as far as to Bethany, and He lifted up
His hands and blessed them (the eleven and them who
were with them) [Luke 24:50]

Jesus Christ brought grace and truth [John 1:17]

Jesus Christ has declared God [John 1:17-18]

Jesus found Philip (and told him to follow Him) [John 1:43]

Jesus went up to Jerusalem at the Jew's Passover [John 2:
13]

Jesus drove those who sold oxen and sheep and doves, and
the changers of money from the temple [John 2:13-15]

Jesus did not commit Himself to them, because He knew all
men, and needed not that any should testify of man: for
He knew what was in man [John 2:23-24]

Jesus and His disciples came into the land of Judea; and
there He tarried with them, and baptized [John 3:22]

Jesus Himself baptized not [John 4:2]

Jesus' disciples marveled that He talked with the woman
(the woman at the well) [John 4:{26}27]

Jesus "told me all things that ever I did: is not this the
Christ?," said the woman at the well to the men of
Samaria [John 4:{26}29]

Jesus was believed on by many of the Samaritans of that
city, because of the saying of the woman (at the well),
and many more believed because of His own word [John
4:{26}39-41]

Jesus Himself testified, that a prophet has no honor in his
own country [John 4:44]

Jesus was received by the Galileans, having seen all the
things He did at Jerusalem at the feast [John 4:{44}45]

Jesus taught in the synagogue in Capernaum [John 6:{53}
59]

Jesus, when His brothers had gone up, then went He also
up to the feast (the Jews' Feast of Tabernacles), not openly, but as it were in secret [John 7:{6}10]

Jesus went up into the temple and taught [John 7:14]

Jesus cried out, as He taught in the temple [John 7:28]

Jesus taught in the temple [John 8:1-2]

Jesus taught in the temple [John 8:20]

Jesus rose from supper, and laid aside His garments; and took a towel, and girded Himself; after that He poured water into a basin, and began to wash the disciples' feet, and to wipe them with the towel werewith He was girded [John 13:3-5]

Jesus "(Lord), do You wash my feet?," Peter said to Him, and continued, after Jesus said he would know (why) hereafter (later), "You shall never wash my feet," and then said, after Jesus told him that if He washed him not, he had no part with Him, "Lord, not my feet only but also my hands and my head!" [John 13:6-10]

Jesus, "whence (where) are You (from)?," Pilate said to Him, but Jesus gave him no answer (Isaiah 53:7) [John 19:9]

Jesus did many other things [John 21:25]

Jesus began to do [Acts 1:1]

Jesus began to teach [Acts 1:1]

Jesus spoke of things pertaining to the Kingdom of God, after His passion (death) [Acts 1:1-3]

Jesus "(Christ) should (would) show light to the people and to the Gentiles," Paul answered King Agrippa, citing Moses and the prophets [Acts 26:{15}23]

Jesus (Christ) also received us [Romans 15:7]

Jesus Christ gives you the grace of God [1 Corinthians 1:4]

Jesus Christ enriches you in everything, in utterance, and in all knowledge [1 Corinthians 1:4-5]

Jesus (Christ) did not send me (Paul) to baptize, but to preach the gospel [1 Corinthians 1:17]

Jesus the Lord, the same night in which He was betrayed, took bread: and when He had given thanks, he brake it, and said, "Take eat: this is My body, which is broken for you: this do in remembrance of Me" [1 Corinthians 11:23-24]

Jesus the Lord, when He had supped, took the cup, saying, "This cup is the new testament in My blood: this do you, as oft as you drink it, in remembrance of Me" [1 Corinthians 11:23-25]

Jesus (Christ) will destroy death, as the last enemy [1 Corinthians 15:{23}26]

Jesus Christ our Lord is the One through whom God, gives us the victory [1 Corinthians 15:57]

Jesus' (Christ) consolation abounds in us [2 Corinthians 1:5]

Jesus Christ our Lord delivers us from the present evil world [Galatians 1:3-4]

Jesus Christ revealed the gospel to Paul [Galatians 1:11-12]

Jesus "(Christ) lives in me," said Paul to Peter and the others [Galatians 2:20]

Jesus "(Christ) loved me," said Paul to Peter and the others [Galatians 2:20]

Jesus "(Christ) gave Himself for me," said Paul to Peter and the others [Galatians 2:20]

Jesus Christ gives the Gentiles the blessing of Abraham [Galatians 3:14]

Jesus (Christ) has made you an heir of God [Galatians 4:7]

Jesus (Christ) has made us free [Galatians 5:1]

Jesus Christ's blood brings us nigh [Ephesians 2:13]

Jesus Christ has made both (Jews and Gentiles) one, and has broken down the middle wall of partition between us; having abolished in His flesh the enmity, even the law of commandments contained in ordinances; for to make in Himself of two one new man, so making peace [Ephesians 2:13-15]

Jesus Christ reconciles both (Jews and Gentiles) to God in one body through the cross [Ephesians 2:{13}16]

Jesus Christ preached peace to you who were far off, and to those who were nigh [Ephesians 2:{13}17]

Jesus Christ gives us access by one Spirit to the father [Ephesians 2:{13}18]

Jesus Christ our Lord completed God's eternal purpose of showing His manifold wisdom by (through) the church to the principalities and powers in heavenly places [Ephesians 3:10-11]

Jesus (Christ) "led captivity captive" (Psalm 68:18) [Ephesians 4:7-8]

Jesus (Christ) "gave gifts to men" (Psalm 68:18) [Ephesians 4:7-8]

Jesus (Christ) gave some, apostles; some, prophets; some, evangelists; and some pastors and teachers [Ephesians 4:{7}11]

Jesus (Christ) gave Himself for us an offering and a sacrifice to God for a sweetsmelling savor [Ephesians 5:2]

Jesus "(Christ) shall give you light" [Ephesians 5:14]

Jesus (Christ) also loved the church [Ephesians 5:25]

Jesus (Christ) gave Himself for it (the church) [Ephesians 5:25]

Jesus (Christ) sanctified and cleansed the church [Ephesians 5:25-26]

Jesus (Christ) will present it (the church) to Himself a glorious church, not having spot, or wrinkle, or any such thing; but that it should be holy and without blemish [Ephesians 5:25-27]

Jesus (Christ) strengthens me, so I can do all things (Paul) [Philippians 4:13]

Jesus' (Christ) circumcision puts off the body of the sins of the flesh [Colossians 2:11]

Jesus (Christ) forgave you [Colossians 3:13]

Jesus (the Lord) shall consume that Wicked (one), who shall be revealed, with the spirit of His mouth, and shall destroy with the brightness of His coming [2 Thessalonians 2:8]

Jesus Christ our Lord Himself, and God, even our Father, who has loved us, and given us everlasting consolation and good hope through grace, will comfort your hearts and establish you in every good word and work [2 Thessalonians 2:16-17]

Jesus Christ, before (in front of) Pontius Pilate, witnessed (made) a good confession (that He came to be a king) (Matthew 27:11; John 18:37) [1 Timothy 6:13]

Jesus Christ abolished death [2 Timothy 1:10]

Jesus Christ has brought life to light through the gospel [2 Timothy 1:10]

Jesus Christ has brought immortality to light through the gospel [2 Timothy 1:10]

Jesus Christ redeems us from every lawless deed [Titus 2:13-14]

Jesus Christ purifies to Himself a peculiar people, zealous of (to do) good works [Titus 2:13-14]

Jesus destroyed him who had the power of death, that is, the devil [Hebrews 2:{9}14]

Jesus Christ has sanctified us, once for all, through the offering of His body [Hebrews 10:10]

Jesus consecrated, by His flesh and blood, a new and living way for us to enter the Holiest [Hebrews 10:19-20]

Jesus (Christ) healed us by His stripes (wounds) (Isaiah 53:5) [1 Peter 2:{21}24]

Jesus (Christ) went and preached to the spirits in prison [1 Peter 3:18-19]

Jesus has given to us all things that pertain to life and godliness [2 Peter 1:2-3]

Jesus (the Son) has anointed you [1 John 2:{24}27]

Jesus (the Son of God) hears us, if we ask anything according to His will [1 John 5:13-14]

Jesus (the Son of God) gives us whatever we ask, if we ask anything according to His will [1 John 5:13-15]

Jesus (the Son of God) has given us an understanding, that we may know Him who is true [1 John 5:20]

Jesus Christ has the revelation (is the one who reveals) which God gave to Him to show to His servants things which must shortly come to pass [Revelation 1:1]

Jesus Christ has made us kings and priests to God and His Father [Revelation 1:5-6]

Jesus (the Lamb), "You have made us to our God kings and priests: and we shall reign on the earth," sang four beasts and four and twenty elders who fell down before the Lamb [Revelation 5:8-10]

Jesus "(the Lamb) shall feed them, and shall lead them to living fountains of waters," an elder said to John [Revelation 7:17]

Jesus "(the Lamb) will overcome them (the beast and the Kings)," an angel said to John [Revelation 17:12-14]

V. His Suffering

Jesus' suffering is well described by Isaiah (Isaiah 53) long before the fact. This passage says that His suffering was all part of God's plan to bring redemption to the world.

I suspect that Jesus is still suffering at our hands because so many reject Him and because those of us who do not are not as committed as we should be. He is still hated (and always will be) by the world, because He reveals its evil works [John 7:7] and refuses to be a part of it. His followers will suffer for the same reasons, and because they refuse to give allegiance to governments or ideologies, reserving final allegiance for Him.

The apostles and others said:

Jesus was led up of (by) the spirit into the wilderness to be tempted of (by) the devil [Matthew 4:1-11] ⊞⊞ Jesus was driven into the wilderness by the Spirit, and He was there in the wilderness forty days, tempted of (by) Satan [Mark 1:{9}12-13] ⊞⊞⊞ Jesus, being full of the Holy Ghost returned from Jordan, and was led by the Spirit into the wilderness, being forty days tempted of (by) the devil [Luke 4:1-2]

Jesus, "if You are the Son of God, command that these stones be made bread," the tempter (the devil) said to Jesus when he came to Him [Matthew 4:{1}3] ⊞⊞ Jesus was tempted by the devil saying to Him, "If You are the Son of God, command this stone that it be made bread" [Luke 4:{1}3-4]

Jesus was taken up into the holy city, and set on a pinnacle of the temple by the devil, who said to Jesus, "If You are the Son of God, cast Yourself down: for it is written, 'He shall give His angels charge concerning you:' and 'In their hands they shall bear You up, lest at any time You dash Your foot against a stone'" (Psalm 91:11-12) [Matthew 4:{1}5-6] ⊞⊞ Jesus was brought to Jerusalem, and set on a pinnacle of the temple by the devil, who tempted Him by saying to Him, "If You are the Son of God, cast yourself down from here: for it is written, 'He shall give His angels charge over You: and in their hands they shall bear You

up, lest at any time You dash Your foot against a stone'"
[Luke 4:{1}9-13]

Jesus was taken up into an exceeding high mountain by the
devil, and shown all the kingdoms of the world, and the
glory of them; and the devil said to Jesus, "All these
things will I give you, if you will fall down and worship
me" [Matthew 4:{7}8-11] ⬚⬚ Jesus was taken by the
devil up into an exceeding high mountain, and showed
all the kingdoms of the world in a moment of time, and
the devil said to Him, "All this power will I give You, and
the glory of them: for that is delivered to me; and to whomsoever I will I give it. If You will worship me, all shall be
yours" [Luke 4{1}5-8]

Jesus "blasphemes," certain of the scribes said within themselves (because Jesus told the man sick of the palsy that
his sins were forgiven) [Matthew 9:2-3] ⬚⬚ Jesus
"speaks blasphemies. Who can forgive sins but God only?,"
certain of the scribes, reasoning in their hearts (because
Jesus told the man sick of the palsy that his sins were
forgiven) [Mark 2:5-7] ⬚⬚⬚ Jesus "speaks blasphemies. Who can forgive sins, but God alone?," the scribes
and the Pharisees began to reason (because Jesus told the
man sick of the palsy that his sins were forgiven) [Luke
5:{12}20-21]

Jesus was laughed to scorn by them (the people at the ruler's house, because the daughter of the ruler was dead,
but Jesus said she was sleeping) [Matthew 9:{22}24]
⬚⬚ Jesus was laughed to scorn by them (those at Jairus'
house, because his daughter was dead, but Jesus said
she was not dead but sleeping) [Mark 5:{36}38-40] ⬚⬚⬚
Jesus was laughed to scorn by them (those at Jairus'
house, because his daughter was dead, and Jesus said she
was not dead but was sleeping) [Luke 8:{50}52-53]

Jesus "casts out devils through the prince of devils," the
Pharisees said [Matthew 9:{30}34]

Jesus "does not cast out devils but by Beelzebub, the prince of
devils," said the Pharisees [Matthew 12:{15}24] ⬚⬚
Jesus "has Beelzebub," and "by the prince of devils casts
He out devils," said the scribes who came down from
Jerusalem [Mark 3:{7}22] ⬚⬚⬚ Jesus "casts out
devils through Beelzebub, the chief of the devils," said
some of the people [Luke 11:{10:41}15]

Jesus began to show His disciples, how that He must go to Jerusalem, and suffer many things of (from) the elders and chief priests and scribes [Matthew 16:21] 📖📖 Jesus began to teach them that the Son of Man (Jesus Himself) must suffer many things [Mark 8:{27}31]

Jesus, "by what authority are You doing these things? And who gave You this authority?," said the chief priests and the elders of the people [Matthew 21:23-24] 📖📖 Jesus, "by what authority do You these things? And who gave You this authority to do these things?," said the chief priests, and the scribes, and the elders [Mark 11:27-29] 📖📖📖 Jesus, "tell us, by what authority do You these things? Or who is he who gave You this authority?," said the chief priests and the scribes with the elders coming upon Him [Luke 20:{19:35}1-2]

Jesus was betrayed to the chief priests by Judas Iscariot for 30 pieces of silver [Matthew 26:14-16]

Jesus was betrayed by Judas [Matthew 26:{19}25]

Jesus came with them (His disciples) to a place called Gethsemane and took with Him Peter and the two sons of Zebedee, and began to be sorrowful and very heavy [Matthew 26: 36-37] 📖📖 Jesus came to a place which was named Gethsemane, and took with Him Peter James and John, and began to be sore amazed, and to be very heavy (troubled) [Mark 14:{30}32-33] 📖📖📖 Jesus went, as He was wont (accustomed), to the Mount of Olives; and His disciples also followed Him [Luke 22:{20:34}39-41]

Jesus went a little farther, and fell on His face, and prayed that if it were possible, the cup (His suffering and death) might pass from Him [Matthew 26:{36}39] 📖📖 Jesus went forward a little, and fell on the ground, and prayed that, if it were possible, the hour might pass from Him and the cup (His suffering and death) taken away from Him [Mark 14:{30}35-36] 📖📖📖 Jesus was withdrawn from them about a stone's cast, and kneeled down, and prayed to the Father that if He were willing, the cup (His suffering and death) be removed from Him [Luke 22: {20:34}41-42]

Jesus came to the disciples, and found them asleep, and went away again the second time, and prayed [Matthew 26:{36}40-42] 📖📖 Jesus came and found them sleeping, and again He went away, and prayed, and spake the same words [Mark 14:{30}37-39]

Jesus came and found them (the disciples) asleep again: for
their eyes were heavy, and He left them, and went away
again, and prayed the third time, saying the same words
[Matthew 26:{36}43-44] ▢▢ Jesus, when He returned,
found them asleep again, (for their eyes were heavy),
neither wist they (did they know) what to answer Him
[Mark 14:{30}40] ▢▢▢ Jesus, being in agony, prayed
more earnestly: and His sweat was as it were great drops
of blood falling down to the ground, and when He rose
up from prayer, and was come to His disciples, He found
them sleeping for (due to) sorrow [Luke 22:{20:35}44-45]

Jesus came to His disciples, and said to them that the hour
was at hand for Him to be betrayed into the hands of
sinners [Matthew 26:45] ▢▢ Jesus came the third
time and said that the hour had come when the Son of
Man was to be betrayed into the hands of sinners [Mark
14:{30}41]

Jesus was forsaken by all the disciples [Matthew 26:{55}56]
▢▢ Jesus' disciples all forsook Him, and fled [Mark
14:{48}50]

Jesus was laid hold of and led away to Caiaphas the high
priest, where the scribes and the elders were assembled
[Matthew 26:57] ▢▢ Jesus was led away to the high
priest: and with him were assembled all the chief priests and
the elders, and the scribes [Mark 14:53] ▢▢▢ Jesus was
taken, and led, and brought into the high priest's house
[Luke 22:{52}54] ▢▢▢▢ Jesus was taken, and bound,
and led away to Annas first; for he was father in law to
Caiaphas, who was the high priest that same year [John
18:12-13]

Jesus "(this fellow) said, 'I am able to destroy the temple of
God, and to build it in three days,'" reported two false
witnesses to the council [Matthew 26:59-61]

Jesus was spat on in His face, and buffeted, and others
smote (struck) Him with the palms of their hands, and
they said, "Prophesy to us, Christ! Who is he who smote
(struck) you?" [Matthew 26:{64}67-68] ▢▢ Jesus was
spit upon by some, had His face covered, and was buffeted, and they said to Him, "Prophesy" [Mark 14:{62}65]
▢▢▢ Jesus was mocked, and smote (beaten), and
when blindfolded was struck on the face by the men
that held Him, and they asked Him, saying, "Prophesy,
who is it that smote (struck) You?," and many other

things blasphemously spake they against Him [Luke 22: 63-65]

Jesus was denied by Peter when he said, "I know not what you say," when a damsel came to him, saying, "You also were with Jesus of Galilee" [Matthew 26:69-70] 📖📖 Jesus was denied by Peter when he said, "I know not, neither understand I what you say," when one of the maids of the high priest came and looked at him and said, "And you also were with Jesus of Nazareth" [Mark 14:67-68] 📖📖📖 Jesus was denied by Peter, who said, "I know Him not," when a maid beheld him, and earnestly looked on him, and said, "This man was also with Him" [Luke 22:{52}56-57] 📖📖📖📖 Jesus was denied by Peter when he said, "I am not," when the damsel who kept the door said to him, "are not you also one of this Man's disciples?" [John 18:{15}17]

Jesus was denied by Peter when he said, with an oath, "I do not know the Man," after another maid saw him, and said to them that were there, "This fellow also was with Jesus of Nazareth" [Matthew 26:71-72] 📖📖 Jesus was denied by Peter again, when a maid saw him again, and began to say to those who stood by, "This is one of them" [Mark 14:{67}69-70] 📖📖📖 Jesus was denied by Peter, who said, "Man, I am not," when another saw Him, and said, "You are also of them" [Luke 22:{52}58] 📖📖📖📖 Jesus was denied by Peter when he said, "I am not," when they said to him, "Are not you also one of His disciples?" [John 18:{23}25]

Jesus was denied by Peter when he began to curse and to swear, saying, "I do not know the Man," when those who stood by came to him and said, "Surely you also are one of them, for your speech betrays you" [Matthew 26:73-74] 📖📖 Jesus was denied by Peter when he began to curse and swear, saying, "I know not this Man of whom you speak," when those who stood by said again to Peter, "Surely you are one of them: for you are a Galilean, and your speech agrees thereto" [Mark 14:{67}70-71] 📖📖📖 Jesus was denied by Peter, who said, "Man, I know not what you say," when another confidently affirmed, saying, "Of a truth this fellow also was with Him, for He is a Galilean" [Luke 22:{52}59-60] 📖📖📖📖 Jesus was denied again by Peter, when a kinsman of the man whose ear Peter cut off, said, "Did not I see you in the garden with Him?" [John 18:{23}26-27]

Jesus was bound and led away and delivered to Pontius Pilate the governor [Matthew 27:1-2] 📖📖 Jesus was bound and carried away, and delivered to Pilate by the chief priests, the elders and scribes and the whole council [Mark 15:1]

Jesus was delivered to Pilate for (due to) envy [Matthew 27:17-18] 📖📖 Jesus was delivered to Pilate by the chief priests for (because of) envy [Mark 15:{5}10]

Jesus was scourged (beaten) by Pilate (Isaiah 50:6) [Matthew 27:26] 📖📖 Jesus was scourged (beaten) by Pilate (Isaiah 50:6) [Mark 15:15] 📖📖📖 Jesus was scourged (beaten) by Pilate (Isaiah 50:6) [John 19:1]

Jesus was stripped by the soldiers, and they put a scarlet robe on Him, and they platted a crown of thorns, and put it on His head, and a reed in His right hand: and they bowed the knee before Him and mocked Him, saying, "Hail, King of the Jews!" [Matthew 27:27-29] 📖📖 Jesus was clothed with purple by the soldiers; and they platted a crown of thorns, and put it about His head, and began to salute Him, "Hail King of the Jews!" [Mark 15:{15}16-18] 📖📖📖 Jesus was set at nought (treated contemptuously) and mocked by Herod and his men of war, who arrayed Him in a gorgeous robe, and sent Him back to Pilate [Luke 23:{8}11] 📖📖📖📖 Jesus had a crown of thorns put on His head by the soldiers, and they put on Him a purple robe, and said, "Hail, king of the Jews!," and they smote (struck) Him with their hands [John 19:{1}2-3]

Jesus was spat on by the soldiers, and they took the reed, and smote (struck) Him on the head, and after they had mocked Him, they took the robe from Him (Isaiah 50:6) [Matthew 27:{27}30-31] 📖📖 Jesus was smote (hit) on the head with a reed by the soldiers, and (they) did spit on Him, and bowing their knees worshipped Him, and when they had mocked Him, they took off the purple from Him (Isaiah 50:6) [Mark 15:{15}19-20]

Jesus was led away by the soldiers to be crucified [Matthew 27:{27}31]

Jesus was given vinegar to drink mingled with gall [Matthew 27:{27}34]

Jesus was reviled by those who passed by, wagging their heads, and saying, "You who destroy the temple and build it in three days, save yourself! If You be the Son of God, come down from the cross" [Matthew 27:{37}39-40] 📖📖 Jesus was railed on by those who passed by, wagging their heads, and saying, "Ah, You who destroy the temple, and build it in three days, save Yourself, and come down from the cross" [Mark 15:{15}29-30]

Jesus was mocked by the chief priests, with the scribes and elders, who said, "He saved others; Himself He cannot save. If He be the King of Israel, let Him now come down from the cross, and we will believe Him. He trusted in God; let Him deliver Him now, if He will have Him: for He said, 'I am the Son of God'" [Matthew 27:{37}41-43] 📖📖 Jesus was mocked by the chief priests also, with the scribes, saying among themselves, "He saved others; Himself He cannot save. Let Christ, the King of Israel descend now from the cross, that we may see and believe" [Mark 15:{15}31-32] 📖📖📖 Jesus "saved others; let Him save Himself, if He be the Christ, the chosen of God," derided the rulers [Luke 23:34-35]

Jesus was mocked by the thieves crucified with Him, who cast the same (taunts) in His teeth [Matthew 27:{27}44] 📖📖 Jesus was reviled by those who were crucified with Him [Mark 15:{15}32]

Jesus was betrayed by Judas Iscariot [Mark 3:{7}19]

Jesus "is beside Himself," said His friends [Mark 3:{7}21]

Jesus began to teach them that the Son of Man (Jesus Himself) must be rejected of (by) the elders, of (by) the chief priests, and scribes [Mark 8:{27}31]

Jesus was feared by the scribes and chief priests, because all the people was astonished at His doctrine, so they sought how they might destroy Him [Mark 11:17-18] 📖📖 Jesus taught daily in the temple, but the chief priests and the scribes and the chief of the people sought to destroy Him, and could not find what they might do: for all the people were very attentive to hear Him [Luke 19:{35}47-48]

Jesus was sent (by the chief priests, and the scribes, and the elders) certain of the Pharisees and the Herodians, to catch Him in His words [Mark 12:{11:33}13]

Jesus was led away to the high priest: and with him were assembled all the chief priests and the elders and the scribes [Mark 14:53]

Jesus held His peace, and answered the high priest nothing [Mark 14:60-61]

Jesus was not received by the Samaritans [Luke 9:{50}52-53]

Jesus was tempted by others, who sought of (from) Him a sign from heaven [Luke 11:{10:41}16]

Jesus began to be urged vehemently by the scribes and the Pharisees, and they tried to provoke Him to speak of many things: laying (in) wait for Him, and seeking to catch something out of His mouth, that they might accuse Him [Luke 11:{10:41}53-54]

Jesus, "get out and depart hence: for Herod will kill You," said certain of the Pharisees to Him [Luke 13:{12}31]

Jesus "receives sinners, and eats with them," the Pharisees and scribes murmured (because the publicans and sinners drew near to Him to hear Him) [Luke 15:{14:3}1-2]

Jesus was derided by the Pharisees, who were covetous [Luke 16:{14:3}14]

Jesus "was gone to be a guest with a man who is a sinner," they all murmured (because He went to eat with Zacchaeus, who was chief among the publicans, and he was rich) [Luke 19:1-7]

Jesus beheld the city (Jerusalem), and wept over it [Luke 19:{35}41]

Jesus was watched, and sent forth spies by the chief priests and the scribes, who should feign themselves just men, that they might take hold of His words, that so they might deliver Him to the power and authority of the governor, and they asked Him saying, "Master, we know that you say and teach rightly, neither accept you the person of any, but teach the way of God truly: is it lawful for us to give tribute to Caesar or no?," ...and they could not take hold of His words before the people: and they marveled at His answer (about whom to pay taxes to), and held their peace [Luke 20:{8}20-26]

Jesus was sought by the chief priests and scribes how they might kill Him; for they feared the people [Luke 22:{20:34} 2]

Jesus, "If You are the Christ, tell us," said the elders of the people, and the chief priests and the scribes, after leading Jesus into their council [Luke 22:{63}66-67]

Jesus, "Are you then the Son of God?," they all said (at the council) [Luke 22:{63}70]

Jesus was led to Pilate by the whole multitude, and they began to accuse Him, saying, "We found this fellow perverting the nation, and forbidding to give tribute to Caesar, saying, that He Himself is Christ, a king" [Luke 23:{22:63}1-2]

Jesus "is without fault," said Pilate to the chief priests and to the people [Luke 23:{22:63}4] 🕮🕮 Jesus "I find no fault in at all," Pilate said to the Jews [John 18:{37}38]

Jesus "stirs up the people, teaching throughout all Jewry, beginning from Galilee to this place," said the chief priests and the crowd more fiercely to Pilate [Luke 23:{22:63}5]

Jesus was sent by Pilate to Herod [Luke 23:{22:63}7]

Jesus was questioned by Herod with many words, but He answered him nothing [Luke 23:8-9]

Jesus was vehemently accused by the chief priests and scribes [Luke 23:{8}10]

Jesus "was brought to me by you, as one who perverts the people: and, behold, I, having examined Him before you, have found no fault in this Man touching those things whereof you accuse Him: no, nor yet (did) Herod: for I sent you back to him; and, lo, nothing worthy of death is done unto Him (was found by Herod); I will therefore chastise Him, and release Him" (Pilate to the chief priests and the rulers and the people) [Luke 23:{8}13-16]

Jesus was delivered by Pilate to their (chief priests, the rulers and the people) will (to be crucified) [Luke 23:13-25]

Jesus was mocked by the soldiers, coming to Him, and offering Him vinegar, and saying, "If You be the King of the Jews, save Yourself" [Luke 23:34-37]

Jesus, "if You be Christ, save Yourself and us," railed one of the malefactors who were hanged with Him [Luke 23:{34} 39]

Jesus "has done nothing amiss," said the other malefactor, who then said to Jesus, "Lord, remember me when you come into Your kingdom" [Luke 23:39-42]

Jesus (the true Light) was in the world, and the world was made by Him, and the world knew Him not [John 1:6-10]

Jesus (the true Light) came to His own, and His own received Him not [John 1:6-11]

Jesus, "what sign show You to us, seeing that You do these things (driving the sellers and the money changers from the temple)," answered the Jews [John 2:{13}18]

Jesus was persecuted by the Jews, and they sought to slay Him, because He had done these things (healed the lame man) on the Sabbath [John 5:16]

Jesus was sought by the Jews the more to kill Him, because He not only had broken the Sabbath, but said also said that God was His Father, making Himself equal with God [John 5:17-18]

Jesus was murmured at by the Jews, because He said, "I am the bread which came down from heaven" [John 6:{35}41]

Jesus knew in Himself that His disciples murmured at it, saying, "This is an hard saying; who can hear it (people must eat His flesh and drink His blood to live forever)" [John 6:53-61]

Jesus should (would) be betrayed by Judas Iscariot, one of the twelve [John 6:70-71]

Jesus walked in Galilee: for He would not walk in Jewry, because the Jews sought to kill Him [John 7:1]

Jesus, "depart hence, and go into Judea (for the Jews' Feast of Tabernacles), that Your disciples also may see the works that You do, for there is no man that does any thing in secret, while he himself seeks to be known openly. If You do these things, show Yourself to the world," said Jesus' brethren to Him, for neither did His brethren believe in Him [John 7:1-5]

Jesus "is a good man," some said: others said, "No, but He deceives the people" [John 7:{6}12]

Jesus marveled the Jews, and they said, "How does this Man know letters, having never learned?" [John 7:14-15]

Jesus, "You have a devil. Who goes about to kill You?," some of them said [John 7:{16}20]

Jesus' hour was not yet come, so, although they sought to take Him, no man laid hands on Him [John 7:{28}30]

Jesus was sent officers by the Pharisees and the chief priests to take Him [John 7:{28}32]

Jesus was laid hands on by no man, though some of them would have taken Him [John 7:{39}44]

Jesus "should not be judged by our law, before it hear him, and knows what He does," Nicodemus said to the Pharisees [John 7:{39}49-51]

Jesus was brought, by the scribes and Pharisees, a woman taken in adultery, and they said to Him, "Master, this woman was caught in adultery, in the very act. Now Moses, in the law commanded us, that such should be stoned: but what say You?," to tempt Him, that they might have (something) to accuse Him [John 8:{1}3-5]

Jesus, as though He heard them not, stooped down, and with His finger wrote on the ground (when being tempted by the scribes and Pharisees about the woman taken in adultery), and He lifted Himself up when they continued asking Him, and He told them that the one without sin should cast the first stone, and again He stooped down, and wrote on the ground [John 8:6-8]

Jesus was left alone, and the woman (the woman caught in adultery) standing in the midst, after those who heard His response to their question, being convicted by their own conscience, went out one by one, beginning at the eldest even to the last [John 8:9]

Jesus, "You bear record of Yourself: Your record is not true," the Pharisees said to Him, after He said that He is the light of the world [John 8:12-13]

Jesus was laid hands on by no man; for His hour was not yet come [John 8:20]

Jesus, "do we not say well that You are a Samaritan and have a devil?," the Jews answered (after Jesus told them that they were not of God) [John 8:{42}48]

Jesus, "now we know that You have a devil," said the Jews to Him (after Jesus said to them that a man who keeps His saying shall never taste of death) [John 8:{49}52]

Jesus, "You are not yet fifty years old, and have You seen Abraham?," the Jews said to Him [John 8:{54}57]

Jesus hid himself, and went out of the temple, going through the midst of them, and so passed by, as they (the Jews) took up stones to throw at Him [John 8:59]

Jesus "is not from God, because He keeps not the Sabbath day," some of the Pharisees said, and others said, "How can a man who is a sinner do such miracles?," and there was a division among them [John 9:{14}16]

Jesus "is a sinner," said the Jews to the man that was blind [John 9:{14}24]

Jesus, "How long do You make us to doubt? If You be the Christ, tell us plainly," the Jews said to Him at the Feast of Dedication in Jerusalem as Jesus walked in the temple [John 10:22-24]

Jesus, "for a good work we stone You not; but for blasphemy; and because You, being a Man, make Yourself God," answered the Jews who took up stones again to stone Him (because Jesus said that He and His Father are one) [John 10:31-33]

Jesus escaped out of their hand, as they (the Jews) sought again to take Him [John 10:{34}39]

Jesus "does many miracles, what do we (shall we do)? If we let Him thus alone, all men will believe on Him: and the Romans shall come and take away both our place and nation," said the chief priests and the Pharisees to a council [John 11:{46}47-48]

Jesus therefore walked no more openly among the Jews; because they took counsel together for (in order) to put Him to death [John 11:53-54]

Jesus was to be taken by the chief priests and the Pharisees at the Jew's Passover feast, so they commanded, that, if any man knew where He was, he should shew (report) it [John 11:55-57]

Jesus should (would) be betrayed by Judas Iscariot [John 12:{3}4]

Jesus was believed on by many Jews, because that by reason of him (Lazarus having been raised from the dead by Jesus), so the chief priests consulted that they might put Lazarus also to death [John 12:{3}9-11]

Jesus was believed on by many of the chief rulers, but because of the Pharisees they did not confess Him, lest they should be put out of the synagogue: for they loved the praise of men more than the praise of God [John 12: 42-43]

Jesus was to be betrayed by Judas Iscariot [John 13:1-2]

Jesus was troubled in spirit (because one of His disciples would betray Him) [John 13:21]

Jesus "(Lord), who is it (who will betray you)?," said one of His disciples, whom Jesus loved; and Jesus, after He had dipped the sop (piece of bread) and said that it would be the one to whom He gave it, gave it to Judas Iscariot [John 13:23-26]

Jesus was struck by an officer with the palm of His hand [John 18:22]

Jesus was sent bound by Annas to Caiaphas the high priest [John 18:{23]24]

Jesus was led from Caiaphas to the hall of judgment [John 18:28]

Jesus "is a malefactor, so we delivered Him up to you (Pilate)," they answered [John 18:{28}30]

Jesus "should be taken by you and judged according to your law," Pilate said to them [John 18:{28}31]

Jesus, "Your own nation and the chief priests have delivered You to me: what have You done?," Pilate answered Jesus [John 18:34-35]

Jesus, "are You a king then?," Pilate therefore said to Him [John 18:36-37]

Jesus "I bring forth to you, that you may know that I find no fault in Him," said Pilate to them [John 19:{1}4]

Jesus came forth then, wearing the crown of thorns, and the purple robe, and Pilate said, "Behold the Man!". When the chief priests therefore and officers saw Him, they cried out, saying, "Crucify Him, crucify Him." Pilate said to them, "You take Him, and crucify Him: for I find no fault in Him" [John 19:5-6]

Jesus, "whence (where) are You (from)?," Pilate said to Him, but Jesus gave him no answer (Isaiah 53:7) [John 19:9]

Jesus, "speak You not to me? Know You not that I have power to crucify You, and have power to release You?," Pilate then said to Jesus [John 19:10-11]

Jesus was brought forth, and sat (set) down in the judgment seat, in a place that is called the Pavement, and it was the preparation of the Passover, and about the sixth hour: and Pilate said to the Jews, "Behold your King!" [John 19:13-14]

Jesus bore His cross to a place called the Place of a Skull, which is called in Hebrew Golgotha: where they crucified Him, and two others with Him [John 19:17-18]

Jesus' side was pierced with a spear, and forthwith came there out blood and water. This was done, that again another Scripture should be fulfilled which says, "They shall look on Him whom they pierced" (Zechariah 12:10) [John 19:33-37]

Jesus shewed Himself alive after His suffering by many infallible proofs to the apostles whom He had chosen [Acts 1:1-3]

Jesus, "God's Son, you (men of Israel) delivered up (to Pilate)" (Peter's response to the people at the temple) [Acts 3:13]

Jesus, "God's Son, was denied by you (men of Israel) in the presence of Pilate, when he was determined to let Him go" (Peter's response to the people at the temple) [Acts 3: 13]

Jesus "has fulfilled those things which God had shewed by the mouth of all His prophets, that the Christ should (would) suffer" (Peter's response to the people at the temple) [Acts 3:{13}18]

Jesus "Christ of Nazareth, who was set at nought (deemed to be of no value) of (by) you builders, is become the head of the corner (cornerstone)" (Peter speaking to the rulers of the people and elders of Israel) (Psalm 118:22; Isaiah 53:3) [Acts 4:10-11]

Jesus "(the Just One) you have been now the betrayers and murderers of," Stephen said to the council [Acts 7:52]

Jesus was being persecuted by Saul [Acts 9:4-5]

Jesus Christ must needs have suffered, as reasoned out of the Scriptures by Paul to the Jews in the synagogue at Thessalonica [Acts 17:1-3]

Jesus of Nazareth was being persecuted by Saul [Acts 22:5-8]

Jesus was being persecuted by (me) Saul (Paul answered King Agrippa) [Acts 26:12-15]

Jesus "the Christ should (would) suffer," Paul answered King Agrippa, citing Moses and the prophets [Acts 26:{15}23]

Jesus our Lord was delivered for our offenses (Isaiah 53:5-6) [Romans 4:24-25]

Jesus the Lord, the same night in which He was betrayed, took bread: and when (after) He had given thanks, he brake it, and said, "Take eat: this is My body, which is broken for you: this do in remembrance of Me" [1 Corinthians 11:23]

Jesus' (Christ) sufferings abound in us [2 Corinthians 1:5]

Jesus (Christ) was made a curse for us: for it is written, "Cursed is everyone who hangs on a tree" (Deuteronomy 21:23) [Galatians 3:13]

Jesus (Christ) suffered [Philippians 3:9-10]

Jesus was made perfect through sufferings [Hebrews 2:{9}10]

Jesus Himself has suffered [Hebrews 2:{9}18]

Jesus (Christ) learned obedience by the things which He
   suffered [Hebrews 5:{5}8]

Jesus (the Son of God) is crucified afresh and put to an open
   shame by those who were once enlightened, and have
   tasted of the heavenly gift, and were made partakers of
   the Holy Ghost, and have tasted the good word of God
   and the powers of the age to come, if they fall away
   [Hebrews 6:4-6]

Jesus for the joy that was set before Him endured the cross
   [Hebrews 12:2]

Jesus despised the shame (of the cross) [Hebrews 12:2]

Jesus endured such contradiction of sinners against Himself
   (Isaiah 53:3) [Hebrews 12:2-3]

Jesus suffered without (outside of) the gate [Hebrews 13:12]

Jesus (Christ) suffered [1 Peter 1:11]

Jesus (Christ) also suffered for us [1 Peter 2:21]

Jesus (Christ) left us an example (of suffering) [1 Peter 2:21]

Jesus (Christ) was reviled [1 Peter 2:{21}23]

Jesus (Christ) suffered [1 Peter 2:{21}23]

Jesus (Christ) also has once suffered for sins [1 Peter 3:18]

Jesus (Christ) has suffered for us in the flesh [1 Peter 4:1]

Jesus (Christ) suffered [1 Peter 4:13]

Jesus (Christ) is evil spoken of on their part (those who
   reproach others for the name of Christ) [1 Peter 4:14]

Jesus (Christ) suffered [1 Peter 5:1]

VI. His Death

Jesus had to die because without the shedding of blood there is no forgiveness [Leviticus 17:11; Hebrews 9:22]. This is God's plan, not yours or mine, and was His plan from the foundation of the world [Revelation 13:8]. For some reason, God believes His thoughts are higher than ours [Isaiah 55:8-9]. I guess this means that His plans are better than ours—sorry.

A. **The apostles and others claimed that Jesus was killed:**

The apostles and others said:

Jesus began to show His disciples that He must be killed [Matthew 16:21]   Jesus began to teach them that the Son of Man (Jesus Himself) must be killed [Mark 8:{27}31]

Jesus was to be taken by subtilty, and killed (consultation by the chief priests, and the scribes, and the elders of the people) [Matthew 26:3-4]   Jesus was to be taken by craft and put to death (result sought by the chief priests and the scribes) [Mark 14:{13:5}1]   Jesus was sought by the chief priests and scribes how they might kill Him, for they feared the people [Luke 22:{20:34}2]

Jesus' "blood be on us, and on our children," all the people answered Pilate [Matthew 27:{22}25]

Jesus, when He had cried again with a loud voice, yielded up the ghost (died) [Matthew 27:50]   Jesus at the ninth hour cried out with a loud voice, and gave up the ghost (died) [Mark 15:34-37]   Jesus cried out with a loud voice, "Father, into Your hands I commend My spirit:" and gave up the ghost (died) [Luke 23:46]   Jesus said, "It is finished:" and bowed His head, and gave up the ghost (died) [John 19:30]

Jesus was already dead [Mark 15:43-44]   Jesus was already dead [John 19:33]

Jesus was to decease (die) in Jerusalem (spoken by Moses and Elijah at Jesus' transfiguration) [Luke 9:{8:50}28-31]

Jesus "of Nazareth was condemned to death," said Cleopas and another man to Jesus [Luke 24:13-20]

Jesus "should die for the nation; and not for that nation only, but that also He should gather together in one the children of God who were scattered abroad. It is expedient for us, that one man should die for the people, and that the whole nation perish not," Caiaphas the high priest prophesied, not saying this on his own authority [John 11:49-52]

Jesus walked no more openly among the Jews; because they took counsel together to put Him to death [John 11:53-54]

Jesus, "by our law, ought to die, because He made Himself the Son of God," the Jews answered Pilate [John 19:5-7]

Jesus, after these things, showed Himself again to His disciples the third time, after that He was risen from the dead [John 21:1-14]

Jesus "of Nazareth was delivered (to death) by the determinate counsel and foreknowledge of God" (Peter's explanation at Pentecost) [Acts 2:22-23]

Jesus "of Nazareth you have taken, and by wicked hands have crucified and slain" (Peter's explanation at Pentecost) [Acts 2:22-23]

Jesus, "God's Son, was killed by you" (Peter's response to the people at the temple) [Acts 3:13-15]

Jesus "you slew by hanging on a tree" (the words of Peter and the other apostles to the council) [Acts 5:30]

Jesus "(the Just One) you have been now the betrayers and murderers of," Stephen said to the council [Acts 7:52]

Jesus "of Nazareth they slew and hanged on a tree" (Peter speaking to Cornelius' household) [Acts 10:38-39]

Jesus "was condemned by they who dwell at Jerusalem, and their rulers, because they knew Him not, nor yet the voices of the prophets which are read every Sabbath day, they have fulfilled them in condemning Him, and though they found no cause of (for) death in Him, yet desired they Pilate that He should be slain" (Paul speaking in the Antioch synagogue) [Acts 13:{23}27-28]

Jesus (Christ) died for the ungodly [Romans 5:6]

Jesus (Christ) died for us while we were yet sinners [Romans 5:8]

Jesus (Christ), God's Son, by His death reconciled us to God [Romans 5:8-10]

Jesus (Christ), being raised from the dead dies no more; death has no more has dominion over Him [Romans 6:9]

Jesus (God's own Son) was not spared by God but delivered up by Him for us all [Romans 8:32]

Jesus (Christ) died [Romans 8:34]

Jesus (Christ) died [Romans 14:9]

Jesus (Christ) died [Romans 14:15]

Jesus (Christ) is sacrificed for us [1 Corinthians 5:7]

Jesus (Christ) died [1 Corinthians 8:11]

Jesus (the Lord) died [1 Corinthians 11:26]

Jesus (Christ) died for our sins according to the Scriptures (Isaiah 53:12) [1 Corinthians 15:3]

Jesus (Christ) the One died for all [2 Corinthians 5:14-15]

Jesus "(Christ) died in vain, if righteousness comes through the law," said Paul to Peter and the others [Galatians 2:21]

Jesus Christ became obedient to death, even the death of the cross [Philippians 2:{5}8]

Jesus (Christ) died [Philippians 3:9-10]

Jesus the Lord was killed by the Jews [1 Thessalonians 2:15]

Jesus died and rose again, even so those also who sleep in Jesus will God bring with Him [1 Thessalonians 4:14]

Jesus Christ our Lord died for us [1 Thessalonians 5:9-10]

Jesus gave Himself a ransom for all, to be testified in due time [1 Timothy 2:6]

Jesus Christ gave Himself for us [Titus 2:13-14]

Jesus tasted death for every man [Hebrews 2:9]

Jesus needs not daily, as those high priests, to offer up sacrifices, first for His own sins, and then for the people's, for this He did once, when he offered up Himself [Hebrews 7:{22}27]

Jesus (Christ) is the mediator of the new testament, that by means of death, for the redemption of the transgressions that were under the first testament [Hebrews 9:14-15]

Jesus (Christ) now once in the end of the world has appeared to put away sin by the sacrifice of Himself [Hebrews 9:{24} 26]

Jesus sanctified the people with His own blood [Hebrews 13:12]

Jesus (Christ) was put to death in the flesh [1 Peter 3:18]

Jesus Christ's blood cleanses us from all sin [1 John 1:7]

Jesus washed us from our sins in His own blood [Revelation 1:5]

Jesus (the Lamb), "You were slain," sung by four beasts and four and twenty elders who fell down before the Lamb [Revelation 5:8-9]

Jesus (the Lamb), "You have redeemed us to God by Your blood out of every kindred, and tongue, and people, and nation," sung by four beasts and four and twenty elders who fell down before the Lamb [Revelation 5:8-9]

Jesus "(the Lamb) was slain," said with a loud voice by many angels, the beasts and the elders: the number of them was ten thousand times ten thousand, and thousands of thousands [Revelation 5:11-12]

Jesus (the Lamb) was slain from the foundation of the world [Revelation 13:8]

B. The apostles and others said that Jesus was killed by crucifixion:

Crucifixion was not only a horrible way to die, but such death was also pronounced a curse by God Himself [Deuteronomy 21:22-23; Galations 3:13].

The apostles and others said:

Jesus was delivered by Pilate to be crucified [Matthew 27:26] ⏹⏹ Jesus was delivered by Pilate to be crucified [Mark 15:15] ⏹⏹⏹ Jesus was delivered by Pilate to their (chief priests, the rulers and the people) will (to be crucified) [Luke 23:13-25] ⏹⏹⏹⏹ Jesus then was delivered therefore by Pilate to them to be crucified, and they took Jesus, and led Him away [John 19:15-16]

Jesus was crucified [Matthew 27:{27}35]

Jesus "was crucified," an angel said to Mary Magdalene and the other Mary [Matthew 28:5] ⌑⌑ Jesus "of Nazareth was crucified," a young man in a long white garment said to Mary Magdalene, Mary the mother of James, and Salome [Mark 16:5-6]

Jesus was led out to be crucified [Mark 15:{15}20]

Jesus was brought to the place Golgotha, which is, being interpreted, The Place of a Skull, and they crucified him the third hour [Mark 15:{15}22-24]

Jesus was crucified with two thieves, and the Scripture was fulfilled, which says, "And He was numbered with the transgressors" (Isaiah 53:12) [Mark 15:{15}27-28] ⌑⌑ Jesus was crucified with the malefactors at the place called Calvary [Luke 23:{28}33]

Jesus "of Nazareth was crucified," said Cleopas and another man to Jesus [Luke 24:13-20]

Jesus said this (that if He be (were) lifted up from the earth, He will draw all men to Him), signifying what death He should (would) die [John 12:30-33]

Jesus had spoken a saying signifying what death He should (would) die [John 18:32]

Jesus "of Nazareth you have taken, and by wicked hands have crucified and slain" (Peter's explanation at Pentecost) [Acts 2:22-23]

Jesus "was crucified by you" (Peter's explanation at Pentecost) [Acts 2:36]

Jesus "Christ of Nazareth, whom you crucified" (Peter to the rulers of the people and elders of Israel) [Acts 4:10]

Jesus "you slew by hanging on a tree" (the words of Peter and the other apostles to the council) [Acts 5:30]

Jesus "of Nazareth they slew and hanged on a tree" (Peter speaking to Cornelius' household) [Acts 10:38-39]

Jesus "was taken down from the tree (cross), when they (those who dwell at Jerusalem, and their rulers) had fulfilled all that was written of (about) Him" (Paul speaking in the Antioch synagogue) [Acts 13:{23}29]

Jesus (Christ) has a cross [1 Corinthians 1:17]

Jesus (Christ) crucified is a stumbling block to the Jews [1 Corinthians 1:23]

Jesus (Christ) crucified is foolishness to the Greeks [1 Corinthians 1:23]

Jesus Christ was crucified [1 Corinthians 2:2]

Jesus (the Lord of glory) would not have been crucified by the princes of this world, if they had known the hidden wisdom of God [1 Corinthians 2:7-8]

Jesus (Christ) was crucified through weakness [2 Corinthians 13:3-4]

Jesus "(Christ) has been crucified," said Paul to Peter and the others [Galatians 2:20]

Jesus Christ has been evidently set forth among you, (as) crucified [Galatians 3:1]

Jesus Christ our Lord has a cross [Galatians 6:14]

Jesus Christ became obedient to death, even the death of the cross [Philippians 2:{5}8]

Jesus (God's Son) made peace through the blood of His cross [Colossians 1:{13}20]

Jesus for the joy that was set before Him endured the cross [Hebrews 12:2]

Jesus (Christ) bore our sins in His own body on the tree [1 Peter 2:{21}24]

C. The apostles and others claimed that Jesus' death was for remission of sins:

Remission means to "forgive, pardon or not exact a penalty for". Jesus' death then means that those who accept that death have been forgiven and will not receive the penalty for being sinners and for sinning, eternal death.

This is also closely related to IIIB, "The apostles and others said that Jesus came to save us and give us life".

The apostles and others said:

Jesus "takes away the sins of the world," said John the Baptist [John 1:29]

Jesus gives forgiveness of sins (the words of Peter and the other apostles to the council) [Acts 5:30-31]

Jesus "of Nazareth brings remission of sins to whosoever believes in Him" (Peter speaking to Cornelius' household) [Acts 10:{38}43]

Jesus Christ, God's own Son, condemned sin in the flesh [Romans 8:2-3]

Jesus (Christ) died for our sins according to the Scriptures (Isaiah 53:12) [1 Corinthians 15:3]

Jesus (Christ) was made to be sin for us; that we might be made the righteousness of God in Jesus [2 Corinthians 5:20-21]

Jesus Christ our Lord gave Himself for our sins (Isaiah 53:12) [Galatians 1:3-4]

Jesus (God's Son) redeems those who were under the law, that we might receive adoption of (as) sons [Galatians 4:4-5]

Jesus Christ, the Beloved, brings us redemption through His blood [Ephesians 1:5-7]

Jesus Christ, the Beloved, brings us forgiveness of sins [Ephesians 1:5-7]

Jesus (God's Son) brings us redemption through His blood [Colossians 1:13-14]

Jesus (God's Son) brings us forgiveness of sins [Colossians 1:13-14]

Jesus (Christ) has forgiven you all trespasses [Colossians 2:{11}13]

Jesus (God's Son) by Himself purged our sins [Hebrews 1:{2}3]

Jesus made reconciliation (with God) for the sins of the people [Hebrews 2:{9}17]

Jesus (Christ) now once in the end of the world has appeared to put away sin by the sacrifice of Himself [Hebrews 9:{24}26]

Jesus (Christ) was once offered to bear the sins of many [Hebrews 9:28]

Jesus Christ, this Man, offered one sacrifice for sins forever [Hebrews 10:{10}12]

Jesus Christ's blood cleanses us from all sin [1 John 1:7]

Jesus Christ is the propitiation (make amends/atone) for our sins: and not for ours only, but also for the sins of the whole world [1 John 2:1-2]

Jesus (God's Son) was sent by God to be the propitiation (to make amends/atone) for our sins [1 John 4:10]

Jesus washed us from our sins in His own blood [Revelation 1:5]

Jesus (the Lamb), "You have redeemed us to God by Your blood out of every kindred, and tongue, and people, and nation," sung by four beasts and four and twenty elders who fell down before the lamb [Revelation 5:8-9]

VII. His Burial

The apostles and others said:

Jesus' body was given by Pilate to a rich man from Arimathea, named Joseph, who also himself was Jesus' disciple: and he wrapped it in a clean linen cloth, and laid it in his own new tomb, which he had hewn out in the rock: and he rolled a great stone to the door of the sepulchre (Isaiah 53:9) [Matthew 27:57-60] ⨅⨅ Jesus' body was granted by Pilate to Joseph of Arimathea (it was the day before the Sabbath), an honorable counsellor, who also waited for the kingdom of God, who took Him down, and wrapped Him in fine linen, and laid Him in a sepulchre which was hewn out of a rock, and rolled a stone to the door of the sepulchre [Mark 15:42-46] ⨅⨅⨅ Jesus' body was taken down (it was the day of the Preparation), and wrapped in linen, and laid in a sepulchre that was hewn in stone, wherein never man before was laid, by a man named Joseph, a counsellor from Arimathea, who also himself waited for the kingdom of God and was a good man, and a just (man), and who had not consented to the counsel and deed of them [Luke 23:50-53] ⨅⨅⨅⨅ Jesus' body was given by Pilate to Joseph of Arimathea, a disciple of Jesus, but secretly for fear of the Jews, who with Nicodemus took the body of Jesus, and wound it in linen clothes with the spices, as the manner of the Jews is to bury, and, because of the Jews' Preparation Day, laid it in a new sepulchre, that was nigh at hand, wherein was never man yet laid [John 19:38-42]

Jesus "was laid in a sepulchre" (Paul speaking in the Antioch synagogue) [Acts 13:{23}29]

Jesus (Christ) was buried [1 Corinthians 15:3-4]

VIII. His Resurrection

If Jesus was not raised from the dead, preaching is vain, faith is vain and there is no resurrection for any [1 Corinthians 15:14-20]. Can there be any doubt that Jesus rose from the dead?

I suspect that the number of those who saw Jesus alive after His resurrection are more than those who witness many historical events that we easily accept. Paul says that He was seen alive by over 500 at once [1 Corinthians 15:6] and by Paul himself and the apostles.

The apostles and others said:

Jesus began to show His disciples that He must be raised again the third day [Matthew 16:21] ▢▢ Jesus began to teach them that the Son of Man (Jesus Himself) after three days must rise again [Mark 8:{27}31]

Jesus "is not here: for He is risen, as He said," an angel said to Mary Magdalene and the other Mary [Matthew 28:5-6] ▢▢ Jesus "of Nazareth is risen," a young man in a long white garment said to Mary Magdalene, Mary the mother of James, and Salome [Mark 16:5-6] ▢▢▢ Jesus "is not here, but is risen; why seek the living among the dead?," two men in shining garments said to the women who had come with Jesus from Galilee and certain others [Luke 24:3-6]

Jesus "is risen from the dead," an angel said to Mary Magdalene and the other Mary [Matthew 28:5-7]

Jesus rose (from the dead) early the first day of the week [Mark 16:9]

Jesus upbraided the eleven with (for) their unbelief and hardness of heart, because they believed not those who had seen Him after He was risen [Mark 16:{6}14]

Jesus' body was not found in the tomb (by the women who came with Him from Galilee and certain others) [Luke 24:1-3]

Jesus' linen clothes laid by themselves in the tomb, and Peter wondered in himself at that which was come to pass [Luke 24:{3}12]

Jesus Himself drew near, and went with them (two men), but their eyes were holden (blinded) that they should (would) know Him [Luke 24:13-16]

Jesus "(the Lord) is risen indeed," said Cleopas and another man to the eleven, and them who were with them [Luke 24:34]

Jesus "(the Lord) has appeared to Simon," said Cleopas and another man to the eleven, and them who were with them [Luke 24:34]

Jesus, after these things, showed Himself again to His disciples the third time, after that He was risen from the dead [John 21:1-14]

Jesus shewed Himself alive after His passion (death) by many infallible proofs to the apostles whom He had chosen [Acts 1:1-3]

Jesus was seen of (by) them (the apostles whom He had chosen) forty days, after His passion (death) [Acts 1:1-3]

Jesus "of Nazareth God has raised up, having loosed the pains of death, because it was not possible that He should be held by it" (Peter's explanation at Pentecost) [Acts 2:22-24]

Jesus "of Nazareth's soul was not to be left in Hell" (Peter's explanation at Pentecost) (Psalm 16:10) [Acts 2:{22}27-31]

Jesus "of Nazareth's flesh did not see corruption" (Peter's explanation at Pentecost) (Psalm 16:10) [Acts 2:{22}27-31]

Jesus "was raised up by God, whereof we all are witnesses" (Peter's explanation at Pentecost) [Acts 2:32]

Jesus, "God's Son, was raised from the dead by God; whereof we are witnesses" (Peter's response to the people at the temple) [Acts 3:13-15]

Jesus, "God's Son, was raised up by God" (Peter's response to the people at the temple) [Acts 3:26]

Jesus was preached (by Peter and John) regarding the resurrection from the dead [Acts 4:1-2]

Jesus "Christ of Nazareth was raised from the dead by God" (Peter speaking to the rulers of the people and elders of Israel) [Acts 4:10]

Jesus the Lord's resurrection was given witness to with great power by the apostles [Acts 4:33]

Jesus "was raised up by the God of our fathers" (the words of Peter and the other apostles to the council) [Acts 5:30]

Jesus appeared to Saul on the road to Damascus [Acts 9:1-19]

Jesus "of Nazareth was raised by God on the third day" (Peter speaking to Cornelius' household) [Acts 10:{38}40]

Jesus "of Nazareth was showed openly, after He rose from the dead, to witnesses chosen before by God" (Peter speaking to Cornelius' household) [Acts 10:{38}40-41]

Jesus "of Nazareth ate and drank with witnesses chosen before by God, after He rose from the dead" (Peter speaking to Cornelius' household) [Acts 10:{38}41]

Jesus "was raised from the dead by God" (Paul speaking in the Antioch synagogue) [Acts 13:{23}30]

Jesus "was seen for many days of (by) them who came up with Him from Galilee to Jerusalem, who are His witnesses to the people" (Paul speaking in the Antioch synagogue) [Acts 13:{23}31]

Jesus "was raised up by God again, as it is also written in the second Psalm, 'You are My Son, this day have I begotten You'" (Psalm 2:7) (Paul speaking in the Antioch synagogue) [Acts 13:33]

Jesus "was raised from the dead, now no more to return to corruption" (Psalm 16:10) (Paul speaking in the Antioch synagogue) [Acts 13:33-35]

Jesus, "whom God raised up again, saw no corruption" (Paul speaking in the Antioch synagogue) [Acts 13:{33}37]

Jesus Christ must needs have risen again from the dead, as reasoned out of the Scriptures by Paul to the Jews in the synagogue at Thessalonica [Acts 17:1-3]

Jesus and the resurrection was preached by Paul to the philosophers of the Epicureans and Stoicks [Acts 17:18]

Jesus "(that Man) was raised by God from the dead, giving assurance to all men that Jesus will judge the world in righteousness," said Paul on Mar's Hill [Acts 17:31]

Jesus "the Christ should (would) be the first that should (would) rise from the dead," Paul answered King Agrippa, citing Moses and the prophets [Acts 26:{15}23]

Jesus Christ our Lord was declared to be the Son of God with power, according to the spirit of holiness, by the resurrection from the dead [Romans 1:3-4]

Jesus our Lord was raised up from the dead [Romans 4:24]

Jesus our Lord was raised again for our justification [Romans 4:24-25]

Jesus (Christ) was raised up from the dead by the glory of the Father [Romans 6:4]

Jesus (Christ), being raised from the dead dies no more; death has no more dominion over Him [Romans 6:9]

Jesus (Christ) was raised from the dead [Romans 8:11]

Jesus (Christ) is risen again [Romans 8:34]

Jesus (Christ) rose, and revived [Romans 14:9]

Jesus Christ our Lord I (Paul) have seen [1 Corinthians 9:1]

Jesus (Christ) rose again the third day according to the Scriptures [1 Corinthians 15:3-4]

Jesus (Christ) was seen of (by) Cephas, then of (by) the twelve: after that, He was seen of (by) above 500 brethren at once; after that, He was seen of (by) James; then of (by) all the apostles, and last of all He was seen of (by) me also (Paul after Jesus' resurrection) [1 Corinthians 15:3-8]

Jesus (Christ) is risen, so there is resurrection of the dead [1 Corinthians 15:13]

Jesus (Christ) is risen, so our preaching is not vain and your faith is also not vain [1 Corinthians 15:14]

Jesus (Christ) was raised up by God, as we have testified [1 Corinthians 15:15]

Jesus (Christ) is risen, so the dead rise [1 Corinthians 15:16]

Jesus (Christ) is risen, so your faith is not futile; you are not yet in your sins [1 Corinthians 15:17]

Jesus (Christ) is risen from the dead [1 Corinthians 15:20]

Jesus (Christ) has become the firstfruits of those who slept (died) [1 Corinthians 15:20]

Jesus the Lord was raised up [2 Corinthians 4:14]

Jesus (Christ) died for them and rose again [2 Corinthians 5:14-15]

Jesus Christ was raised from the dead by God [Galatians 1:1]

Jesus (Christ) was raised from the dead by God [Ephesians 1:20]

Jesus' (Christ) resurrection has power [Philippians 3:9-10]

Jesus (God's Son) is the firstborn of every creature [Colossians 1:{13}15]

Jesus (God's Son) is the firstborn from the dead [Colossians 1:{13}18]

Jesus (Christ) was raised from the dead by God [Colossians 2:11-12]

Jesus was raised from the dead by God [1 Thessalonians 1:9-10]

Jesus died and rose again, even so those also who sleep in Jesus will God will bring with Him [1 Thessalonians 4:14]

Jesus Christ was raised from the dead [2 Timothy 2:8]

Jesus (God's Son) is the firstbegotten [Hebrews 1:{2}6]

Jesus (the Son), "You remain" (Psalm 102:26) [Hebrews 1:{2}
11]

Jesus our Lord was brought again from the dead by the God
of peace [Hebrews 13:20]

Jesus Christ was resurrected from the dead [1 Peter 1:3]

Jesus (Christ) was raised up from the dead by God [1 Peter
1:{19}21]

Jesus (Christ) was quickened (raised from the dead) by the
Spirit [1 Peter 3:18]

Jesus Christ was resurrected [1 Peter 3:21]

Jesus Christ is the first begotten from the dead [Revelation
1:5]

IX. His Return

There are many Scriptures that speak of the day of Jehovah, in that day, the last day or the day of the Lord. Some Scriptures [1 Corinthians 5:5; 2 Corinthians 1:14; Philippians 1:10, 2:16] state that Jesus has a "day". Are these the same? No doubt.

The second time Jesus comes to earth it will be as KING OF KINGS AND LORD OF LORDS [Revelation 19:11-16]. He will take vengeance on those who have rejected Him. This will be a truly awe inspiring sight, but to many it will be a time of great fear [Revelation 6:14-17].

The apostles and others said:

Jesus "shall so come in like manner as you have seen Him go into heaven," said two men in white apparel to the apostles whom He had chosen [Acts 1:10-11]

Jesus Christ our Lord is coming [1 Corinthians 1:7]

Jesus (the Lord) will come [1 Corinthians 11:26]

Jesus (Christ), the firstfruits, will come [1 Corinthians 15:23]

Jesus (Christ) shall appear [Colossians 3:4]

Jesus is coming from heaven [1 Thessalonians 1:10]

Jesus Christ our Lord with you in His presence at His coming is our joy [1 Thessalonians 2:19]

Jesus Christ our Lord is coming with all His saints [1 Thessalonians 3:13]

Jesus died and rose again, even so those also who sleep in Jesus will God bring with Him [1 Thessalonians 4:14]

Jesus (the Lord) Himself shall descend from heaven [1 Thessalonians 4:16]

Jesus (the Lord) Himself shall descend with a shout [1 Thessalonians 4:16]

Jesus (the Lord) Himself shall descend with the voice of the archangel [1 Thessalonians 4:16]

Jesus (the Lord) Himself shall descend with the trump of God [1 Thessalonians 4:16]

Jesus Christ our Lord is coming [1 Thessalonians 5:23]

Jesus the Lord shall be revealed from heaven with His mighty angels [2 Thessalonians 1:7]

Jesus the Lord shall be revealed in flaming fire taking vengeance on those who know not God [2 Thessalonians 1:7-8]

Jesus the Lord shall be revealed in flaming fire taking vengeance on those who obey not the gospel of our Lord Jesus Christ [2 Thessalonians 1:7-8]

Jesus the Lord, in the day when He comes, shall be glorified in His saints [2 Thessalonians 1:{7}10]

Jesus the Lord, in the day when He comes, shall be admired in (by) all those who believe [2 Thessalonians 1:{7}10]

Jesus Christ our Lord is coming, and we will be gathered together to Him [2 Thessalonians 2:1]

Jesus' (Christ) day shall not come, except (until) there come a falling away first, and that man of sin be revealed, the son of perdition; who opposes and exalts himself above all that is called God, or that is worshipped; so that he as God sits in the temple of God, showing himself that he is God [2 Thessalonians 2:2-3]

Jesus shall consume that Wicked (one), who shall be revealed, with the spirit of His mouth, and shall destroy with the brightness of His coming [2 Thessalonians 2:8]

Jesus Christ our Lord will appear, shown by God in His own times (when He is ready) [1 Timothy 6:14-15]

Jesus Christ will judge the quick (living) and the dead at His appearing and His kingdom [2 Timothy 4:1]

Jesus Christ will appear [Titus 2:13]

Jesus (Christ) shall appear the second time without sin unto salvation, to those who look for Him [Hebrews 9:28]

Jesus Christ will appear [1 Peter 1:7]

Jesus Christ will be revealed [1 Peter 1:13]

Jesus Christ our Lord is coming [2 Peter 1:16]

Jesus (the Son) shall appear [1 John 2:{24}28]

Jesus (the Son) will come [1 John 2:{24}28]

Jesus Christ is coming with clouds; and every eye shall see Him, and they also who pierced Him: and all kindreds (people) of the earth shall wail because of Him [Revelation 1: 5-7]

X. His Character

The character of Jesus is an example of the character He wants in His followers: humility, compassion, completion of assignments, servant attitude, sinlessness, truth in judgment and love. This character is attested to by most of the statements in this book.

The apostles and others said:

Jesus, when He saw the multitudes, was moved with compassion on them, because they fainted, and were scattered abroad, as sheep having no shepherd [Matthew 9:{35}36]

Jesus began to upbraid the cities wherein most of His mighty works were done, because they repented not [Matthew 11:{7}20]

Jesus was moved with compassion toward them (a great multitude) [Matthew 14:14]

Jesus had compassion on two blind men [Matthew 20:34]

Jesus "is a just Man, have nothing to do with Him: for I have suffered many things this day in a dream because of Him," said Pilate's wife to Pilate [Matthew 27:{17}19]

Jesus "is a just Person," Pilate said to the multitude [Matthew 27:{22}24]

Jesus was moved with compassion [Mark 1:41]

Jesus looked round about on them with anger, being grieved for the hardness of their hearts [Mark 3:{2:19}5]

Jesus saw much people in the desert, and was moved with compassion toward them, because they were as sheep not having a shepherd [Mark 6:34]

Jesus sighed deeply in His spirit (because the Pharisees began to question with Him, seeking of (from) Him a sign from heaven, tempting Him) [Mark 8:{1}11-12]

Jesus beholding him (a man with great possessions), loved him [Mark 10:21]

Jesus increased in wisdom and stature, and in favor with God and man [Luke 2:52]

Jesus (the Lord) had compassion on her (the widow with the dead son) [Luke 7:13]

Jesus, when the time was come that He should (would) be received up, steadfastly set His face to go to Jerusalem [Luke 9:{50}51]

Jesus rebuked His disciples James and John for suggesting they command fire to come down from heaven, and consume them (the Samaritans for not receiving Him) [Luke 9:{50}52-56]

Jesus beheld the city (Jerusalem), and wept over it [Luke 19: {35}41]

Jesus "certainly was a righteous Man," said the centurion when he saw what was done, glorifying God [Luke 23:46-47]

Jesus (the Word) was full of grace [John 1:14]

Jesus (the Word) was full of truth [John 1:14]

Jesus "was zealous for God's house," the disciples remembered (Psalm 69:9) [John 2:{13}17]

Jesus loved Martha, and her sister, and Lazarus [John 11:5]

Jesus groaned in the spirit, and was troubled, when He saw Mary and the Jews weeping [John 11:33]

Jesus wept [John 11:35]

Jesus again groaned in Himself [John 11:38]

Jesus loved His own who were in the world to the end [John 13:1]

Jesus, "God's Son, is the Just" (Peter's response to the people at the temple) [Acts 3:13-14]

Jesus "of Nazareth went about doing good" (Peter speaking to Cornelius' household) [Acts 10:38]

Jesus Christ loves us [Romans 8:35-39]

Jesus Christ our Lord has God's love in Him [Romans 8:39]

Jesus' (Christ) love constrains us [2 Corinthians 5:14]

Jesus (Christ) knew no sin [2 Corinthians 5:20-21]

Jesus (Christ) was meek [2 Corinthians 10:1]

Jesus (Christ) was gentle [2 Corinthians 10:1]

Jesus' (Christ) love passes knowledge [Ephesians 3:19]

Jesus has the truth in Him [Ephesians 4:21]

Jesus (Christ) also has loved us [Ephesians 5:2]

Jesus Christ made Himself of (to have) no reputation [Philippians 2:5-7]

Jesus Christ humbled Himself [Philippians 2:{5}8]

Jesus Christ became obedient to death, even the death of the cross [Philippians 2:{5}8]

Jesus (the Son), "You loved righteousness" (Psalm 45:7) [Hebrews 1:{8}9]

Jesus (the Son), "You hated iniquity" (Psalm 45:7) [Hebrews 1:{8}9]

Jesus was made perfect through sufferings [Hebrews 2:{9}10]

Jesus is a merciful and faithful High Priest in things pertaining to God [Hebrews 2:{9}17]

Jesus Christ was faithful to Him who appointed Him [Hebrews
3:1-2]

Jesus the Son of God, our great High Priest, can be touched
with the feeling of our infirmities [Hebrews 4:14-15]

Jesus the Son of God, our great High Priest, was without sin
[Hebrews 4:14-15]

Jesus (Christ) in the days of His flesh, when He had offered
up prayers and supplications with strong crying and tears
to Him who was able to save Him from death, and was heard
in that (because) He feared [Hebrews 5:{5}7]

Jesus (Christ) was perfected [Hebrews 5:{5}9]

Jesus is holy [Hebrews 7:{22}26]

Jesus is harmless [Hebrews 7:{22}26]

Jesus is undefiled [Hebrews 7:{22}26]

Jesus, the Son, is consecrated forever more [Hebrews 7:28]

Jesus despised the shame (of the cross) [Hebrews 12:2]

Jesus Christ is the same yesterday [Hebrews 13:8]

Jesus Christ is the same today [Hebrews 13:8]

Jesus Christ is the same forever [Hebrews 13:8]

Jesus (Christ) was as a lamb without blemish and without spot
[1 Peter 1:19]

Jesus (Christ) "did no sin" (Isaiah 53:9) [1 Peter 2:21-22]

Jesus (Christ) "had no guile in His mouth" (Isaiah 53:9) [1 Peter
2:21-22]

Jesus (Christ) committed Himself to Him who judges righteously [1 Peter 2:{21}23]

Jesus (Christ) reviled not again [1 Peter 2:{21}23]

Jesus (Christ) threatened not [1 Peter 2:{21}23]

Jesus (Christ) is just [1 Peter 3:18]

Jesus (the Son) is righteous [1 John 2:{24}29]

Jesus (the Son of God) is true [1 John 5:20]

Jesus Christ the Lord has mercy [Jude 21]

Jesus Christ loved us [Revelation 1:5]

Jesus' "(the Lamb) great day of wrath has come, and who is
able to stand? Fall on us (mountains and rocks) and hide
us from the face of Him who sits on the throne and from
the wrath of the Lamb!," said the kings of the earth, and
the great men, and the rich men, and the chief captains,
and the mighty men, and every bondman, and every free
man; all of them had hidden themselves in the dens and
in the rocks of the mountains [Revelation 6:15-17]

Jesus (the king on a white horse) was called faithful [Revelation 19:11-16]

Jesus (the king on a white horse) was called true [Revelation 19:11-16]

XI. His Glory

A. The apostles and others said that Jesus returned to His Father in heaven and is sitting at God's right hand.

Jesus is not only in heaven at God's right hand, he is also there advocating and interceding for us [Romans 8:34; Hebrews 7:25; 1 John 2:1]!

The apostles and others said:

Jesus (the Lord) was received up into heaven [Mark 16:19]

Jesus (the Lord) sat on the right hand of God (after being received up into heaven) [Mark 16:19]

Jesus was parted from them (the eleven and those who were with them), and carried up into heaven [Luke 24: {36}51]

Jesus knew that His hour was come that He should depart out of this world to the father [John 13:1]

Jesus knew that he went (was going) to God [John 13:3]

Jesus was taken up [Acts 1:1-2]

Jesus, when He had spoken these things, while they (the apostles whom He had chosen) beheld, was taken up, and a cloud received Him out of their sight [Acts 1:{1} 9]

Jesus "was taken up from you into heaven," said two men in white apparel to the apostles whom He had chosen [Acts 1:10-11]

Jesus "was taken up from us," said Peter to the disciples [Acts 1:{21}22]

Jesus "was by (to) the right hand of God exalted" (Peter's explanation at Pentecost) [Acts 2:32-33]

Jesus "Christ must be received by heaven until the times of restitution of all things" (Peter's response to the people at the temple) [Acts 3:20-21]

Jesus "has been exalted by God to His right hand" (the words of Peter and the other apostles to the council) [Acts 5: 30-31]

Jesus, "the Son of Man, is standing at the right hand of God," said Stephen describing what he saw at his martyrdom [Acts 7:55-56]

Jesus (Christ) is even at the right hand of God [Romans 8: 34]

Jesus (Christ) also makes intercession for us [Romans 8: 34]

Jesus (Christ) was set at His own right hand by God [Ephesians 1:20]

Jesus (Christ) "ascended on high" (Psalm 68:18) [Ephesians 4: 7-8]

Jesus (Christ) is also the One who ascended up far above all heavens [Ephesians 4:7-10]

Jesus (Christ) is above, sitting on the right hand of God [Colossians 3:1]

Jesus (God's Son) sat down at the right hand of the Majesty on high [Hebrews 1:{2}3]

Jesus (the Son), "sit at My right hand" (Psalm 110:1) [Hebrews 1:{8}13]

Jesus ever lives to make intercession for those who come to God by (through) Him [Hebrews 7:{22}25]

Jesus (our High Priest) is set on the right hand of the throne of the Majesty in the heavens [Hebrews 8:1]

Jesus (Christ) is not entered into the holy places made with hands, which are the figures of the true; but into heaven itself [Hebrews 9:24]

Jesus (Christ) appears in the presence of God for us [Hebrews 9:24]

Jesus Christ, this Man, sat down on the right hand of God [Hebrews 10:{10}12]

Jesus is set down at the right hand of the throne of God [Hebrews 12:2]

Jesus Christ is gone into heaven [1 Peter 3:21-22]

Jesus Christ is on the right hand of God [1 Peter 3:21-22]

Jesus Christ is our Advocate with the Father [1 John 2:1]

Jesus "(the Lamb) is in the midst of the throne," an elder said to John [Revelation 7:17]

B. The apostles and others said that Jesus has been and will be glorified:

The apostles and others said:

Jesus took Peter, James, and John his brother, and brought them up to a high mountain apart, and was transfigured before them: and His face did shine as the sun, and His raiment was white as the light [Matthew

17:1-2] ⏏⏏ Jesus took Peter, and James, and John, and led them up into an high mountain apart by themselves: and He was transfigured before them, and His raiment became shining, exceeding white as snow (the Transfiguration) [Mark 9:2-3] ⏏⏏⏏ Jesus took Peter, John and James and went up into a mountain to pray, and as He prayed, the fashion of His countenance was altered, and His raiment was white and glistening (the Transfiguration) [Luke 9:{8:50}28-29]

Jesus was set on an ass and a very great multitude spread their garments in the way; others cut down branches from the trees, and strawed (spread) them in the way, and the multitude that went before, and that followed cried, saying: "Hosanna to the son of David: blessed is He who comes in the name of the Lord; Hosanna in the Highest" (the Triumphal Entry) [Matthew 21:6-9] ⏏⏏ Jesus sat on the colt and many spread their garments in the way: and others cut down branches off the trees, and strawed (spread) them in the way, and they that went before, and they that followed cried, saying: "Hosanna; blessed is He who comes in the name of the Lord: blessed be the kingdom of our father David, that comes in the name of the Lord: Hosanna in the Highest" (the Triumphal Entry) [Mark 11:6-11] ⏏⏏⏏ Jesus was set on the colt, and as He went, they spread their clothes in the way, and when He was come nigh, even now at the descent of the Mount of Olives, the whole multitude of the disciples began to rejoice and praise God with a loud voice for all the mighty works that they had seen; saying: "Blessed is the King who comes in the name of the Lord: peace in heaven, and glory in the highest" (the Triumphal Entry) [Luke 19:35-38] ⏏⏏⏏ Jesus was met by much people that were come to the feast, when they heard that He was coming to Jerusalem, and they took branches of palm trees, and cried, "Hosanna: blessed is the King of Israel He who comes in the name of the Lord" (the Triumphal Entry) [John 12:12-13]

Jesus, "Master, grant to us that we may sit, one on Your right hand and the other on Your left hand, in Your glory," said James and John, the sons of Zebedee [Mark 10:{32} 35-37]

Jesus "shall be great," an angel said to Mary [Luke 1:31-32]

Jesus was glorified of (by) all [Luke 4:14-15]

Jesus (the Word) had glory as of the only begotten of the Father [John 1:14]

Jesus manifested forth His glory by this beginning of miracles (by turning the water into wine) [John 2:11]

Jesus spake concerning the Spirit, whom those who believe on Him should (would) receive: for the Holy Ghost was not yet given; because Jesus was not yet glorified [John 7:39]

Jesus was glorified [John 12:16]

Jesus "was made both Lord and Christ by God" (Peter's explanation at Pentecost) [Acts 2:36]

Jesus, "God's Son, was glorified by God" (Peter's response to the people at the temple) [Acts 3:13]

Jesus "has been exalted by God to His right hand" (the words of Peter and the other apostles to the council) [Acts 5:30-31]

Jesus "has been exalted by God to be a Prince" (the words of Peter and the other apostles to the council) [Acts 5:30-31]

Jesus "has been exalted by God to be a Savior" (the words of Peter and the other apostles to the council) [Acts 5:30-31]

Jesus (Christ) and we, God's children, are joint heirs of God: if so be that we suffer with Jesus, that we may be glorified together [Romans 8:16-17]

Jesus (Christ) is far above all principality, and power, and might, and dominion, and every name that is named [Ephesians 1:20-21]

Jesus (Christ) is the head over all things to the church, His body [Ephesians 1:20-23]

Jesus Christ has been highly exalted by God [Philippians 2:{5}9]

Jesus Christ has been given, by God, a name which is above every name [Philippians 2:{5}9]

Jesus shall have every knee bow to His name [Philippians 2:10]

Jesus Christ shall have every tongue confess that He is Lord (Isaiah 45:23) [Philippians 2:11]

Jesus (God's Son) is the head of the body, the church [Colossians 1:{13}18]

Jesus (Christ) is the head of all principality and power [Colossians 2:8-10]

Jesus the Lord, in the day when He comes, shall be glorified in His saints [2 Thessalonians 1:{7}10]

Jesus the Lord, in the day when He comes, shall be admired in (by) all those who believe [2 Thessalonians 1: {7}10]

Jesus (God's Son) is the brightness of God's glory [Hebrews 1:{2}3]

Jesus (the Son), "I will make Your enemies Your footstool" (Psalm 110:1) [Hebrews 1:{8}13]

Jesus was crowned with glory and honor [Hebrews 2:9]

Jesus Christ our Lord is the Lord of glory [James 2:1]

Jesus (Christ) was given glory by God [1 Peter 1:{19}21]

Jesus Christ glorifies God [1 Peter 4:11]

Jesus' (Christ) glory shall be revealed [1 Peter 4:13]

Jesus Christ our Lord is majestic [2 Peter 1:16]

Jesus Christ our Lord received from God the Father honor and glory [2 Peter 1:16-17]

Jesus (One like the Son of Man) was clothed with a garment down to the foot and girt about the paps (chest) with a golden girdle [Revelation 1:13]

Jesus' (One like the Son of Man) head and His hairs were white like wool, as white as snow [Revelation 1:13-14]

Jesus' (One like the Son of Man) eyes were as a flame of fire [Revelation 1:13-14]

Jesus' (One like the Son of Man) feet were like fine brass [Revelation 1:13-15]

Jesus' (One like the Son of Man) voice was as the sound of many waters [Revelation 1:13-15]

Jesus (One like the Son of Man) had in His right hand seven stars [Revelation 1:13-16]

Jesus (One like the Son of Man) had a sharp two-edged sword that went out of His mouth [Revelation 1:13-16]

Jesus' (One like the Son of Man) countenance was as the sun shining in its strength [Revelation 1:13-16]

Jesus (the Lamb) "has prevailed to open the book, and to loose the seven seals thereof," an elder said to John [Revelation 5:5-9]

Jesus (the Lamb), "You are worthy to take the book, and to open the seals thereof," sung by four beasts and four and twenty elders who fell down before the Lamb [Revelation 5:8-9]

Jesus "(the Lamb) is worthy to receive power, and riches, and wisdom, and strength, and honor, and glory, and blessing," said with a loud voice by many angels, the beasts and the elders: the number of them was ten thousand times ten thousand [Revelation 5:11-12]

Jesus "(the Lamb) is to have blessing, and honor, and glory, and power forever and ever," said every creature which is in heaven, and on the earth, and under the earth, and such as are in the sea [Revelation 5:13]

Jesus "(the Lamb) will be married" (voice of a great multitude) [Revelation 19:7-9]

Jesus' testimony is the spirit of prophecy [Revelation 19:10]

Jesus' (the king on a white horse) eyes were as a flame of fire [Revelation 19:11-16]

Jesus (the king on a white horse) had a name written, that no man knew, but He Himself [Revelation 19:11-16]

Jesus (the king on a white horse) was clothed with a vesture (garment) dipped in blood [Revelation 19:11-16]

Jesus (the king on a white horse) has a sharp sword that goes out of His mouth, that with it He should smite the nations [Revelation 19:11-16]

Jesus "(the Lamb) has a bride, a wife," an angel (one of the seven angels who had the seven vials full of the seven last plagues) said to John [Revelation 21:9]

Jesus (the Lamb) has the Book of Life [Revelation 21:27]

Jesus' (the Lamb) servants shall serve Him, see His face, and His name shall be on their foreheads [Revelation 22:3-4]

XII. Other

A. The apostles and others said that Jesus was human and of Jewish lineage and was in the line of the promises and the kings:

His suffering and death also attest to His humanity.

The apostles and others said:

Jesus Christ is the Son of David [Matthew 1:1]

Jesus Christ is the Son of Abraham [Matthew 1:1]

Jesus was born of Mary [Matthew 1:16]

Jesus Christ "is to be born of a virgin," said an angel to Joseph (Isaiah 7:14) [Matthew 1:18-25] ▢▢ Jesus "shall be called the Son of God, because the Holy Ghost shall come upon you, and the power of the Highest shall overshadow you" an angel said to Mary after she said to the angel, "How shall this be, seeing I know not a man?" (Isaiah 7:14) [Luke 1:{31}34-35]

Jesus "was to be the Son of Mary," said an angel to Joseph [Matthew 1:20-21]

Jesus was Mary's firstborn Son [Matthew 1:20-25]

Jesus was born in Bethlehem of Judea in the days of Herod the king (Micah 5:2) [Matthew 2:1] ▢▢ Jesus (Christ) was born in Bethlehem of Judea, wrapped in swaddling clothes and laid in a manger [Luke 2:1-12]

Jesus "(Christ) was to be born in Bethlehem of Judea," the chief priests and scribes responded to Herod (Micah 5:2) [Matthew 2:4-5]

Jesus (the young Child) was taken to Egypt with His mother by night by Joseph: and was there until the death of Herod: that it might be fulfilled which was spoken of (about) the Lord by the prophet, saying, "Out of Egypt have I called My son" (Hosea 11:1) [Matthew 2:14-15]

Jesus (the young Child) came into the land of Israel and dwelt in a city called Nazareth: that it might be fulfilled which was spoken by the prophets, "He shall be called a Nazarene" [Matthew 2:21-23]

Jesus was hungry (after fasting 40 days and 40 nights) [Matthew 4:1-2]

Jesus "is the carpenter's son" (the people of His own country) [Matthew 13:{51}54-55] ⊞⊞ Jesus "is the carpenter" (the people of His own country) [Mark 6:{5:36}3]

Jesus "mother is called Mary" (the people of His own country) [Matthew 13:{51}54-55] ⊞⊞ Jesus "is the son of Mary" (the people of His own country) [Mark 6: {5:36}3]

Jesus' "brothers are James, and Joses, and Simon, and Judas" (the people of His own country) [Matthew 13:{51} 54-55] ⊞⊞ Jesus "is the brother of James, and Joses, and of Juda, and Simon" (the people of His own country) [Mark 6:{5:36}3]

Jesus' "sisters are all with us" (the people of His own country) [Matthew 13:{51}54-55] ⊞⊞ Jesus' "sisters are here with us" (the people of His own country) [Mark 6:{5:36}3]

Jesus was hungry [Matthew 21:{12}18]

Jesus "will be your Son," an angel said to Mary [Luke 1: 30-31]

Jesus, when eight days were accomplished, was circumcised [Luke 2:21]

Jesus, the name the child was called, was the name the angel gave Him before He was conceived in the womb [Luke 2:21]

Jesus was brought to Jerusalem to be presented to the Lord, when the days of her (Mary's) purification according to the law of Moses, were accomplished (as it is written in the law of the Lord, "Every male who opens the womb shall be called holy to the Lord") (Exodus 13: 2) [Luke 2:{21}22-23]

Jesus (the child) grew, and waxed strong in spirit, filled with wisdom [Luke 2:{27}40]

Jesus (the child) had the grace of God upon Him [Luke 2: {27}40]

Jesus (the child) was subject to them (His parents) [Luke 2:{43}51]

Jesus was (as was supposed) the son of Joseph [Luke 3: 23]

Jesus "is Joseph's son" (those in the synagogue at Nazareth) [Luke 4:{14}22]

Jesus (the Word) was made flesh, and dwelt among us [John 1:14]

Jesus was wearied from His journey [John 4:6]

Jesus "is the son of Joseph, whose father and mother we know. How is it then that He says, 'I came down from heaven'?" (the Jews) [John 6:42]

Jesus, knowing that all things were now accomplished that the Scripture might be fulfilled, said, "I thirst" [John 19:28]

Jesus "of Nazareth ate and drank with witnesses chosen before by God, after He rose from the dead" (Peter speaking to Cornelius' household) [Acts 10:{38}41]

Jesus Christ our Lord was made (born) of the seed of David according to the flesh [Romans 1:3]

Jesus Christ, God's own Son, was sent by God in the likeness of sinful flesh, for (because of) sin [Romans 8:2-3]

Jesus (Christ) came, concerning the flesh, from the fathers (Israelites) [Romans 9:5]

Jesus (Christ) we have known after the flesh [2 Corinthians 5:16]

Jesus (Christ) "is the seed of Abraham" [Galatians 3:16]

Jesus (God's Son) was made (born) of a woman [Galatians 4:4]

Jesus (God's Son) was made (born) under the law [Galatians 4:4]

Jesus Christ has made both (Jews and Gentiles) one, and has broken down the middle wall of partition between us, having abolished in His flesh the enmity, even the law of commandments contained in ordinances, for to make in Himself of two one new man, so making peace [Ephesians 2:13-15]

Jesus Christ was made in the likeness of men [Philippians 2:5-7]

Jesus Christ was found in fashion as a man [Philippians 2:{5}8]

Jesus Christ is the Man [1 Timothy 2:5]

Jesus Christ is of the seed of David [2 Timothy 2:8]

Jesus was made a little lower than the angels [Hebrews 2:9]

Jesus took part of the same (flesh and blood) [Hebrews 2:{9}14]

Jesus had to be made like His brethren in all things [Hebrews 2:{9}17]

Jesus Himself was tempted [Hebrews 2:{9}18]

Jesus the Son of God, our great High Priest, was in all points tempted as we are [Hebrews 4:14-15]

Jesus (Christ) in the days of His flesh, when He had offered up prayers and supplications with strong crying and
tears to Him who was able to save Him from death, and
was heard in that (because) He feared [Hebrews 5:{5}7]
Jesus (our Lord) sprang out of Judah [Hebrews 7:14]
Jesus consecrated, by His flesh and blood, a new and living way for us to enter the Holiest [Hebrews 10:19-20]
Jesus Christ is confessed as having come in the flesh by
every spirit that is of God [1 John 4:2]
Jesus Christ, as having come in the flesh, is not confessed by every spirit that is not of God, and this is the
spirit of antichrist [1 John 4:3]
Jesus Christ, is come in the flesh, is confessed not by many
deceivers who are entered into the world; this is an antichrist [2 John 7]

B. The apostles and others made other statements about Jesus:

The apostles and others said:

Jesus marveled (at the centurion's faith) [Matthew 8:10]
ꀊꀊ Jesus marvelled at him (the centurion, because
of his faith) [Luke 7:8-9]
Jesus was besought by the whole city that He would
depart out of their coasts (after casting the devils out
of two and into some swine) [Matthew 8:34] ꀊꀊ
Jesus' action (casting unclean spirit(s) out of a man
and into some swine) made them afraid (people of the
city and the country), and they began to pray Him to
depart out of their coasts [Mark 5:13-17] ꀊꀊꀊ
Jesus' action (casting devils out of a man and into
some swine) took them (the whole multitude of the
country of the Gadarenes round about) with great fear,
so they besought Him to depart from them [Luke 8:{35}
37]
Jesus knew their (the scribes) thoughts (that He was blaspheming) [Matthew 9:4]
Jesus "is the prophet of Nazareth of Galilee," said the multitude [Matthew 21:{6}11]

Jesus was taken for (perceived as) a prophet by the multitude, and because of this the chief priests and Pharisees feared the multitude [Matthew 21:{42}46]

Jesus perceived their (the Pharisees) wickedness [Matthew 22:18]

Jesus was not answered a word by any man, neither durst (did) any man from that day forth ask Him any more questions [Matthew 22:{41}46]

Jesus had a woman pour an alabaster box of very precious ointment on His head [Matthew 26:6-7] ◫◫ Jesus had a woman pour an alabaster box of ointment of spikenard on His head [Mark 14:{13:5}3] ◫◫◫ Jesus' feet were anointed by Mary with a pound of very costly ointment of spiknard, and she wiped His feet with her hair [John 12:3]

Jesus had been ministered to by many women from Galilee (who were at the crucifixion, looking on from afar) [Matthew 27:{54}55]

Jesus came into Galilee, preaching the gospel of the kingdom of God [Mark 1:14]

Jesus perceived in His spirit that they (some of the scribes) so reasoned ("Who can forgive sins but God alone?") within themselves [Mark 2:{5}8] ◫◫ Jesus perceived their (the scribes and the Pharisees) thoughts ("Who can forgive sins but God alone?") [Luke 5:22]

Jesus had many publicans and sinners as His followers, and He sat at meat with them [Mark 2:15]

Jesus' disciples did not fast [Mark 2:{17}18] ◫◫ Jesus disciples did not fast often or make prayers [Luke 5:{31}33]

Jesus knew that virtue had gone out of Him (after being touched by the woman with an issue of blood) [Mark 5:30]

Jesus' disciples were astonished at His words (the difficulty of a rich man to enter the kingdom of God) [Mark 10:24]

Jesus' disciples were astonished out of measure, saying among themselves, "Who then can be saved?" [Mark 10:26]

Jesus knew their hypocrisy (the Pharisees and the Herodians) [Mark 12:{11:33}15]

Jesus, after answering the question, "Which is the first commandment of all?," had no man that durst (dared) ask Him any question [Mark 12:28-34]

Jesus was about thirty years of age (at His baptism) [Luke 3:23]

Jesus was brought up in Nazareth [Luke 4:{14}16]

Jesus knew their (the scribes and Pharisees) thoughts (watching Him to see whether He would heal on the Sabbath day: that they might find an accusation against Him) [Luke 6:{3}8]

Jesus "is a great prophet risen up among us" and "God has visited His people," said the people of Nain, after the raising of the widow's son [Luke 7:{9}16]

Jesus' feet were washed with the tears of a woman who was a sinner, and she did wipe them with the hairs of her head, and kissed His feet and anointed them with the ointment [Luke 7:{22}37-38]

Jesus was ministered of (from) the substance of Mary called Magdalene, Joanna, Susanna and many others [Luke 8:{7:40}2-3]

Jesus perceived the thought (disputing about which of them would be the greatest) of their (His disciples) heart [Luke 9:47]

Jesus knew their thoughts (that He cast out devils by Beelzebub) [Luke 11:{10:41}17]

Jesus could not be answered to (about) these things (whether it was lawful to heal on the Sabbath day) [Luke 14:{3}6]

Jesus "rebuke Your disciples," some of the Pharisees said (for rejoicing and praising God during the Triumphal Entry) [Luke 19:{35}39]

Jesus perceived their craftiness, when they (the chief priests and the scribes) asked Him whether it was lawful to pay taxes to Caesar [Luke 20:{8}21-23]

Jesus was strengthened by an angel who appeared to Him from heaven [Luke 22:{20:34}43]

Jesus "must increase, but I must decrease," answered John the Baptist [John 3:22-30]

Jesus, "Sir, I perceive that You are a prophet," the woman (at the well) said to Him [John 4:{17}19]

Jesus perceived that they were about to come and take Him by force, to make Him king, so He departed again to a mountain Himself alone [John 6:15]

Jesus knew from the beginning who they were who believed not, and who should (would) betray Him [John 6:64]

Jesus was not spoken openly of by any man for fear of the Jews [John 7:{1}13]

Jesus "is He whom they seek to kill, but lo, He speaks boldly, and they say nothing to Him. Do the rulers know indeed that this is the very Christ? Howbeit we know this Man whence He is (Where He is from): but when the Christ comes, no one knows whence He is (where He is from)," said some of them of (from) Jerusalem [John 7:{21}25-27]

Jesus "speaks like no other man," the officers answered the chief priests and Pharisees who asked them, "Why have you not brought Him (Jesus)?" [John 7:{39}45-46]

Jesus "is not believed on by any of the rulers or of the Pharisees. This people who know not the law are cursed" the Pharisees answered the officers [John 7:{39}47-48]

Jesus was believed on by many, as He spake these words (that the Father had sent Him and that He spoke what His Father taught Him) [John 8:{28}30]

Jesus was asked by His disciples, "Master, who did sin, this man, or his parents, that he was born blind?" [John 9: 2-3]

Jesus "is a prophet," said the man born blind from birth [John 9:{14}17]

Jesus, "are we blind also?," said some of the Pharisees to Him [John 9:39-41]

Jesus went away beyond Jordan; and there He abode, and many believed on Him there [John 10:{34}40-42]

Jesus "(Lord), if you had been here, my brother had not died, but I know, that even now, whatever You will ask of God, God will give it (to) You," said Martha, Lazarus' sister [John 11:20-22]

Jesus, "Lord, if You had been here, my brother had not died," said Mary, Lazarus' sister [John 11:32]

Jesus was believed on by many of the Jews, who had seen the things which Jesus did [John 11:45]

Jesus knew who should (would) betray Him [John 13:10-11]

Jesus knew all things that should (would) come upon Him [John 18:4]

Jesus saw His mother, and His mother's sister, Mary the wife of Cleophas, and Mary Magdalene standing by the cross, and said to His mother, "Woman, behold your son!" and then said to the disciple whom He loved,

"Behold your mother!", and from that hour that disciple took her into his own home [John 19:25-26]

Jesus "(the Lord) has been taken away out of the sepulchre, and we do not know where they have laid Him," said Mary Magdalene to Simon Peter and the other disciple, whom Jesus loved [John 20:1-2]

Jesus "(my Lord) they have taken away, and I do not know where they have laid Him," she (Mary Magdalene) said to the two angels in white sitting, the one at the head, and the other at the feet, where the body of Jesus had lain, after they said to her, "Why weep you?" [John 20:11-13]

Jesus was standing (there), and she, (Mary Magdalene) knew not that it was Jesus [John 20:14]

Jesus, after eight days came, the doors being shut, and stood in the midst (of His disciples) [John 20:{24}26]

Jesus "(Lord); You know that I love You," said Simon Peter, after Jesus said to him, "Simon, son of Jonas, love you me more than these?" [John 21:15]

Jesus "(Lord); You know that I love You," he (Simon Peter) said, after Jesus said to him again the second time, "Simon, son of Jonas, love you me" [John 21:{15}16]

Jesus "(Lord), You know all things; You know that I love You," said Simon, after Jesus said to him the third time, "Simon son of Jonas, love you me?" [John 21:17]

Jesus spake this, signifying by what death he (Simon Peter) should (would) glorify God [John 21:{17}19]

Jesus did not say to him (Peter), "He (the disciple whom Jesus loved, who also leaned on His breast at supper) shall not die" [John 21:20-23]

Jesus "Christ was preached to you before" (Peter's response to the people at the temple) [Acts 3:20]

Jesus must not be spoken or taught about," they (the council) commanded them (Peter and John) [Acts 4:13-18]

Jesus "should not be spoken about," they (the council) commanded them (Peter and the other apostles) [Acts 5:40]

Jesus "of Nazareth shall destroy this place and change the customs which Moses delivered to us," said the Synagogue of the Libertines (and others) to the council about what Stephen allegedly said [Acts 6:9-14]

Jesus, "Lord, receive my spirit," called out Stephen as he was stoned to death [Acts 7:59-60]

Jesus Christ's name was preached by Philip to those in the city of Samaria [Acts 8:5-12]

Jesus the Lord was the name in which people in Samaria were baptized [Acts 8:16]

Jesus was preached by Philip to a man of Ethiopia [Acts 8:26-35]

Jesus the Lord was preached to the Grecians by some men of (from) Cyprus and Cyrene [Acts 11:20]

Jesus, the Lord's word, was heard by all who dwelt in Asia, both Jews and Greeks [Acts 19:10]

Jesus "I know, and Paul I know; but who are You?," said an evil spirit to certain of the vagabond Jews, exorcists who called on the name of the Lord Jesus over those who had evil spirits, saying, "We adjure you by Jesus whom Paul preaches" [Acts 19:13-15]

Jesus the Lord's name was magnified to all Jews and Greeks dwelling at Ephesus, and fear fell on them all [Acts 19:17]

Jesus Christ our Lord gives us access by faith into this grace wherein we stand [Romans 5:1-2]

Jesus (Christ) died to sin once [Romans 6:9-10]

Jesus (Christ) and we, God's children, are joint heirs of God: if so be that we suffer with Jesus, that we may be glorified together [Romans 8:16-17]

Jesus (Christ) is the end of the law for righteousness to everyone who believes [Romans 10:4]

Jesus' (Christ) mind is ours [1 Corinthians 2:16]

Jesus (Christ) is sinned against when we wound a brother's weaker conscience [1 Corinthians 8:11-12]

Jesus (Christ) is one body [1 Corinthians 12:12]

Jesus' (Christ) body is made up of you (us) [1 Corinthians 12:27]

Jesus (the Son) Himself will be subject to Him (God) who put all things under Him (Jesus), that God may be all in all [1 Corinthians 15:28]

Jesus' life may be manifested in our mortal flesh [2 Corinthians 4:11]

Jesus (Christ) has no concord with Belial (lawlessness, Satan?) [2 Corinthians 6:15]

Jesus Christ our Lord was rich (while in heaven) [2 Corinthians 8:9]

Jesus Christ our Lord became poor (by becoming a man and entering this world) for your sakes [2 Corinthians 8:9]

Jesus (Christ) lives by the power of God [2 Corinthians 13:
3-4]

Jesus "(Christ) is not the minister of sin," said Paul to Peter
and the others [Galatians 2:17]

Jesus (Christ) was put on by as many of you as have been
baptized into Christ [Galatians 3:27]

Jesus (Christ) will profit you nothing, if you become circumcised, for I testify again to every man that is circumcised, that he is a debtor to do the whole law [Galatians
5:2-3]

Jesus Christ the Lord's God is the Father of glory [Ephesians
1:17]

Jesus' (Christ) mystery has now been revealed by the Spirit
to His holy apostles and prophets; that the gentiles
should be fellowheirs (with the Jews), and of the same
body, and partakers of His promise in Christ by (in) the
gospel [Ephesians 3:3-6]

Jesus' (Christ) riches are unsearchable [Ephesians 3:8]

Jesus (Christ) descended first into the lower parts of the
earth [Ephesians 4:7-9]

Jesus (Christ) fills all things [Ephesians 4:7-10]

Jesus (Christ) is preached by some even of (from) envy and
strife; of (from) contention, not sincerely [Philippians 1:
15-16]

Jesus (Christ) is preached by some also of (from) good will,
of (from) love [Philippians 1:15-17]

Jesus Christ the Lord shall change our vile body, that it
may be fashioned like His glorious body [Philippians 3:
20-21]

Jesus (Christ) in you, the hope of glory, is the mystery made
known among the Gentiles [Colossians 1:27]

Jesus (Christ) is the body (reality?) [Colossians 2:17]

Jesus Christ has now appeared [2 Timothy 1:10]

Jesus is able to succor (help) those who are tempted [Hebrews
2:{9}18]

Jesus (Christ) is a Son over His own house; whose house
we are [Hebrews 3:6]

Jesus the Son of God, our great High Priest, has passed
into the heavens [Hebrews 4:14]

Jesus, the forerunner, has entered within the veil [Hebrews
6:19-20]

Jesus was made a surety (the guarantee) of a better testament [Hebrews 7:22]

Jesus is separate from sinners [Hebrews 7:{22}26]

Jesus (our High Priest) has obtained a more excellent ministry, by how much also He is the Mediator of a better covenant [Hebrews 8:{1}6]

Jesus (Christ), through the eternal Spirit, offered Himself without spot to God [Hebrews 9:14]

Jesus' (Christ) blood shall purge your conscience from dead works to serve the Living God [Hebrews 9:14]

Jesus Christ's Spirit was in the prophets [1 Peter 1:10-11]

Jesus (Christ) was manifested in these last times for you [1 Peter 1:19-20]

Jesus Christ was used by God to call us to His eternal glory [1 Peter 5:10]

Jesus' (the Son) denial by a person means that person has not the Father [1 John 2:23]

Jesus' (the Son) acknowledgment by a person means that person has the Father [1 John 2:23]

Jesus (the Son of God) was manifested, that He might destroy the works of the devil [1 John 3:8]

Jesus Christ came by water and blood [1 John 5:6]

Jesus (the Son of God) is come [1 John 5:20]

APPENDIX A
Bible Book References

The following are the same scripture citations as in **Part 1: Statements Jesus Made About Himself**, but they are listed with the book of the bible in which they are located and are stated consecutively. Examining these will give one some feeling about various emphases by the author.

Part 1: Statements Jesus Made About Himself

Matthew

"I"

Matthew 3:
want to fulfill all righteousness [15]

Matthew 4:
will make you fishers of men, if you follow Me (to Simon and Andrew) [19]

Matthew 5:
am not come to destroy the Law or the prophets; I am come to fulfil [17]

Matthew 7:
will profess to those that work iniquity, "I never knew you: depart from me" [21-23]

Matthew 8:
will; "be clean" (healing a leper) [3]
have nowhere to lay my head (Son of Man) [20]

Matthew 9:
have the power on earth to forgive sins (proved by forgiving the sins of a man sick of the palsy and then healing him) (Son of Man) [1-6]
am the Son of Man (proved by forgiving the sins of the man sick of the palsy and then healing him) [1-6]

say to you, "Arise, take up your bed, and go to your house,"
(healing a man sick of the palsy) [6]

am not come to call the righteous, but sinners to repentance
[13]

Matthew 10:

send you forth as sheep in the midst of wolves...and you shall
be hated by all men for My name's sake [16-22]

will confess before My Father who is in heaven whoever confesses me before men [32]

will deny before My Father who is in heaven whoever denies
me before men [33]

am not come to send peace on earth, but a sword [34]

am come to set a man at variance against his father, and the
daughter against her mother, and the daughter in law
against her mother in law, and a man's foes shall be
those of his own household [35-36]

Matthew 11:

came eating and drinking (Son of Man) [19]

thank You, Father, Lord of heaven and earth, because You
have hidden these things from the wise and prudent and
have revealed them to babes [25]

have been delivered all things of (by) My Father [27]

the Son, am not known by any man, but the Father [27]

the Son, and he to whomsoever the Son will reveal the Father,
are the only ones who know the Father [27]

will give the heavy laden rest [28]

am meek and lowly in heart [29]

want you to take My yoke upon you, and learn of Me, for My
yoke is easy and My burden is light [29-30]

Matthew 12:

am One greater than the temple [6]

am Lord even of the Sabbath (Son of Man) [8]

cast out devils by the Spirit of God, not by Beelzebub [25-28]

will be three days and three nights in the heart of the earth
(Son of Man) [40]

am greater than Jonah [41]

am greater than Solomon [42]

Matthew 13:
  speak to them in parables: because they seeing see not; and
    hearing they hear not, neither do they understand [13]
  sow the good seed (Son of Man) [37]
  shall send forth My angels, and they shall gather out of My
    kingdom all things that offend, and those which do iniqui-
    ty, and shall cast them into a furnace of fire: there shall be
    wailing and gnashing of teeth (Son of Man) [41-42]

Matthew 15:
  am not sent but to the lost sheep of the house of Israel [24]
  have compassion on the multitude, because they continue
    with Me now three days, and have nothing to eat: and I
    will not send them away fasting, lest they faint in the way
    [32]

Matthew 16:
  am the Son of Man [13]
  also say to you that you are Peter, and upon this rock I will
    build My church [18]
  will give to you the keys of the kingdom of heaven: and what-
    ever you shall bind on earth shall be bound in heaven:
    and whatever you shall loose on earth shall be loosed in
    heaven (to Peter) [19]
  shall come in the glory of My Father with His angels; and then
    I shall reward every man according to his works (Son of
    Man) [27]
  will come in My kingdom (Son of Man) [28]

Matthew 17:
  want you to tell this vision (the Transfiguration) to no man,
    until I am risen from the dead (Son of Man) [9]
  shall also suffer of them (Son of Man) [12]
  shall be betrayed into the hands of men (Son of Man) [22]
  shall be killed by them (the hands of men) (Son of Man) [23]
  shall be raised again the third day (Son of Man) [23]

Matthew 18:
  have come to save that which was lost (Son of Man) [11]
  am there in the midst of two or three who are gathered togeth-
    er in My name [20]

Matthew 19:
do not want you to forbid the little children to come to me; for
of such is the kingdom of heaven [14]
shall sit on the throne of My glory [28]

Matthew 20:
shall be betrayed to the chief priests and to the scribes, and
they shall condemn Me to death (Son of Man) [18]
shall be delivered to the Gentiles by the chief priests and the
scribes to be mocked and scourged (beaten) and crucified
(Son of Man) [18-19]
shall rise again the third day (Son of Man) [19]
am to be baptized (His suffering and death) [23]
came not to be ministered to, but to minister (Son of Man)
[28]
came to give my life a ransom for many (Son of Man) [28]

Matthew 21:
the Lord, have need of them (an ass and a colt) [2-3]
also will ask you one thing, which if you tell me, I in like wise
will tell you by what authority I do these things; "The
baptism of John, was it from heaven, or of men?" (to the
chief priests and elders) [23-25]
will not tell you by what authority I do these things (because
the chief priests and elders refused to answer Jesus' question about John's baptism) [23-27]

Matthew 23:
send you prophets, and wise men, and scribes [34]
often would have gathered your children together, O Jerusalem,
even as a hen gathers her chickens under her wings, and
you would not! [37]

Matthew 24:
want you to take heed that no man deceive you, for many
shall come in My name, saying, "I am Christ;" and shall
deceive many [4-5]
have told you before they (false Christs and false prophets)
shall arise [23-25]
shall come as the lightning comes out of the east and shines
even to the west (Son of Man) [27]

shall come in the clouds of heaven with power and great glory, and all the tribes of the earth shall see me (Son of Man) [30]

shall send my angels (as He returns) with a great sound of a trumpet, and they shall gather together My elect from the four winds, from one end of heaven to the other (Son of Man) [30-31]

shall come as the days of Noah were, before the flood, they were eating and drinking, marrying and giving in marriage (Son of Man) [37-39]

am coming at an hour when you think not (do not expect) (Son of Man) [44]

Matthew 25:

shall sit on the throne of My glory when I come in My glory, and all the holy angels (come) with Me (Son of Man) [31]

shall separate them (the nations) one from another, as a shepherd divides his sheep from the goats: I shall set the sheep on My right hand, but the goats on the left; then shall the King (Jesus Himself) say to them on His right hand, "Come, blessed of My Father, inherit the kingdom prepared for you from the foundation of the world:" then shall He say also unto them on the left hand, "Depart from Me, you cursed, into everlasting fire," and these shall go into everlasting punishment: but the righteous into life eternal (Son of Man) [31-46]

Matthew 26:

will be betrayed to be crucified in two days (Son of Man) [2]

was done a good work by this woman, for in pouring this fragrant oil on My body, she did it for My burial [10-12]

the Master, will keep the passover at your (a man's) house with My disciples, for My time is at hand [18]

say to you, "One of you shall betray Me" [21]

shall be betrayed by him who dips his hand with Me in the dish [23]

go as it is written of Me (Son of Man) [24]

want you to take, eat (the bread); this is (represents) My body [26]

want you to drink all of it (this cup), for this is (represents) My blood of the new testament (covenant), which is shed for many for the remission of sins [27-28]

say to you, (His disciples), "I will not drink henceforth of this
fruit of the vine, until that day when I drink it new with
you in My Father's kingdom" [29]

(the Shepherd) "will be smitten, and the sheep of the flock will
be scattered abroad," for it is written (Zechariah 13: 7) [31]

after I am risen again, will go before you into Galilee [32]

say to you, Peter, that this night, before the cock crow, you
will deny Me thrice [34]

will go and pray yonder [36]

am exceedingly sorrowful, even unto death [38]

ask of You, O My Father, "If it be possible, let this cup pass
from Me: nevertheless not as I will, but as You will" [39]

ask of You, Father, "If this cup may not pass away from Me,
except I drink it, Your will be done" [42]

am being betrayed into the hands of sinners, behold the hour
is at hand (Son of Man) [45]

if I now pray to My Father, shall be given more than twelve
legions of angels, but how then shall the Scriptures be
fulfilled, that thus it must be [53-54]

sat daily with you teaching in the temple, and you laid no hold
on Me, but all this was done that the Scriptures of the prophets might be fulfilled [55-56]

am, as you said, the Christ the Son of God (response to the
high priest) [63-64]

shall sit at the right hand of power (Son of Man) [64]

shall come in the clouds of heaven (Son of Man) [64]

Matthew 27:

am forsaken by My God (Psalm 22:1) [46]

"will rise again after three days" (chief priests and Pharisees
testifying about what Jesus had said) [62-63]

Matthew 28:

shall be seen in Galilee by My brethren [10]

have been given all power in heaven and in earth [18]

am with you alway, even to the end of the world [20]

Mark

"I"

Mark 1:
will make you to become fishers of men, if you come after Me
(to Simon and Andrew) [17]
came forth to preach [38]
will; "be clean" (healing a leper) [41]

Mark 2:
came not to call the righteous, but sinners to repentance [17]
am Lord also of the Sabbath (Son of Man) [28]

Mark 5:
say to you, Damsel, "Arise" (raising Jairus' daughter from the
dead) [41]

Mark 8:
have compassion on the multitude, because they have now
been with Me three days and have nothing to eat: and if I
send them away fasting to their own houses, they will faint
by the way: for divers (some or many) of them have come
from far [2]
shall be ashamed of whomever is ashamed of Me and My words
in this adulterous and sinful generation, when I come in the
glory of My Father with the holy angels (Son of Man) [38]

Mark 9:
must suffer many things and be set at nought (given no value)
(Son of Man) [12]
charge you, deaf and dumb spirit, "come out of him and enter
no more into him" [25]
am delivered into the hands of men, and they shall kill Me
(Son of Man) [31]
shall rise the third day, after I am killed (Son of Man) [31]

Mark 10:
want you to let the little children to come to Me, and forbid
them not: for of such is the kingdom of God [14]
shall be delivered to the chief priests, and to the scribes; and
they shall condemn Me to death (Son of Man) [33]

shall be delivered by the chief priests and scribes to the Gentiles: they shall mock Me, and shall scourge (beat) Me, and shall spit on Me, and shall kill Me (Son of Man) [33-34]

shall rise again the third day (Son of Man) [34]

drink the cup (His suffering and death) [38]

am baptized (His suffering and death) [38]

came not to be ministered to, but to minister (Son of Man) [45]

came to give My life a ransom for many (Son of Man) [45]

Mark 11:

the Lord, have need of it (a colt) [2-3]

will also ask of you one question, and answer Me, and I will tell you by what authority I do these things; "The baptism of John, was it from heaven, or of men?," answer Me (to the chief priests, and the scribes, and the elders) [27-30]

will not tell you by what authority I do these things (because the chief priests, scribes and elders refused to answer Jesus' question about John's baptism) [27-33]

Mark 13:

want you to take heed lest any man deceive you: for many shall come in My name, saying, "I am Christ;" and shall deceive many [5-6]

have foretold you all (end time) things, so take heed [23]

shall come in the clouds with great power and glory (Son of Man) [26]

shall send My angels (as He returns), and shall gather together My elect from the four winds, from the uttermost part of earth to the uttermost part of heaven (Son of Man) [26-27]

speak words that shall not pass away [31]

(the Son) do not know that day and that hour (coming of the Son of Man) [26-32]

say to you, I say to all, "Watch" (for His return) [37]

Mark 14:

was done a good work by this woman, for she is come aforehand to anoint My body to the burying [6-8]

the Master, say (to the goodman of the house), "Where is the guestchamber, where I shall eat the passover with My disciples?" [14]

say to you, "One of you who eats with Me shall betray Me" [18]

shall be betrayed by one of the twelve, who dips with Me in the dish [18-20]

go as it is written of Me (Son of Man) [21]

want you to take, eat (this bread): this is (represents) My body [22]

shed My blood for many; this is (represents) my blood of the new testament (covenant) [23-24]

say to you (the twelve apostles), "I will drink no more of the fruit of the vine, until that day that I drink it new in the kingdom of God" [25]

(the Shepherd) "will be smitten, and the sheep shall be scattered," for it is written (Zechariah 13:7) [27]

after I am risen, will go before you into Galilee [28]

say to you, Peter, that this day, even in this night, before the cock crow twice, you shall deny Me thrice [30]

am exceedingly sorrowful unto death [34]

ask of You, Father, "Take away this cup from Me: nevertheless, not what I will, but what You will" [36]

am betrayed into the hands of sinners, the hour is come (Son of Man) [41]

was daily with you in the temple teaching, and you took Me not: but the Scriptures must be fulfilled [49]

am the Christ, the Son of the Blessed (response to the high priest) [61-62]

will sit at the right hand of the Power (Son of Man) [62]

will come in the clouds of heaven (Son of Man) [62]

Mark 15:

am forsaken by My God (Psalm 22:1) [34]

Luke

"I"

Luke 2:

must be about My Father's business (when Jesus was twelve years old) [49]

Luke 4:

"have the Spirit of the Lord upon me" (Isaiah 61.1-2) [17-21]

"was anointed by the Lord to preach the gospel to the poor" (Isaiah 61.1-2) [17-21]

"was sent by the Lord to heal the brokenhearted, to preach
deliverance to the captives, and recovering of sight to the
blind, to set at liberty them that are bruised, to preach
the acceptable year of the Lord" (Isaiah 61:1-2) [17-21]

must preach the kingdom of God to the other cities also: for
therefore am I sent [43]

Luke 5:

will, "be clean" (healing a leper) [13]

am the Son of Man (proved by forgiving the sins of a man sick
of the palsy and then healing him) [23-24]

have power on earth to forgive sins (proved by forgiving the
sins of a man sick of the palsy and then healing him) (Son
of Man) [23-24]

say to you, "Arise, and take up your couch, and go into your
house," (healing a man sick of the palsy) [24]

came not to call the righteous, but sinners, to repentance [32]

Luke 6:

am Lord also of the Sabbath (Son of Man) [5]

Luke 7:

say to you, young man, "Arise" (raising a widow's son) [14]

have made the blind see, the lame walk, the lepers are cleansed,
the deaf hear, the dead are raised [21-22]

have preached the gospel to the poor [21-22]

have come eating and drinking (Son of Man) [34]

Luke 8:

perceive that virtue (power) is gone out of me (after being
touched by a woman with an issue of blood) [46]

say to you, maid, "Arise" (raising Jairus' daughter from the
dead) [54]

Luke 9:

must suffer many things and be rejected by the elders and
chief priests and scribes (Son of Man) [22]

must be slain (Son of Man) [22]

must be raised the third day (Son of Man) [22]

shall be ashamed of him who is ashamed of Me and of My words,
when I shall come in My own glory, and in My Father's, and of
the holy angels (Son of Man) [26]

shall be delivered into the hands of men (Son of Man) [44]

am not come to destroy men's lives, but to save them (Son of
    Man) [56]
have not where to lay my head (Son of Man) [58]

Luke 10:
    beheld Satan as lightning fall from heaven (after the seventy
        returned) [18]
    give you power to tread on serpents and scorpions, and over
        all the power of the enemy (to the seventy) [19]
    thank You, O Father, Lord of heaven and earth, that You have
        hid these things from the wise and prudent, and have re-
        vealed them to babes [21]
    have been delivered all things of (by) My Father [22]
    the Son, am not known by any man, but the Father [22]
    the Son, and he to whom the Son reveals the Father, are the
        only ones who know who the Father is [22]

Luke 11:
    cast out devils with the finger of God, not, as you say, by
        Beelzebub [17-20]
    shall become a sign to this generation (Son of Man) [30]
    am greater than Solomon [31]
    am greater than Jonah [32]
    say to you (a lawyer), "It (the blood of Abel to the blood of
        Zacharias) shall be required of this generation" [51]

Luke 12:
    shall confess before the angels of God whoever confesses Me
        before men (Son of Man) [8]
    shall deny before the angels of God whoever denies Me be-
        fore men (Son of Man) [9]
    am coming at an hour when you think not (do not expect)
        (Son of Man) [40]
    am come to send fire on the earth [49]
    have a baptism to be baptized with; and how am I straitened
        till it (anxious for it to) be accomplished [50]
    am come to give peace on earth? I tell you, "No"; but rather
        division [51]

Luke 13:
    cast out devils, and I do cures today and tomorrow [32]
    shall be perfected the third day [32]

must walk today, and tomorrow, and the day following: for it
cannot be that a prophet perish out of Jerusalem [33]

often would have gathered your children together, O Jerusalem,
as a hen gathers her brood under her wings, and you would
not! [34]

say to you (Pharisees), "You shall not see Me, until the time
comes when you shall say, 'Blessed is He who comes in
the name of the Lord'" [35]

Luke 17:

shall be in My day as the lightning, that lightens out of the
one part under heaven, shines to the other part under
heaven (Son of Man) [24]

must first suffer many things (Son of Man) [24-25]

must first be rejected of (by) this generation (Son of Man) [24-
25]

will be revealed in the day when people eat, drink, marry wives,
are given in marriage, buy, sell, plant, and build (Son of Man)
[27-30]

Luke 18:

wonder if I shall find faith on the earth when I come (Son of
Man) [8]

want you to let the little children to come to Me, and forbid
them not; for of such is the kingdom of God [16]

go up to Jerusalem, and all things that are written by the prophets concerning Me shall be accomplished (Son of Man)
[31]

shall be delivered to the Gentiles, and shall be mocked, and
spitefully entreated, and spit on, and they shall scourge
(beat) Me, and put Me to death (Son of Man) [32-33]

shall rise again the third day (Son of Man) [33]

Luke 19:

am come to seek and to save that which was lost (Son of
Man) [10]

Luke 20:

will also ask you one thing; and answer Me: "The baptism of
John, was it from heaven, or of men?" (to the chief priests
and the scribes and the elders) [1-4]

will not tell you by what authority I do these things (because the chief priests and the scribes and the elders refused to answer Jesus' question about John's baptism) [1-8]

Luke 21:

want you to take heed that you be not deceived: for many shall come in My name, saying, "I am Christ;" and, "The time draws near:" therefore go not after them [8]

will give you (those who are persecuted) a mouth and wisdom, which all your adversaries shall not be able to gainsay (oppose) nor resist [15]

shall come in a cloud with power and great glory (Son of Man) [27]

Luke 22:

the Master, say to you (the master of the house), "Where is the guestchamber, where I shall eat the passover with My disciples?" [11]

have desired to eat this passover with you before I suffer [15]

say to you (the twelve apostles), "I will not drink of the fruit of the vine, until the kingdom of God shall come" [18]

want you to do this (eat the bread) in remembrance of Me: this is (represents) My body which is given for you [19]

shed My blood for you: this cup is (represents) the new testament (covenant) in My blood [20]

have a betrayer whose hand is with Me on the table [21]

go, as it was determined (Son of Man) [22]

am among you as he who serves [27]

have temptations (trials) [28]

appoint to you a kingdom, as My Father appointed to Me [29]

have prayed for you, Simon, that your faith fail not: and when you are converted, strengthen your brethren [31-32]

tell you, Peter, "The cock shall not crow this day, before you shall thrice deny that you know Me" [34]

say to you (the twelve apostles), "What is written must yet be accomplished in me, 'And He was reckoned among the transgressors': for the things concerning Me have an end" (Isaiah 53:12) [37]

ask of You, Father, "If You be willing, remove this cup from Me: nevertheless not My will, but Yours, be done" [42]

am being betrayed by your kiss? (to Judas) (Son of Man) [48]

was with you daily in the temple, you stretched forth no hands against Me: but this is your hour, and the power of darkness [53]

shall sit on the right hand of the power of God (Son of Man) [69]

Luke 23:

ask you to forgive them (those who crucified Him→ us?), Father; for they know not what they do [34]

say to you (one of the malefactors crucified with Jesus), "Today you shall be with Me in paradise" [43]

commend My spirit into Your hands, Father [46]

Luke 24:

"must be delivered into the hands of sinful men, and be crucified" (two men at the tomb reporting what Jesus had said to women who had come with Him from Galilee and certain other women) (Son of Man) [7]

"must rise again the third day" (two men at the tomb reporting what Jesus had said to women who had come with Him from Galilee and certain other women) (Son of Man) [7]

(the Christ) ought to have suffered (must suffer) these things, and to enter into My glory [26]

have flesh and bones, as you (the eleven) see Me have (after His resurrection from the dead) [39]

spoke these words to you while I was yet with you, that all things must be fulfilled, which were written in the Law of Moses, and in the Prophets, and the Psalms, concerning Me [44]

(the Christ) had to suffer, thus it is written [46]

(the Christ) had to rise from the dead the third day, thus it is written [46]

send the Promise of My Father upon you (Acts 2:4) [49]

John

"I"

John 2:

will raise this temple (His body) up in three days, after it is destroyed [19-21]

John 3:

say to you, "We speak that (what) we do know, and testify that (what) we have seen; and you receive not our witness" (to Nicodemus) [11]

came down from heaven and am in heaven (Son of Man) [13]

must be lifted up (Son of Man) [14]

(God's only begotten Son) was given by God, that whoever believes in Me should not perish, but have everlasting life [16]

(God's Son) was not sent into the world by Him (God) to condemn the world; but that the world through Him might be saved [17]

John 4:

would have given you living water [10]

shall give him a well of water springing up into eternal life, and he shall never thirst [14]

who speak to you am the Messiah (response to the woman at the well) [25-26]

have meat to eat that you know not of [32]

do the will of Him who sent Me [34]

finish the work of Him who sent Me [34]

sent you (His disciples) to reap whereon you bestowed no labor [38]

John 5:

say to you, "Rise, take up your bed, and walk" (healing a man with an infirmity) [8]

work, and My Father works [17]

(the Son) can do nothing of Myself, but what I see the Father do: for whatever He does, I also do likewise [19]

(the Son) am loved by the Father, and He shows Me all things that He does [20]

(the Son) quicken (give life to) whom I will [21]

(the Son) have been committed all judgment by the Father, who judges no man [22]

(the Son of God) will be heard by the dead: and they that hear shall live [25]

(the Son) have life in myself, as given by the Father, who has life in Himself [26]

(the Son) have been given authority by the Father to execute judgment also, because I am the Son of Man [26-27]

can of My own self do nothing: as I hear, I judge: and My judgment is just; because I seek not My own will, but the will
of the Father who has sent Me [30]

have greater witness than that of John: for the works which
the Father has given Me to finish, the same works that I
do, bear witness of Me, that the Father has sent Me [36]

am testified of (to) by the Scriptures [39]

receive not honor from men [41]

am come in My Father's name, and you receive Me not [43]

will not accuse you to the Father: there is one that accuses
you, even Moses, in whom you trust (to the Jews) [45]

John 6:

will give you the meat which endures to everlasting life (Son
of Man) [27]

am the bread of life [35]

said to you, that you also have seen Me, and believe not [36]

will in no wise cast out him who comes to Me [37]

came down from heaven, not to do My own will, but the will
of Him who sent Me [38]

should lose nothing of all the Father who sent Me has given
Me, but should raise it up again at the last day, for this
is His will [39]

will raise every one up at the last day, who sees Me, the Son,
and believes on Me, for this is the will of Him who sent
Me [40]

will raise him up at the last day whom the Father who sent
Me, draws to Me [44]

am that bread of life [48]

am the living bread which came down from heaven: if any
man eat of this bread, he shall live forever: and the bread
that I will give is My flesh, which I will give for the life of
the world [51]

will raise up at the last day whoever eats My flesh, and drinks
My blood, and he will have eternal life [54]

dwell in him, and he in Me, who eats My flesh and drinks My
blood [56]

was sent by the living Father [57]

live by the Father [57]

speak to you the words that are spirit and that are life [63]

John 7:
> am hated by the world, because I testify of it, that the works
> thereof are evil [7]
> go not up yet to this feast (Feast of Tabernacles); for My time
> is not yet full come [8]
> have a doctrine that is not Mine, but His who sent Me [16]
> have done one work, and you all marvel [21]
> have made a man every whit whole on the Sabbath day [23]
> am not come of Myself [28]
> know Him: for I am from Him, and He has sent Me [29]
> am with you yet a little while, and then I go to Him who sent
> Me [33]
> will be where you cannot come [34]

John 8:
> do not condemn you: go, and sin no more (to a woman caught
> in adultery) [11]
> am the light of the world [12]
> am He (the light of the world/from above/have true judgment
> {in fact, God}) [12-24]
> know whence I came, and whither I go [14]
> judge no man [15]
> have true judgment: for I am not alone, but I and the Father
> who sent Me [16]
> am One who bears witness of Myself [18]
> was sent by the Father who bears witness of Me [18]
> go My way, and you shall seek me, and shall die in your sins:
> whither I go, you cannot come [21]
> am from above [23]
> am not of this world [23]
> have many things to say and to judge of (about) you [26]
> speak to the world those things which I have heard of (from)
> Him who sent Me [26]
> am the Son of Man (proved when Jesus was lifted up) [28]
> do nothing of Myself; but as My Father has taught Me, I speak
> these things [28]
> have not been left alone by the Father [29]
> do always those things that please the Father [29]
> the Son, if I shall make you free, you shall be free indeed [36]
> know that you are Abraham's seed (descendant); but you seek
> to kill Me, because My word has no place in you [37]
> speak what I have seen with My Father [38]

a man who has told you the truth, which I have heard of (from)
    God, you seek now to kill [40]
proceeded forth and came from God [42]
came of Myself [42]
was sent by God [42]
tell you the truth, you believe Me not [45]
do not have a devil (as you say) [48-49]
honor My Father, and you do dishonor Me [49]
do seek not My own glory [50]
am honored by My Father; of whom you say, that He is your
    God [54]
know My Father [54-55]
keep My Father's word [54-55]
say to you (the Jews), before Abraham was, I am, (Exodus
    3:14) [58]

John 9:

must work the works of Him who sent Me [4]
am the light of the world, as long as I am in the world [5]
say to you, go, wash in the pool of Siloam (healing a man born
    blind) [7]
whom you have seen and who is talking with you, am the Son
    of God (response to the man born blind) [35-37]
am come into this world for judgment (to judge) [39]

John 10:

am the door of the sheep [7]
am the door (of the sheep): by Me if any man enter in, he shall
    be saved, and shall go in and out, and find pasture [9]
have come that they (the sheep) might have life, and that they
    might have it more abundantly [10]
am the good shepherd: the good shepherd gives His life for the
    sheep [11]
am the good shepherd [14]
know My sheep [14]
am known by the Father, and I know the Father [15]
lay down My life for the sheep [15]
have other sheep, which are not of this fold: them also I must
    bring [16]
am loved by My Father, because I lay down My life, that I might
    take it again [17]
lay down My life of Myself: no man takes it from Me [18]

have power to lay down My life, and I have power to take it again: this commandment have I received of (from) My Father [18]

told you (that I am the Christ), and you believed not [24-25]

do works in My Father's name; they bear witness of Me [25]

said to you (the Jews), "You believe not (even though My works bear witness of Me)", because you are not of My sheep [26]

give My sheep eternal life, and they shall never perish, neither shall any man pluck them out of My hand [27-28]

was given My sheep by My Father who is greater than all; no man is able to pluck them out of My Father's hand [27-29]

and My Father are one [30]

have shown you many good works from My Father, for which of those works do you stone Me [32]

have been sanctified by the Father [36]

have been sent into the world by the Father [36]

said, "I am the Son of God" (response to the Jews in the temple who said He blasphemed) [36]

have the Father in Me [38]

am in the Father [38]

John 11:

the Son of God, will be glorified thereby (raising of Lazarus) [4]

go, that I may awake him (Lazarus) out of sleep (raise him from the dead) [11-14]

am the resurrection [25]

am the life [25]

thank You, Father, that you have heard Me [41]

knew that You hear Me always, Father [41-42]

said this, that they may believe that You have sent Me, Father [41-42]

John 12:

will not always be with you [8]

should (shall) be glorified: the hour is come (Son of Man) [23]

now have a troubled soul [27]

came to this hour for this cause (to be a sacrifice), so shall I say, "Father, save Me from this hour?" [27]

want You to glorify Your name, Father [28]

if I be lifted up from the earth, will draw all men to Me [32]

am come a light into the world, that whoever believes on Me should (would) not abide in darkness [46] judge him not who hears my words, and believes not [47]

came not to judge the world, but to save the world [47]

have spoken the word which will judge, in the last day, he that rejects Me, and receives not My words [48]

have not spoken of Myself; but the Father who sent Me, He gave Me a command, what I should say, and what I should speak [49]

know that His (the Father's) commandment is life everlasting [50]

speak, even as the Father said to Me [50]

John 13:

am your Master [13]

am your Lord [13]

am your Lord [14]

am your Master [14]

have given you an example (washing the Disciple's feet), that you should do as I have done to you [15]

know whom I have chosen: but that the Scripture may be fulfilled, "He who eats bread with Me has lifted up his heel against Me" (Psalm 41:9) [18]

say to you, that one of you shall betray Me [21]

shall be betrayed by him to whom I shall give a sop (piece of bread), when I have dipped it [21-26]

am glorified, and God is glorified in Me (Son of Man) [31]

now say to you, little children, "Yet a little while I am with you; you shall seek Me: and as I said to the Jews, where I go, you cannot come" [33]

give to you a new commandment, that you love one another; as I have loved you [34]

say to you, Peter, "The cock shall not crow till you have denied Me thrice" [37-38]

John 14:

would have told you if My Father's house did not have many mansions [2]

go to prepare a place for you, and if I go and prepare a place for you, I will come again [2-3]

will receive you to Myself; that where I am, there you may be also [3]

am the way [6]

am the truth [6]

am the life [6]

am the only one a man goes through to get to the Father [6]

am in the Father [10]

have the Father in Me [10]

do not speak words to you of Myself: but the Father who dwells
in Me, He does the works [10]

am in the Father [11]

have the Father in Me [11]

do works [12]

go to My Father [12]

will do whatever you ask in My name, that the Father may be
glorified in the Son [13]

will do anything you ask in My name [14]

will pray the Father, and He shall give you another Comforter,
that He may abide with you forever; even the Spirit of
truth; whom the world cannot receive, because it sees Him
not, neither knows Him [16-17]

will not leave you comfortless: I will come to you [18]

live, and because I live, you shall live also [19]

am in My Father [20]

am in you [20]

love him who keeps My commandments [21]

will manifest Myself to him who keeps My commandments [21]

and My Father will love him, and we will come to Him, and
make Our abode with him who loves Me and keeps My
words [23]

have spoken these things to you, being yet present with you
[25]

leave My peace with you, My peace I give to you: not as the
world gives, give I to you, so let not your heart be troubled, neither let it be afraid [27]

go away and come again to you [28]

am going to the Father [28]

am not as great as My father [28]

have told you before it come to pass, that, when it is come to
pass, you might believe (His return to the Father) [29]

will not talk much with you hereafter: for the prince of this
world comes, and (he) has nothing in Me [30]

love the Father [31]

do as the Father gave Me commandment [31]

John 15:

am the true vine [1]

have spoken the word to you that has made you clean [3]

am the vine [5]

have loved you [9]

have kept My Father's commandments [10]

abide in My Father's love [10]

have spoken these things to you, that My joy may remain in you, and that your joy might be full [11]

have loved you [12]

count you as My friends, if you do whatever I command you [14]

henceforth call you not servants; for the servant knows not what his lord does: but I have called you friends (His disciples) [15]

have made known to you all things that I have heard of (from) My Father [15]

have chosen you and ordained you, that you should go and bring forth fruit [16]

command you that you love one another [17]

was hated by the world before it hated you [18]

have come and spoken to them, so they now have no cloke (excuse) for their sin (those who are of the world) [18-22]

am hated without cause (by those who are of the world) (Psalm 69:4) [18-25]

have chosen you out of the world, therefore the world hates you [19]

said to you, "The servant is not greater than his lord" [20]

did among them the works which no other man did [24]

will send the Comforter, even the Spirit of truth, to you from the Father [26]

shall be testified of by the Spirit of truth [26]

John 16:

have spoken these things to you, that you should not be offended [1]

have told you these things, that when the time shall come, you may remember that I told you of them [4]

did not say these things to you at the beginning, because I was with you, but now I go My way to Him who sent Me [4-5]

have said these things to you, so sorrow has filled your heart [6]

tell you the truth; "It is expedient for you that I go away: for if I go not away, the Comforter will not come to you; but if I depart, I will send Him to you" [7]

go to My Father, and you see Me no more [10]

have yet many things to say to you, but you cannot bear them
now [12]

shall be glorified by the Spirit of truth, for He shall receive of
Mine, and shall show it to you [13-14]

have all things that the Father has [15]

go to the Father, so a little while, and you shall not see Me:
and again, a little while, and you shall see Me [16]

say to you, that you shall weep and lament, but the world
shall rejoice: and you shall be sorrowful, but your sorrow (at His death) shall be turned into joy (at His resurrection) [20]

will see you again, and your heart shall rejoice [22]

say to you, "Whatever you shall ask the Father in My name,
He will give it (to) you" [23]

have spoken these things to you in proverbs: but the time
comes, when I shall no more speak to you in proverbs, but
I shall show you plainly of the Father [25]

say not to you, that I will pray the Father for you at that day:
for the Father Himself loves you, because you have loved
Me, and have believed that I came out from God [26-27]

came forth from the Father, and am come into the world [28]

leave the world, and go to the Father [28]

am not alone, because the Father is with me [32]

have spoken these things to you, that in Me you might have
peace [33]

have overcome the world, so be of good cheer [33]

John 17 (Jesus prayer prior to His arrest):

ask You, Father, now that the hour is come; to glorify Your
Son, that Your Son also may glorify You [1]

(Your Son) was given by You, Father, power over all flesh, that
I should give eternal life to as many as You have given Me
[1-2]

was sent by You, Father, the only true God [3]

have glorified You on the earth, Father [4]

have finished the work which You gave Me to do, Father [4]

had the glory with You, Father, before the world was [5]

have manifested Your name, Father, to the men You gave Me
out of the world [6]

have given to them (the men You have gave Me), Father, the
words which You gave Me [8]

came out from You, Father [8]

pray for them, Father: I pray not for the world, but for them
    You have given Me; for they are Yours, and all Mine are
    yours, and Yours are Mine [9-10]
am glorified in them (the men You gave Me), Father [9-10]
am no more in the world [11]
come to You, Holy Father [11]
and You are one, Holy Father [11]
while I was with them in the world, kept them in Your name,
    Holy Father: those You gave Me, and none of them is lost,
    but the son of perdition; that the Scripture might be
    fulfilled [12]
come to You, Holy Father [13]
speak these things in the world, Holy Father, that they (those
    You gave Me) might have My joy fulfilled in themselves [13]
have given them (those You gave Me) Your word, Holy Father
    [14]
am not of the world [14]
pray not, Holy Father, that You should take them (those You
    gave Me) out of the world, but that You should keep them
    from the evil [15]
am not of the world [16]
was sent by You, Holy Father, into the world [18]
have sent them (those You gave Me), Holy Father, into the world
    [18]
sanctify Myself [19]
do not pray for these alone (those You gave Me), but for them
    also who shall believe on Me through their word [20]
have You, Father, in Me [21]
am in You, Father [21]
have been sent by You, Father [21]
was given glory by You, Father [22]
have given them (those You gave Me) the glory which You gave
    Me, Father [22]
and You are one, Father [22]
am in them (those You gave Me), Father [23]
have You in Me, Father [23]
have been sent by You, Father [23]
have been loved by You, Father [23]
will that they also, whom You have given Me, Father, be with
    Me where I am [24]
have been given glory by You, Father [24]
was loved by You, Father, before the foundation of the world
    [24]

have known You, righteous Father [25]

have been sent by You, righteous Father [25]

have declared to them (those You gave Me) Your name, righteous Father, and will declare it: that the love wherewith You have loved Me may be in them, and I in them [26]

John 18:

am He (Jesus of Nazareth) [5]

have told you that I am He (Jesus of Nazareth) [7-8]

"have lost none of them whom You gave Me" (saying of Jesus) [9]

shall drink the cup which My Father has given me [11]

spoke openly to the world [20]

ever (always) taught in the synagogues, whither the Jews always resort [20]

ever (always) taught in the temple, whither the Jews always resort [20]

have said nothing in secret [20]

have a kingdom but it is not of this world: if My kingdom were of this world, then would My servants fight, that I should not be delivered to the Jews [36]

am, as you say, a king (responding to Pilate): to this end I was born, and for this cause came I into the world, that I should bear witness to the truth [37]

John 19:

thirst (during His crucifixion) [28]

have finished it (His sacrifice) [30]

John 20:

am not yet ascended to My Father, so touch Me not: but go to My brethren, and say to them, "I ascend to My Father, and your Father; and to My God and your God" (to Mary Magdalene) [17]

have been sent by My Father, even so send I you [21]

John 21:

say to you, Simon, son of Jonas, feed My lambs [15]

say to you, Simon, son of Jonas, feed My sheep [16]

say to you, Simon, son of Jonas, feed My sheep [17]

Acts

"I"

Acts 1:
 shall be witnessed to by you (the apostles) in Jerusalem, and
 in all Judea, and in Samaria, and to the uttermost part of
 the earth [8]

Revelation

"I"

Revelation 1:
 am the Alpha and the Omega, the Beginning and the Ending
 [8]
 am [8]
 was [8]
 am to come [8]
 am the Almighty [8]
 am Alpha and the Omega, the first and the last [11]
 am the first and the last [17]
 am He who lives [18]
 am He who was dead [18]
 am He who is alive forevermore [18]
 have the keys of hell and of death [18]
 have the seven stars, the angels of the seven churches, in My
 right hand and am in the midst of the seven golden candlesticks, the seven churches [12-20]

Revelation 2:
 know your works (church of Ephesus), and your labor, and
 your patience, and how you cannot bear them who are
 evil [2]
 have somewhat against you (church of Ephesus), because you
 have left your first love [4]
 will come to you (church of Ephesus) quickly, and will remove
 your candlestick out of his (its) place, except (unless) you
 repent [5]
 also hate the deeds of the Nicolaitanes (some kind of false doctrine) [6]

will give to him who overcomes to eat of the tree of life, which
   is in the midst of the paradise of God [7]
am the first and the last [8]
was dead [8]
am alive [8]
know your works (church in Smyrna), and tribulation, and
   poverty [9]
know the blasphemy of them who say they are Jews and are
   not, but the a synagogue of Satan [9]
will give you (church in Smyrna) a crown of life, if you are faithful unto death [10]
have the sharp sword with two edges [12]
know your works (church in Pergamos), and where you dwell,
   even where Satan's seat is [13]
have a few things against you (church in Pergamos), because
   you have there them who hold the doctrine of Balaam, who
   taught Balac to cast a stumbling block before the children
   of Israel, to eat things sacrificed to idols, and to commit fornication [14]
hate the doctrine of the Nicolaitanes (some kind of false doctrine) [15]
will come to you (church in Pergamos) quickly, and will fight
   against them (Nicolaitanes) with the sword of My mouth,
   unless you repent [16]
will give to him who overcomes to eat of the hidden manna
   [17]
will give to him who overcomes a white stone, and in the
   stone a new name written, which no man knows save he
   who receives it [17]
the Son of God, have eyes like unto a flame of fire, and feet
   like fine brass [18]
know your works (church in Thyatira), and charity, and service, and faith, and your patience [19]
have a few things against you (church in Thyatira), because
   you suffer that woman Jezebel, who calls herself a prophetess, to teach and to seduce My servants to commit
   fornication, and to eat things sacrificed to idols [20]
gave her (Jezebel) space to repent of her fornication; and she
   repented not [21]
will cast her (Jezebel) into a bed, and them who commit adultery with her into great tribulation, except they repent of
   their deeds [22]
will kill her children (Jezebel's) with death [23]

am He who searches the reins (inward parts) and hearts [23]

will give to every one of you (church in Thyatira) according to
   your works [23]

say to you, and to the rest in Thyatira, as many as have not
   this doctrine, and who have not known the depths of Satan,
   as they speak; "I will put upon you none other burden" [24]

will come [25]

will give him who overcomes, and keeps My works unto the
   end, power over the nations [26]

received of (from) My Father, power over the nations [26-27]

will give him who overcomes, and keeps My works until the
   end, the morning star [26-28]

Revelation 3:

have the seven Spirits of God [1]

have the seven stars [1]

know your works (church in Sardis), that you have a name
   that you live, and (but) are dead [1]

have not found your works (church in Sardis) perfect before
   God [2]

will come upon you (church in Sardis) as a thief, if you shall
   not watch [3]

will clothe him who overcomes in white garments [5]

will not blot the name of him who overcomes out of the Book
   of Life [5]

will confess the name of him who overcomes before My Father,
   and before His angels [5]

am holy [7]

am true [7]

have the key of David [7]

am He that opens, and no man shuts [7]

am He that shuts and no man opens [7]

know your works (church in Philadelphia): for you have little
   strength, and have kept My word, and have not denied My
   name [8]

have set before you (church in Philadelphia) an open door, and
   no man can shut it [8]

will make them of the synagogue of Satan, who say they are
   Jews, and are not, but do lie, behold, I will make them to
   come and worship before your (church in Philadelphia) feet
   [9]

have loved you (church in Philadelphia) [9]

also will keep you (church in Philadephia) from the hour of
temptation, which shall come upon all the world, to try
them who dwell upon the earth, because you have kept
the word of My patience [10]

come quickly [11]

will make him who overcomes a pillar in the temple of My
God, and He shall go no more out [12]

will write on him who overcomes the name of My God, and
the name of the city of My God, which is new Jerusalem,
which comes down out of heaven from My God [12]

will write on him who overcomes My new name [12]

am the Amen [14]

am the faithful and true witness [14]

am the beginning of the creation of God [14]

know your works (church of the Laodiceans), that they are
neither cold nor hot [15]

would that you (church of the Laodiceans) were cold or hot; so
then because you are lukewarm, and neither cold nor hot,
I will spew you out of my mouth [15-16]

counsel you (church of the Laodiceans) to buy of (from) Me gold
tried in the fire, that you may be rich; and white raiment,
that you may be clothed [18]

rebuke and chasten as many as I love [19]

stand at the door and knock [20]

will, if any man hear My voice and open the door, come in to
him, and will sup (eat) with him [20]

will grant to him who overcomes to sit with Me in My throne
[21]

overcame, and am set down with My Father in His throne
[22]

Revelation 16:

come as a thief (without further notice) [15]

Revelation 22:

come quickly [7]

come quickly [12]

have My reward with me (when I come), to give to every man
according as his work shall be (Isaiah 40:10) [12]

am Alpha and Omega, the beginning and the end, the first
and the last [13]

Jesus, have sent My angel to testify to you these things in
the churches [16]

am the root and offspring of David [16]
am the bright and morning star [16]
surely come quickly [20]

Part 2:   **Statements Made By Jesus' Apostles and Others About Jesus**

Matthew

"Jesus"

Matthew 1:
Christ is the Son of David [1]
Christ is the Son of Abraham [1]
was born of Mary [16]
is called Christ [16]
Christ was a child of the Holy Ghost [18]
Christ "is to be born of a virgin," said an angel to Joseph (Isaiah 7:14) [18-25]
Christ "is of the Holy Ghost," said an angel to Joseph [{18}20]
"was to be the Son of Mary," said an angel to Joseph [20-21]
was Mary's firstborn Son [20-25]
"shall save His people from their sins," said an angel to Joseph [21]
"shall be called Immanuel, which being interpreted is, God with us," said an angel to Joseph (Isaiah 7:14) [21-23]

Matthew 2:
was born in Bethlehem of Judea in the days of Herod the king (Micah 5:2) [1]
"was born King of the Jews, for we have seen His star in the East, and are come to worship Him," said wise men from the East [1-2]
"(Christ) was to be born in Bethlehem of Judea, for so it is written by the prophet," the chief priests and scribes responded to Herod (Micah 5:2) [4-5]
(the young Child) was taken to Egypt with His mother by night by Joseph: and was there until the death of Herod: that it might be fulfilled which was spoken of (about) the Lord by the prophet, saying, "Out of Egypt have I called My son" (Hosea 11:1) [14-15]
(the young Child) came into the land of Israel and dwelt in a city called Nazareth: that it might be fulfilled which was spoken by the prophets, "He shall be called a Nazarene" [21-23]

Matthew 3:

was baptized by John in the Jordan [13-16]

saw the Spirit of God descending like a dove and lighting upon Him (at His baptism) [16]

"is My beloved Son" (a voice from heaven at Jesus' baptism) [16-17]

"in You I am well pleased" (a voice from heaven at Jesus' baptism) [16-17]

Matthew 4:

was led up of (by) the spirit into the wilderness to be tempted of (by) the devil [1-11]

was hungry (after fasting 40 days and 40 nights) [1-2]

"if You are the Son of God, command that these stones be made bread," the tempter (the devil) said to Jesus when he came to Him [{1}3]

was taken up into the holy city, and set on a pinnacle of the temple by the devil, who said to Jesus, "If You are the Son of God, cast Yourself down: for it is written, 'He shall give His angels charge concerning you:' and 'In their hands they shall bear You up, lest at any time You dash Your foot against a stone'" (Psalm 91:11-12) [{1}5-6]

was taken up into an exceeding high mountain by the devil, and shown all the kingdoms of the world, and the glory of them; and the devil said to Jesus, "All these things will I give you, if you will fall down and worship me" [{7}8-11]

dwelt in Capernaum [13]

began to preach [17]

asked Simon called Peter, and Andrew his brother, James the son of Zebedee, and John his brother to follow Him [18-22]

went about all Galilee, teaching in their synagogues [23]

went about all Galilee, preaching the gospel of the kingdom [23]

went about all Galilee, healing all manner of sickness and all manner of disease among the people [23]

was brought all sick people who were taken with divers diseases and torments, and those who were possessed with devils, and those who were lunatick, and those who had the palsy; and He healed them [23-24]

Matthew 5:

taught them (the multitudes on a mountain) [{4:23}1-2]

Matthew 7:

doctrine astonished them, for He taught them as one having authority (sermon on the mountain) [28-29]

Matthew 8:

cleansed a leper [1-3]

told him (the leper) to tell no one (about his cleansing) [4]

healed a centurion's paralyzed servant, who lay at home sick of the palsy, grievously tormented [5-13]

marveled (at the centurion's faith) [10]

touched Peter's wife's mother's hand, and the fever left her [14-15]

was brought many who were possessed with devils: and He cast out the spirits with His word [{14}16]

healed all who were sick [{14}16]

fulfilled that which was spoken by Esaias the prophet, saying, "Himself took our infirmities and bare our sicknesses" [{14}16-17]

rebuked the winds and the sea; and there was a great calm [{18}23-27]

made the men (His disciples) marvel (by calming the winds and the sea) [{18}27]

"is even obeyed by the winds and the sea. What manner of man is this?," said the men (Jesus' disciples) [{18}27]

cast devils out of two who were possessed by them [28-33]

"what have we to do with You, Son of God? Are You come hither to torment us before the time?," cried out two who were devil possessed [28-29]

gave permission to the devils to go into the herd of swine, and when they were come out, they went into the herd of swine: and, behold, the whole herd of swine ran violently down a steep place into the sea, and perished in the waters [{29}31-32]

was besought by the whole city that He would depart out of their coasts (after casting the devils out of two and into some swine) [34]

Matthew 9:

healed a man sick of the palsy [1-8]

"blasphemes," certain of the scribes said within themselves (because Jesus told the man sick of the palsy that his sins were forgiven) [2-3] knew their (the scribes) thoughts (that He was blaspheming) [4]

raised from the dead the daughter of a certain ruler [18-26]

healed a woman who was diseased with an issue of blood twelve years, when she touched the hem of His garment [19-22]

was laughed to scorn by them (the people at the ruler's house, because the daughter of the ruler was dead, but Jesus said she was sleeping) [{22}24]

healed two blind men [27-31]

cast a devil out of a dumb man possessed with a devil [{30} 32-34]

"casts out devils through the prince of devils," the Pharisees said [{30}34]

went about all the cities and villages, teaching in their synagogues [35]

went about all the cities and villages, preaching the gospel of the kingdom [35]

went about all the cities and villages, healing every sickness and every disease among the people [35]

when He saw the multitudes, was moved with compassion on them, because they fainted, and were scattered abroad, as sheep having no shepherd [{35}36]

Matthew 10:

called His twelve disciples to Him and gave them power against unclean spirits, to cast them out, and to heal all manner of sickness and all manner of disease [{9:35}1]

twelve apostles are these; The first, Simon, who is called Peter, and Andrew his brother; James the son of Zebedee, and John his brother; Philip and Bartholomew; Thomas and Matthew the publican; James the son of Alphaeus, and Lebbaeus, whose surname was Thaddaeus; Simon the Canaanite, and Judas Iscariot, who also betrayed Him [{9:35}1-3]

Matthew 11:

departed thence to teach and to preach in their cities [1]

did works [2]

began to upbraid the cities wherein most of His mighty works were done, because they repented not [{7}20]

Matthew 12:

Restored whole the withered hand of a man on a Sabbath day
[{1}9-13]

healed all those in the multitudes [15]

charged the multitudes that they should not make Him known
[15-16]

healed one possessed with a devil, blind, and dumb (mute)
[{15}22]

amazed all the people [{15}22-23]

"does not cast out devils but by Beelzebub the prince of devils,"
said the Pharisees [{15}24]

Matthew 13:

spoke many things to them in parables [1-3]

spoke to them in parables [10]

put forth another parable to them [24]

put forth another parable to them [31]

spoke another parable to them [33]

spoke all these things to the multitude in parables [34]

finished these parables [53]

when He had come to His own country, taught them in their
synagogue [{51}54]

astonished those of His own country with His wisdom and mighty
works [{51}54]

"is the carpenter's son" (the people of His own country) [{51}
54-55]

"mother is called Mary" (the people of His own country) [{51}
54-55]

"brothers are James, and Joses, and Simon, and Judas" (the
people of His own country) [{51}54-55]

"sisters are all with us" (the people of His own country) [{51}
54-55]

offended them (the people of His own country) [57]

did not many mighty works there (His own country) because
of their unbelief [{57}58]

Matthew 14:

fed about 5,000 men, beside women and children, with five loaves
and two fish [13-21]

was moved with compassion toward them (a great multitude)
[14]

healed the sick in the multitude [14]

took the five loaves, and the two fish, and looking up to heaven, He blessed, and brake (them), and gave the loaves to His disciples [{16}19]

when He had sent the multitudes away, went up into a mountain apart to pray [22-23]

went to them (His disciples), walking on the sea [22-33]

stretched forth His hand, and caught him (Peter), as he was beginning to sink [30-31]

"of a truth You are the Son of God," said those in the boat after Jesus had walked on the water [{31}33]

made the diseased who touched the hem of His garment perfectly whole [{31}35-36]

Matthew 15:

offended the Pharisees (because He said that it is what comes out of the mouth that defiles a man not what goes into it) [{1}12]

made whole the daughter of a woman of Canaan who was grievously vexed with a devil [21-28]

healed the lame, blind, dumb, maimed and many others [29-30]

made the multitude wonder, when they saw the dumb to speak, the maimed to be whole, the lame to walk, and the blind to see [29-31]

fed 4,000 men, beside women and children, with seven loaves and a few fish [32-39]

commanded the multitude to sit down on the ground, and He took the seven loaves and the fish, and gave thanks, and brake them, and gave (them) to His disciples [{34}35-36]

Matthew 16:

told them (His disciples) to beware of the doctrine of the Pharisees and Sadducees [{8}12]

"You are the Christ," said Peter when Jesus asked His disciples, "Whom do men say that I the Son of Man am [13-16]

"You are the Son of the living God," said Peter (when Jesus asked His disciples who men said that He was) [13-16]

charged His disciples that they should tell no man that He was Jesus the Christ [20]

began to show His disciples, how that He must go to Jerusalem, and suffer many things of (from) the elders and chief priests and scribes [21]

began to show His disciples that He must be killed [21]

began to show His disciples that He must be raised again the
third day [21]

Matthew 17:

took Peter, James, and John his brother, and brought them
up to a high mountain apart, and was transfigured before
them: and His face did shine as the sun, and His raiment
was white as the light) [1-2]

talked with Moses and Elijah (at the Transfiguration) [{1}3]

"is My beloved Son" (voice out of the cloud at Jesus' Transfiguration) [{1}5]

"in You I am well pleased" (voice out of the cloud at Jesus'
Transfiguration) [{1}5]

charged them (Peter, James and John), that they should tell
the vision to no man, until the Son of Man (Jesus Himself) be
risen again from the dead [9]

rebuked the devil, and he departed out of him (a child) [14-
21]

Matthew 19:

was followed by great multitudes: and He healed them [2]

laid His hands on the little children [13-15]

Matthew 20:

"grant that these my two sons may sit, the one on Your right
hand, and the other on the left, in Your kingdom," said
the mother of Zebedee's sons [{17}21]

gave sight to two blind men [29-34]

had compassion on two blind men [34]

Matthew 21:

rode into Jerusalem on an ass, that it might be fulfilled which
was spoken by the prophet, saying, "Tell the daughter of
Sion, 'Behold, your King comes to you, meek, and sitting
on an ass, a colt the foal of an ass'" (Zechariah 9:9) (the
Triumphal Entry) [1-9]

was set on an ass and a very great multitude spread their
garments in the way; others cut down branches from the
trees, and strawed (spread) them in the way, and the
multitude that went before, and that followed cried, saying: "Hosanna to the son of David: blessed is He who comes
in the name of the Lord; Hosanna in the Highest" (the
Triumphal Entry) [6-9]

"is the prophet of Nazareth of Galilee," said the multitude [{6} 11]

went into the temple of God and cast out all them who sold and bought in the temple [12]

healed the blind and the lame who came to Him in the temple [{12}14]

did wonderful things, as seen by the chief priests and scribes [{12}15]

made the chief priests and scribes sore displeased (by the wonderful things He did, and by the children crying out in the temple and saying, "Hosanna to the Son of David") [{12}15]

was hungry [{12}18]

caused a fig tree to wither away [18-22]

was teaching in the temple [23-24]

"by what authority are You doing these things? And who gave You this authority?," said the chief priests and the elders of the people [23-24]

was taken for (perceived as) a prophet by the multitude, and because of this the chief priests and Pharisees feared the multitude [{42}46]

Matthew 22:

spoke to them again by parables [1]

perceived their (the Pharisees) wickedness [18]

made them (Pharisees) marvel (because of His response about the payment of taxes) [{18}21-22]

astonished the multitude at His doctrine [23-33]

had silenced the Sadducees [{29}34]

was not answered a word by any man, neither durst (did) any man from that day forth ask Him any more questions [{41} 46]

Matthew 26:

was to be taken by subtilty, and killed (consultation by the chief priests, and the scribes, and the elders of the people) [3-4]

had a woman pour an alabaster box of very precious ointment His head [6-7]

was betrayed to the chief priests by Judas Iscariot for 30 pieces of silver [14-16]

was betrayed by Judas [{19}25]

as they were eating (the Passover meal), took bread, and blessed it, and brake it, and gave it to the disciples [26]

took the cup (at the Passover meal), and gave thanks, and gave it to them (His disciples) [{26}27]

came with them (His disciples) to a place called Gethsemane and took with Him Peter and the two sons of Zebedee, and began to be sorrowful and very heavy [36-37]

went a little farther, and fell on His face, and prayed that if it were possible, the cup (His suffering and death) might pass from Him [{36}39]

came to the disciples, and found them asleep, and went away again the second time, and prayed [{36}40-42]

came and found them (the disciples) asleep again: for their eyes were heavy, and He left them, and went away again, and prayed the third time, saying the same words [{36}43-44]

came to His disciples, and said to them that the hour was at hand for Him to be betrayed into the hands of sinners [45]

was forsaken by all the disciples [{55}56]

was laid hold of and led away to Caiaphas the high priest, where the scribes and the elders were assembled [57]

"(this fellow) said, 'I am able to destroy the temple of God, and to build it in three days,'" reported two false witnesses to the council [59-61]

held His peace (was silent) before the high priest (Isaiah 53: 7) [63]

was spat on in His face, and buffeted, and others smote (struck) Him with the palms of their hands, and they said, "Prophesy to us, You Christ! Who is he who smote (struck) you?" [{64} 67-68]

was denied by Peter when he said, "I know not what you say," when a damsel came to him, saying, "You also were with Jesus of Galilee" [69-70]

was denied by Peter when he said, with an oath, "I do not know the Man," after another maid saw him, and said to them that were there, "This fellow was also with Jesus of Nazareth" [71-72]

was denied by Peter when he began to curse and to swear, saying, "I know not the Man," when those who stood by came to him and said, "Surely you also are one of them; for your speech betrays you" [73-74]

Matthew 27:

was bound and led away and delivered to Pontius Pilate the governor [1-2]

"are You the King of the Jews?," the governor (Pilate) asked Him [11]

when He was accused of (by) the chief priests and elders, and when Pilate said to Him, "Hear You not how many things they testify against You?," answered never a word [11-14]

"who is called Christ" (Pilate to the multitude) [17]

was delivered to Pilate for (due to) envy [17-18]

"is a just Man, have nothing to do with Him: for I have suffered many things this day in a dream because of Him," said Pilate's wife to Pilate [{17}19]

"is called Christ," Pilate said to the multitude [22]

"is a just Person," Pilate said to the multitude [{22}24]

"blood be on us, and on our children," all the people answered Pilate [{22}25]

was scourged (beaten) by Pilate (Isaiah 50:6) [26]

was delivered by Pilate to be crucified [26]

was stripped by the soldiers, and they put a scarlet robe on Him, and they platted a crown of thorns, and put it on His head, and a reed in His right hand: and they bowed the knee before Him and mocked Him, saying, "Hail, King of the Jews!" [27-29]

was spat on by the soldiers, and they took the reed, and smote (struck) Him on the head, and after they had mocked Him, they took the robe from Him (Isaiah 50:6) [{27}30-31]

was led away by the soldiers to be crucified [{27}31]

was given vinegar to drink mingled with gall [{27}34]

was crucified [{27}35]

garments were parted (divided) by them, casting lots: that it might be fulfilled which was spoken by the prophet, "They parted (divided) My garments among them, and on (for) My vesture (clothing) they cast lots" (Psalm 22:18) [{27}35]

had set up over His head (on the cross) His accusation written, "THIS IS JESUS THE KING OF THE JEWS" [37]

was reviled by those who passed by, wagging their heads, and saying, "You who destroy the temple and build it in three days, save yourself! If You be the Son of God, come down from the cross" [{37}39-40]

was mocked by the chief priests, with the scribes and elders, who said, "He saved others; Himself He cannot save. If He be the King of Israel, let Him now come down from the cross, and we will believe Him. He trusted in God; let Him deliver Him now, if He will have Him: for He said, 'I am the Son of God'" [{37}41-43] was mocked by the thieves crucified with Him, who cast the same (taunts) in His teeth [{27}44]

when He had cried again with a loud voice, yielded up the ghost (died) [Matthew 27:50]

"truly was the Son of God," said the centurion, and they that were with him, fearing greatly, as they watched Jesus, and when they saw the earthquake and those things that were done [54]

had been ministered to by many women from Galilee (who were at the crucifixion, looking on from afar) [{54}55]

body was given by Pilate to a rich man from Arimathea, named Joseph, who also himself was Jesus' disciple: and he wrapped it in a clean linen cloth, and laid it in his own new tomb, which he had hewn out in the rock: and he rolled a great stone to the door of the sepulchre (Isaiah 53:9) [57-60]

Matthew 28:

"was crucified," an angel said to Mary Magdalene and the other Mary [5]

"is not here: for He is risen, as He said," an angel said to Mary Magdalene and the other Mary [5-6]

"is risen from the dead," an angel said to Mary Magdalene and the other Mary [5-7]

"goes before you (His disciples) into Galilee," an angel said to Mary Magdalene and the other Mary [5-7]

Mark

"Jesus"

Mark 1:

Christ is the Son of God [1]

"Christ will baptize you with the Holy Spirit" (John the Baptist) [{1}8]

was baptized of (by) John in Jordan [9]

coming up out of the water, saw the heavens opened and the Spirit like a dove descending upon Him (at His baptism) [9-10]

"You are My beloved Son" (voice from heaven at Jesus' baptism) [9-11]

"in You I am well pleased" (voice from heaven at Jesus' baptism)
[9-11]

was driven into the wilderness by the Spirit, and He was there
in the wilderness forty days, tempted of (by) Satan [{9}12-
13]

came into Galilee, preaching the gospel of the kingdom of God
[14]

called Simon and Andrew his brother, James the son of Zebedee,
and John his brother, and they went after Him [16-20]

went into Capernaum, and straightway on the Sabbath day
He entered the synagogue, and taught [{17}21]

astonished them at His doctrine: for He taught them as one
that had authority (in the synagogue at Capernaum) [{17}
22]

"of Nazareth, let us alone; what have we to do with You? Are
You come to destroy us? I know You who You are, the Holy
One of God," a man with an unclean spirit cried out [23-
24]

rebuked an unclean spirit, and it cried out with a loud voice
and came out of him (a man with an unclean spirit) [23-
28]

amazed them all, insomuch that they questioned among themselves, saying "What thing is this? What new doctrine is
this? For with authority, commands He even the unclean
spirits, and they do obey Him" (those in the synagogue at
Capernaum who saw Jesus cast an unclean spirit out of
a man) [25-27]

took Simon's wife's mother's hand, and lifted her up; and immediately the fever left her [{25}29-31]

healed many who were sick of (with) divers (various) diseases
[{25}34]

cast out many devils [{25}34]

suffered not (did not allow) the devils to speak, because they
knew Him [{25}34]

departed into a solitary place, and there prayed [{25}35]

preached in their synagogues throughout all Galilee [{25}39]

cast out devils [{25}39]

cleansed a leper [40-45]

was moved with compassion [41]

straitly charged him (the leper) to say nothing to any man
(about his cleansing) [{41}43-44]

Mark 2:

preached the word to them [{1:45}2]

healed a man sick of the palsy [3-12]

"speaks blasphemies. Who can forgive sins but God only?," certain of the scribes, reasoning in their hearts (because Jesus told the man sick of the palsy that his sins were forgiven) [5-7]

perceived in His spirit that they (some of the scribes) so reasoned ("Who can forgive sins but God alone?") within themselves [{5}8]

taught the multitude [{8}13]

had many publicans and sinners as His followers, and He sat at meat with them [15]

disciples did not fast [{17}18]

Mark 3:

restored whole the withered hand of a man on a Sabbath day [{2:19}1-5]

looked round about on them with anger, being grieved for the hardness of their hearts [{2:19}5]

had healed many; insomuch that they pressed upon Him for to touch Him, as many as had plagues [{7}10]

"You are the Son of God," cried out unclean spirits, when they saw Him, and they fell down before Him [{7}11]

straitly charged the unclean spirits that they should not make Him known [{7}11-12]

called to Him whom He would, and He ordained twelve, that they should be with Him, and that He might send them forth to preach, and to have power to heal sicknesses, and to cast out devils: and Simon He surnamed Peter; and James the son of Zebedee, and John the brother of James; and He surnamed them Boanerges, which is, The sons of thunder: and Andrew, and Philip, and Bartholomew, and Matthew, and Thomas, and James the son of Alphaeus, and Thaddaeus, Simon the Canaanite; and Judas Iscariot [{7}13-19]

was betrayed by Judas Iscariot [{7}19]

"is beside Himself," said His friends [{7}21]

"has Beelzebub," and "by the prince of devils casts He out devils," said the scribes who came down from Jerusalem [{7}22]

Mark 4:

began to teach by the sea side, and He taught them many things by parables [{3:7}2]

with many such parables, spake the word to them, as they were able to hear it, but without a parable spake He not to them [{3:7}33-34]

when they were alone, expounded (explained) all things (that He had said in parables) to His disciples [{3:7}34]

rebuked the wind and the sea, and the wind ceased, and there was a great calm [{3:7}34-41]

made them (His disciples) fear exceedingly (by calming the wind and the sea) [{3:7}39-41]

"is even obeyed by the wind and the sea. What manner of man is this?," they (Jesus' disciples) said to one another [{3:7}34-41]

Mark 5:

cast (an) unclean spirit(s) out of a man [1-20]

"what have I to do with You, Son of the most high God? I adjure You by God, that You torment me not," cried out a man with an unclean spirit [7]

gave the unclean spirit(s) leave to enter the swine, and the unclean spirit(s) went out, and entered into the swine: and the herd ran violently down a steep place into the sea (there were about 2,000), and were choked in the sea [12-13]

action (casting unclean spirit(s) out of a man and into some swine) made them afraid (people of the city and the country), and they began to pray Him to depart out of their coasts [13-17]

made all men of Decapolis marvel (because He cast unclean spirits out of a man) [20]

raised from the dead the daughter of one of the rulers of the synagogue, Jairus by name [21-43]

healed a woman who had an issue of blood twelve years, when she touched His garment [25-34]

knew that virtue had gone out of Him (after being touched by the woman with an issue of blood) [30]

was laughed to scorn by them (those at Jairus' house, because his daughter was dead, but Jesus said she was not dead but sleeping) [{36}38-40] charged them (Peter, James, John, and the father and mother of the damsel) straitly that no man should know it (raising Jairus' daughter from the dead) [{36}43]

Mark 6:

began to teach in the synagogue on the Sabbath [{5:36}2]

astonished many (of His own country), so they said, "From whence has this Man these things? And what wisdom is this which is given to him, that even such mighty works are wrought by His hands" [{5:36}2]

"is the carpenter" (the people of His own country) [{5:36}3]

"is the son of Mary" (the people of His own country) [{5:36}3]

"is the brother of James, and Joses, and of Juda, and Simon" (the people of His own country) [{5:36}3]

"sisters are here with us" (the people of His own country) [{5:36} 3]

offended them (the people of His own country) [{5:36}3]

could there do no mighty work (His own country), save that He laid His hands on a few sick folk, and healed them, and He marvelled because of their unbelief [{4}5-6]

went round about the villages, teaching [{4}6]

called the twelve to Him, and began to send them forth two by two; and gave them power over unclean spirits [{4}7]

fed about 5,000 men with five loaves of bread and two fish [32-44]

saw much people in the desert, and was moved with compassion toward them, because they were as sheep not having a shepherd [34]

began to teach (much people in the desert) many things [34]

when He had taken the five loaves and the two fish, looked up to heaven, and blessed, and brake the loaves, and gave them to His disciples to set before them; and the two fish divided He among them all [{34}41]

came to them (His disciples), walking on the sea [{34}45-52]

healed the sick who touched Him (border of His garment?) [{34}56]

Mark 7:

cast forth (out) a devil from the young daughter of a Syro-Phoenician woman [24-30]

healed a deaf man with an impediment in his speech [{27}31-37] charged that they should tell no one (about the healing of a deaf man with an impediment in his speech) [{27}36]

astonished them beyond measure, so they were saying, "He has done all things well: He makes both the deaf to hear, and the dumb (mute) to speak" [{27}37]

Mark 8:

fed 4,000 with seven loaves and a few fish [1-10]

commanded the people to sit down on the ground: and He took the seven loaves, and gave thanks, and brake (the loaves), and gave (them) to His disciples to set before them (the people); and He blessed a few small fish, and commanded them (His disciples) to set them also before them (the people) [{1}6-7]

sighed deeply in His spirit (because the Pharisees began to question with Him, seeking of (from) Him a sign from heaven, tempting Him) [{1}11-12]

gave sight to a blind man [{17}22-26]

"You are the Christ," said Peter when Jesus asked His disciples, "Whom do men say that I am? [27-29]

charged them (His disciples) that they should tell no one about Him (that He was the Christ) [{27}29-30]

began to teach them that the Son of Man (Jesus Himself) must suffer many things [{27}31]

began to teach them that the Son of Man (Jesus Himself) must be rejected of (by) the elders, and of (by) the chief priests, and scribes [{27}31]

began to teach them that the Son of Man (Jesus Himself) must be killed [{27}31]

began to teach them that the Son of Man (Jesus Himself) after three days must rise again [{27}31]

rebuked Peter, because Peter began to rebuke Him for saying that He must suffer and be killed [{27}31-33]

Mark 9:

took Peter, and James, and John, and led them up into an high mountain apart by themselves: and He was transfigured before them, and His raiment became shining, exceeding white as snow (the Transfiguration) [2-3]

talked with Moses and Elias (at the Transfiguration) [4]

"is My beloved Son" (voice out of the cloud at Jesus' Transfiguration) [{5}7] charged them (Peter, James and John) that they should tell no man what things they had seen (the Transfiguration), till the Son of Man (Jesus Himself) were risen from the dead [{8}9]

rebuked a foul (deaf and dumb) spirit in a child, and it came out of him [14-29]

Mark 10:

as He was wont (accustomed), taught them again [{9:39}1]

took the young children up in His arms, put His hands on them, and blessed them [13-16]

beholding him (a man with great possessions), loved him [21]

disciples were astonished at His words (the difficulty of a rich man to enter the kingdom of God) [24]

disciples were astonished out of measure, saying among themselves, "Who then can be saved?" [26]

took again the twelve, and began to tell them what things should (would) happen to Him [32]

"Master, grant to us that we may sit, one on Your right hand, and the other on Your left hand, in Your glory," said James and John, the sons of Zebedee [{32}35-37]

gave sight to blind Bartimaeus [46-52]

Mark 11:

sat on the colt and many spread their garments in the way: and others cut down branches off the trees, and strawed (spread) them in the way, and they that went before, and they that followed cried, saying: "Hosanna; blessed is He who comes in the name of the Lord: blessed be the kingdom of our father David, that comes in the name of the Lord: Hosanna in the Highest" (the Triumphal Entry) [6-11]

entered into Jerusalem, and into the temple: and when he had looked round about on all things, and now the eventide was come, He went out to Bethany with the twelve [11]

caused a fig tree to wither away [12-22]

went into the temple, and began to cast out them who sold and bought in the temple, and overthrew the tables of the moneychangers, and the seats of them who sold doves; and would not suffer (let) that any man should carry any vessel through the temple [15]

was feared by the scribes and chief priests, because all the
people was astonished at His doctrine, so they sought
how they might destroy Him [17-18]

"by what authority do You these things? And who gave You
this authority to do these things?," said the chief priests,
and the scribes, and the elders [27-29]

Mark 12:

began to speak to them by (with) parables [{11:33}1]

was sent (by the chief priests, and the scribes, and the elders)
certain of the Pharisees and of the Herodians, to catch
Him in His words [{11:33}13]

knew their hypocrisy (the Pharisees and the Herodians) [{11:33}
15]

after answering the question, "Which is the first commandment
of all?," had no man that durst (dared) ask Him any question [28-34]

taught in the temple [35]

Mark 14:

was to be taken by craft and put to death (result sought by
the chief priests and the scribes) [{13:5}1]

had a woman pour an alabaster box of ointment of spikenard on His head [{13:5}3]

as they did eat (the Passover meal), took bread, and blessed
and brake it, and gave to them (the twelve) [22]

took the cup (at the Passover meal), and when He had given
thanks, He gave it to them (the twelve) [{22}23]

came to a place which was named Gethsemane, and took
with Him Peter and James and John, and began to be
sore amazed, and to be very heavy (troubled) [{30}32-33]

went forward a little, and fell on the ground, and prayed that,
if it were possible, the hour might pass from Him and the
cup (His suffering and death) taken away from Him [{30}
35-36]

came and found them sleeping, and again He went away, and
prayed, and spake the same words [{30}37-39]

when He returned, found them asleep again, (for their eyes
were heavy), neither wist they (did they know) what to
answer Him [{30}40]

came the third time and said that the hour had come when
the Son of Man was to be betrayed into the hands of sinners [{30}41]

disciples all forsook Him, and fled [{48}50]

was led away to the high priest: and with him were assembled all the chief priests and the elders and the scribes [53]

held His peace, and answered the high priest nothing [60-61]

was spit upon by some, had His face covered, and was buffeted, and they said to Him, "Prophesy" [{62}65]

was denied by Peter when he said, "I know not, neither understand I what you say," when one of the maids of the high priest came and looked at him and said, "And you also were with Jesus of Nazareth" [67-68]

was denied by Peter again, when a maid saw him again, and began to say to those who stood by, "This is one of them" [{67}69-70]

was denied by Peter when he began to curse and to swear, saying, "I know not this Man of whom you speak," when those who stood by said again to Peter, "Surely you are one of them: for you are a Galilean, and your speech agrees thereto" [{67}70-71]

Mark 15:

was bound and carried away, and delivered to Pilate by the chief priests, the elders and scribes and the whole council [1]

"are You the King of the Jews?," Pilate asked Him [2]

while being accused of many things by the chief priests, and when Pilate asked Him again, saying, "Answer You nothing? Behold how many things they witness against You," answered nothing (Isaiah 53:7) [3-5]

was delivered to Pilate by the chief priests for (because of) envy [{5}10]

was scourged (beaten) by Pilate (Isaiah 50:6) [15]

was delivered by Pilate to be crucified [15]

was clothed with purple by the soldiers, and they platted a crown of thorns, and put it about His head, and began to salute Him, "Hail King of the Jews!" [{15}16-18]

was smote (hit) on the head with a reed by the soldiers, and (they) did spit on Him, and bowing their knees worshiped Him, and when they had mocked Him, they took off the purple from Him (Isaiah 50:6) [{15}19-20]

was led out to be crucified [{15}20]

was brought to the place Golgotha, which is, being interpreted, The Place of a Skull, and they crucified him the third hour [{15}22-24]

had the superscription of His accusation written over (on the cross), "THE KING OF THE JEWS" [{15}26]

was crucified with two thieves, and so the Scripture was fulfilled, which says, "And He was numbered with the transgressors" (Isaiah 53:12) [{15}27-28]

was railed on by those who passed by, wagging their heads, and saying, "Ah, You who destroy the temple, and build it in three days, save Yourself, and come down from the cross" [{15}29-30]

was mocked by the chief priests also, with the scribes, saying among themselves, "He saved others; Himself He cannot save. Let Christ, the King of Israel descend now from the cross, that we may see and believe" [{15}31-32]

was reviled by those who were crucified with Him [{15}32]

at the ninth hour cried out with a loud voice, and gave up the ghost (died) [34-37]

"truly was the Son of God," said the centurion, who stood over against Him, when he saw that Jesus cried out and gave up the ghost (died) [{37}39]

body was granted by Pilate to Joseph of Arimathea (it was the day before the Sabbath), an honorable counsellor, who also waited for the kingdom of God, who took Him down, and wrapped Him in fine linen, and laid Him in a sepulchre which was hewn out of a rock, and rolled a stone to the door of the sepulchre [42-46]

was already dead [43-45]

Mark 16:

"of Nazareth was crucified," a young man in a long white garment said to Mary Magdalene, Mary the mother of James, and Salome [5-6]

"of Nazareth is risen," a young man in a long white garment said to Mary Magdalene, Mary the mother of James, and Salome [5-6]

"is going before you into Galilee: there shall you see Him, as He said to you," a young man in a long white garment said to Mary Magdalene, Mary the mother of James, and Salome [{6}7]

rose (from the dead) early the first day of the week [9]

appeared first (after He rose from the dead) to Mary Magdalene, out of whom He had cast seven devils [9]

after that, appeared in another form to two of them, as they walked [{9}12]

afterward appeared to the eleven as they sat at meat [{9}14]

upbraided the eleven with (for) their unbelief and hardness of heart, because they believed not those who had seen Him after He was risen [{9}14]

(the Lord) was received up into heaven [19]

(the Lord) sat on the right hand of God (after being received up into heaven) [19]

(the Lord) worked with them (the eleven), confirming the word with signs following (after He was received up into heaven) [20]

Luke

"Jesus"

Luke 1:

"shall be your Son," an angel said to Mary [30-31]

"shall be great," an angel said to Mary [31-32]

"shall be called the Son of the Highest," an angel said to Mary [31-32]

"shall be given the throne of His Father David by the Lord God," an angel said to Mary [31-32]

"shall reign over the house of Jacob forever," an angel said to Mary [31-33]

"shall have a kingdom with no end," an angel said to Mary [31-33]

"shall be called the Son of God, because the Holy Ghost shall come upon you, and the power of the Highest shall over-shadow you" an angel said to Mary after she said to the angel, "How shall this be, seeing I know not a man?" (Isaiah 7:14) [{31}34-35]

Luke 2:

(Christ) was born in Bethlehem of Judea, wrapped in swad-dling clothes and laid in a manger [1-12]

"(a Savior) is Christ the Lord, born to you this day in the city of David," said an angel to the shepherds [11]

when eight days were accomplished, was circumcised [21]

the name the child was called, was the name the angel gave
Him before He was conceived in the womb [21]

was brought to Jerusalem to be presented to the Lord, when
the days of her (Mary's) purification according to the law
of Moses were accomplished (as it is written in the law of
the Lord, "Every male who opens the womb shall be called
holy to the Lord") (Exodus 13:2) [{21}22-23]

is the Lord's Christ was revealed to Simeon by the Holy Ghost
[25-32]

"is set for the fall and rising again of many in Israel," said
Simeon to Mary, Jesus' Mother [{27}34]

"is set for a sign which shall be spoken against that the
thoughts of many hearts may be revealed," said Simeon to
Mary, Jesus' mother [{27}34-35]

(the child) grew, and waxed strong in spirit, filled with wisdom
[{27}40]

(the child) had the grace of God upon Him [{27}40]

when He was 12 years old, was found sitting in the midst of
the doctors in the temple, both listening to them, and asking them questions, and all who heard Him were astonished at His understanding and answers [42-47]

(the child) was subject to them (His parents) [{43}51]

increased in wisdom and stature, and in favor with God and
man [52]

Luke 3:

was baptized [21]

had the Holy Ghost descend in bodily shape like a dove
upon Him (at His baptism) [21-22]

"You are My beloved Son" (voice from heaven at Jesus' baptism) [21-22]

"in You I am well pleased" (voice from heaven at Jesus'
baptism) [21-22]

was about thirty years of age (at His baptism) [23]

was (as was supposed) the son of Joseph [23]

Luke 4:

being full of the Holy Ghost returned from Jordan, and was
led by the Spirit into the wilderness, being forty days
tempted of (by) the devil [1-2]

was tempted by the devil saying to Him, "If You are the Son
of God, command this stone that it be made bread" [{1}3-
4]

was taken by the devil up into an exceeding high mountain, and showed all the kingdoms of the world in a moment of time, and the devil said to Him, "All this power will I give You, and the glory of them: for that is delivered to me; and to whomsoever I will I give it. If You will worship me, all shall be yours" [{1}5-8]

was brought to Jerusalem, and set on a pinnacle of the temple by the devil, who tempted Him by saying to Him, "If You are the Son of God, cast yourself down from here: for it is written, 'He shall give His angels charge over You: and in their hands they shall bear You up, lest at any time You dash Your foot against a stone'" (Psalm 91:11-12) [{1}9-13]

returned in the power of the Spirit to Galilee [14]

taught in their synagogues [14-15]

was glorified of (by) all [14-15]

was brought up in Nazareth [{14}16]

went into the synagogue at Nazareth on the Sabbath day, and stood up to read [{14}16]

made them (those in the synagogue at Nazareth) wonder at the gracious words which proceeded out of His mouth [{14}22]

"is Joseph's son" (those in the synagogue at Nazareth) [{14}22]

filled them (those in the synagogue at Nazareth) with wrath, when they heard these things, and they rose up and thrust Him out of the city, and they led Him to the brow of the hill whereon their city was built, that they might cast Him down headlong, but He passing through the midst of them went on His way [{14}28-30]

came down to Capernaum, a city of Galilee, and was teaching them on the Sabbath days [{14}31]

astonished them (in Capernaum) at His doctrine: for His word was with power [Luke 4:{14}32]

"of Nazareth let us alone; what have we to do with You? Are You come to destroy us? I know You, who You are; the Holy One of God," a man with a spirit of an unclean devil cried out with a loud voice [33-34]

rebuked an unclean devil and it came out of him (the man with a spirit of an unclean devil) [33-37]

amazed all, and they spake among themselves, saying, "What a word is this! For with authority and power He commands the unclean spirits, and they come out" (people in Capernaum who saw Jesus cast an unclean devil out of a man) [35-36] rebuked the fever in Simon's wife's mother, and it left her [{35}38-39]

laid His hands on every one of the sick, and healed them [{35} 40]

made devils come out of many [{35}41]

"You are Christ the Son of God," cried out devils, as they came out of many [{35}41]

rebuked the devils, suffering them not to speak: for they knew that He was Christ [{35}41]

preached in the synagogues of Galilee [{35}44]

Luke 5:

taught the people out of the ship [{4:35}3]

"depart from me; for I am a sinful man, O Lord," Simon Peter said in astonishment after catching many fish at Jesus' command [{4:35}4-9]

cleansed a man full of leprosy [12-14]

charged him (the man full of leprosy) to tell no one (about his cleansing) [12-14]

was teaching [{12}17]

healed a man sick of the palsy [18-26]

"speaks blasphemies. Who can forgive sins, but God alone?," the scribes and the Pharisees began to reason (because Jesus told the man sick of the palsy that his sins were forgiven) [{12}20-21]

perceived their (the scribes and the Pharisees) thoughts ("Who can forgive sins but God alone?") [22]

amazed them all (by healing the man sick of the palsy) [{22}26]

disciples did not fast often or make prayers [{31}33]

spake a parable to them [{31}36]

Luke 6:

taught in the synagogue on another Sabbath [{3}6]

restored the withered right hand of a man on a Sabbath [6-11]

knew their (the scribes and Pharisees) thoughts (watching Him to see whether He would heal on the Sabbath day: that they might find an accusation against Him) [{3}8]

filled them (the scribes and Pharisees) with madness (because He healed the man with a withered hand on the Sabbath) [9-11]

went out into a mountain to pray, and continued all night in prayer to God [{11}12] called to Him His disciples: and of (from) them He chose twelve, whom also He named apostles; Simon, (whom He also named Peter), and Andrew his brother, James and John, Philip and Bartholomew, Matthew and Thomas, James the son of Alphaeus, and Simon called the Zelotes, Judas, the brother of James, and Judas Iscariot, who also was the traitor [{11}13-17]

healed those with diseases and those who were vexed with unclean spirits [{11}17-19]

power healed those who sought to touch Him [{11}19]

spake a parable to them [{11}39]

Luke 7:

healed a centurion's sick, ready to die servant [1-10]

marvelled at him (the centurion because of his faith) [8-9]

(the Lord) raised the widow's son from the dead [11-16]

(the Lord) had compassion on her (the widow with the dead son) [13]

"is a great prophet risen up among us" and "God has visited His people," said the people of Nain, after the raising of the widow's son [{9}16]

in that same hour, cured many of their infirmities and plagues, and of evil spirits; and to many who were blind He gave sight [{19}21]

feet were washed with the tears of a woman who was a sinner, and she did wipe them with the hairs of her head, and kissed His feet and anointed them with the ointment [{22}37-38]

"forgives sins also," they who sat at meat with Him began to say within themselves [{40}49]

Luke 8:

went throughout every city and village, preaching and showing the glad tidings of the kingdom of God [{7:40}1]

healed Mary called Magdalene, out of whom went seven devils, Joanna the wife of Chusa Herod's steward, Susanna, and many others who had been healed of evil spirits and infirmities [{7:40}2-3]

was ministered of (from) the substance of Mary called Magdalene, Joanna, Susanna and many others [{7:40}2-3]

spake to much people by (with) a parable [{7:40}4]

rebuked the wind and the raging of the water: and they ceased, and there was a calm [{7:40}22-25] made them (His disciples) afraid and wonder (by calming the wind and the sea) [{7:40}25]

"commands even the winds and water, and they obey Him. What manner of man is this!," they (Jesus' disciples) said to one another [{7:40}25]

"what have I to do with You, Son of God most high? I beseech You, torment me not," said with a loud voice by a man with devils [26-28]

cast devils out of a man [26-39]

suffered (allowed) the unclean spirits to enter the swine, then went the devils out of the man, and entered into the swine: and the herd ran violently down a steep place into the lake, and were choked [{30}31-33]

action (casting devils out of a man and into some swine) took them (the whole multitude of the country of the Gadarenes round about) with great fear, so they besought Him to depart from them [{35}37]

raised from the dead the only daughter of a man named Jairus, a ruler of the synagogue [41-56]

healed a woman having an issue of blood twelve years, when she touched the border of His garment [43-48]

was laughed to scorn by them (those at Jairus' house, because his daughter was dead, and Jesus said she was not dead but was sleeping) [{50}52-53]

charged Jairus' daughter's parents that they should tell no man what was done (His raising her from the dead) [{50}56]

Luke 9:

called His twelve disciples together, and gave them power and authority over all devils, and to cure diseases, and He sent them to preach the kingdom of God, and to heal the sick [{8:50}1-2]

received the people, and spake to them of (about) the kingdom of God [{8:50}11]

healed the people who had need of healing [{8:50}11]

fed about 5,000 men with five loaves and two fish [{8:50}12-17]

took the five loaves and the two fish, and looking up to heaven, He blessed them, and brake (them), and gave (them) to the disciples to set before the multitude [{8:50}16]

was alone praying [{8:50}18]

"You are the Christ of God," said Peter when Jesus asked His disciples, "But whom say you that I am?" [{8:50}20]

straitly charged them (His disciples), and commanded them to
   tell no man that thing (that He was the Christ) [{8:50}21]

took Peter, John and James and went up into a mountain to
   pray, and as He prayed, the fashion of His countenance
   was altered, and His raiment was white and glistening
   (the Transfiguration) [{8:50}28-29]

talked with two men, Moses and Elias (at the Transfiguration)
   [{8:50}28-31]

was to decease (die) in Jerusalem (spoken by Moses and Elijah
   at Jesus' Transfiguration) [{8:50}28-31]

"is My beloved Son" (voice out of the cloud at Jesus'
   Transfiguration) [35-36]

rebuked an unclean spirit, healing a child who was thrown
   down and torn by the devil [37-42]

made everyone wonder at all the things He did [43]

perceived the thought (disputing about which of them would
   be the greatest) of their (His disciples) heart [47]

when the time was come that He should (would) be received
   up, steadfastly set His face to go to Jerusalem [{50}51]

was not received by the Samaritans [{50}52-53]

rebuked His disciples James and John for suggesting they
   command fire to come down from heaven, and consume
   them (the Samaritans for not receiving Him) [{50}52-56]

Luke 10:

(the Lord) appointed other seventy also, and sent them two
   and two before His face into every city and place, where
   He himself would come [1]

rejoiced in spirit [21]

Luke 11:

was praying [{10:41}1]

was casting a devil out of a dumb (mute) man [{10:41}14]

made the people wonder (by casting a devil out of a dumb
   (mute) man) [{10:41}14]

"casts out devils through Beelzebub, the chief of the devils,"
   said some of the people [{10:41}15]

was tempted by others, who sought of (from) Him a sign from
   heaven [{10:41}16]

knew their thoughts (that He cast out devils by Beelzebub)
   [{10:41}17]

began to be urged vehemently by the scribes and the Pharisees,
   and they tried to provoke Him to speak of many things: laying

(in) wait for Him, and seeking to catch something out of His mouth, that they might accuse Him [{10:41}53-54]

Luke 12:

spake a parable to them [{10:41}16]

(Lord) "speak You this parable to us, or even to all?," Peter said to Him [{10:41}41]

Luke 13:

spake also this parable [{2}6]

was teaching in one of the synagogues on the Sabbath [{2}10]

healed, on the Sabbath, a (Satan-bound) woman who had a spirit of infirmity eighteen years, and was bowed together, and could in no wise lift up herself [10-17]

adversaries were ashamed (after His answer to the ruler of the synagogue about healing the Satan-bound woman on the Sabbath) [{12}17]

went through the cities and villages, teaching, and journeying toward Jerusalem [{12}22]

"get out and depart hence: for Herod will kill You," said certain of the Pharisees to Him [{12}31]

Luke 14:

healed a man with dropsy on the Sabbath day [1-6]

could not be answered again to (about) these things (whether it was lawful to heal on the Sabbath day) [{3}6]

put forth a parable to those who were bidden, when He marked how they chose out the chief rooms (to honor themselves) [{3}7]

Luke 15:

"receives sinners, and eats with them," the Pharisees and scribes murmured (because the publicans and sinners drew near to Him to hear Him) [{14:3}1-2]

spake this parable to them [{14:3}3]

Luke 16:

was derided by the Pharisees, who were covetous [{14:3}14]

Luke 17:

cleansed ten lepers [11-19]

Luke 18:

spake a parable to them to this end, that men ought always
to pray, and not to faint [{17:17}1]

spake this parable to certain (people) who trusted in themselves
that they were righteous, and despised others [{17:17}9]

was brought also infants, that He would touch them [15-17]

gave sight to a certain blind man [35-43]

Luke 19:

"was gone to be guest with a man who is a sinner," they all
murmured (because He went to eat with Zacchaeus, who
was chief among the publicans, and he was rich) [1-7]

added and spake a parable, because He was nigh to Jerusalem,
and because they thought that the kingdom of God should
appear immediately [{9}11]

was set on the colt, and as He went, they spread their clothes in
the way, and when He was come nigh, even now at the
descent of the Mount of Olives, the whole multitude of
the disciples began to rejoice and praise God with a loud
voice for all the mighty works that they had seen; saying:
"Blessed be the King who comes in the name of the Lord:
peace in heaven, and glory in the highest" (the Triumphal
Entry) [35-38]

"rebuke Your disciples," some of the Pharisees said (for rejoicing and praising God during the Triumphal Entry) [{35}39]

beheld the city (Jerusalem), and wept over it [{35}41]

went into the temple, and began to cast out those who sold
therein, and those who bought [{35}45]

taught daily in the temple, but the chief priests and the scribes
and the chief of the people sought to destroy Him, and
could not find what they might do:. for all the people were
very attentive to hear Him [{35}47-48]

Luke 20:

taught the people in the temple [{19:35}1]

preached the gospel in the temple [{19:35}1]

"tell us, by what authority do You these things? Or who is he
who gave You this authority?," said the chief priests and the
scribes with the elders coming upon Him [{19:35}1-2]

began to speak this parable [8-9]

was watched, and sent forth spies by the chief priests and
the scribes, who should feign themselves just men, that
they might take hold of His words, that so they might

deliver Him to the power and authority of the governor, and they asked Him saying, "Master, we know that you say and teach rightly, neither accept you the person of any, but teach the way of God truly: is it lawful for us to give tribute to Caesar or no?," ...and they could not take hold of His words before the people: and they marveled at His answer (about whom to pay taxes to), and held their peace [{8}20-26]

perceived their craftiness, when they (the chief priests and the scribes) asked Him whether it was lawful to pay taxes to Caesar [{8}21-23]

Luke 21:

was teaching in the temple [{20:34}37-38]

Luke 22:

was sought by the chief priests and scribes how they might kill Him; for they feared the people [{20:34}2]

took the cup (at the Passover meal), and gave thanks [{20:34}14-17]

took bread (at the Passover meal), and gave thanks, and brake it, and gave it to them (the twelve apostles) [{20:34}19]

likewise also took the cup after supper (at the Passover meal) [{20:35}20]

went, as He was wont (accustomed), to the Mount of Olives; and His disciples also followed Him [{20:34}39-41]

was withdrawn from them about a stone's cast, and kneeled down, and prayed to the Father that if He were willing, the cup (His suffering and death) be removed from Him [{20:34}41-42]

was strengthened by an angel who appeared to Him from heaven [{20:34}43]

being in agony, prayed more earnestly: and His sweat was as it were great drops of blood falling down to the ground, and when He rose up from prayer, and was come to His disciples, He found them sleeping for (due to) sorrow [{20:35}44-45]

healed the cut-off ear of the servant of the high priest [47-51]

was taken, and led, and brought into the high priest's house [{52}54]

was denied by Peter, who said, "Woman, I know Him not," when a certain maid beheld him, and earnestly looked on him, and said, "This man was also with Him" [{52}56-57] was denied by Peter, who said, "Man, I am not," when another saw Him, and said, "You are also of them" [{52}58]

was denied by Peter, who said, "Man, I know not what you say," when another confidently affirmed, saying, "Of a truth this fellow also was with Him, for He is a Galilean" [{52}59-60]

was mocked, and smote (beaten), and when blindfolded was struck on the face by the men that held Him, and they asked Him, saying, "Prophesy, who is it that smote You?", and many other things blasphemously spake they against Him [63-65]

"If You are the Christ, tell us," said the elders of the people, and the chief priests and the scribes, after leading Jesus into their council [{63}66-67]

"Are you then the Son of God?," they all said (at the council) [{63}70]

Luke 23:

was led to Pilate by the whole multitude, and they began to accuse Him, saying, "We found this fellow perverting the nation, and forbidding to give tribute to Caesar, saying, that He Himself is Christ a king" [{22:63}1-2]

"are You the King of the Jews?," Pilate asked Him [{22:63}3]

"is without fault," said Pilate to the chief priests and to the people [{22:63}4]

"stirs up the people, teaching throughout all Jewry, beginning from Galilee to this place," said the chief priests and the people more fiercely to Pilate [{22:63}5]

was sent by Pilate to Herod [{22:63}7]

was questioned by Herod with many words, but He answered him nothing [8-9]

was vehemently accused by the chief priests and scribes [{8}10]

was set at nought (treated contemptuously) and mocked by Herod and his men of war, who arrayed Him in a gorgeous robe, and sent Him again to Pilate [{8}11]

"was brought to me by you, as one who perverts the people: and, behold, I, having examined Him before you, have found no fault in this Man touching those things whereof you accuse Him: no, nor yet (did) Herod: for I sent you back to him; and, lo, nothing worthy of death is done unto Him (was found by Herod); I will therefore chastise

Him, and release Him" (Pilate to the chief priests and the rulers and the people) [{8}13-16]

was delivered by Pilate to their (chief priests, the rulers and the people) will (to be crucified) [13-25]

was crucified with the malefactors at the place called Calvary [{28}33]

"saved others; let Him save Himself, if He be Christ, the chosen of God," derided the rulers [34-35]

was mocked by the soldiers, coming to Him, and offering Him vinegar, and saying, "If You be the King of the Jews, save Yourself" [34-37]

had a superscription written over Him (on the cross) in letters of Greek, and Latin, and Hebrew: THIS IS THE KING OF THE JEWS" [{34}38]

"if You be Christ, save Yourself and us," railed one of the malefactors who were hanged with Him [{34}39]

"has done nothing amiss," said the other malefactor, who then said to Jesus, "Lord, remember me when you come into Your kingdom" [39-42]

cried out with a loud voice, "Father, into Your hands I commend My spirit:" and gave up the ghost (died) [46]

"certainly was a righteous Man," said the centurion when he saw what was done, glorifying God [46-47]

body was taken down (it was the day of the Preparation), and wrapped in linen, and laid in a sepulchre that was hewn in stone, wherein never man before was laid, by a man named Joseph, a counsellor from Arimathea, who also himself waited for the kingdom of God and was a good man, and a just (man), and who had not consented to the counsel and deed of them [50-53]

Luke 24:

body was not found in the tomb (by the women who came with Him from Galilee and certain others) [1-3]

"is not here, but is risen; why seek the living among the dead?," two men in shining garments said to the women who had come with Jesus from Galilee and certain others [3-6]

linen clothes laid by themselves in the tomb and Peter wondered in himself at that which was come to pass [{3}12]

Himself drew near, and went with them (two men), but their eyes were holden (blinded) that they should (would) not know Him [13-16]

"of Nazareth was a prophet," said Cleopas and another man
to Jesus [13-19]

"of Nazareth was mighty in deed," said Cleopas and another
man to Jesus [13-19]

"of Nazareth was mighty in word," said Cleopas and another
man to Jesus [13-19]

"of Nazareth was condemned to death," said Cleopas and
another man to Jesus [13-20]

"of Nazareth was crucified," said Cleopas and another man to
Jesus [13-20]

(after His resurrection) beginning at Moses and all the prophets,
expounded to them (Cleopas and another man) in all the
Scriptures the things concerning Himself [{15}27]

took bread, and blessed it, and brake (it), and gave (it) to them,
and their eyes were opened, and they knew Him [{15}30-
31]

vanished out of their sight [{15}31]

"talked with us by the way, and opened to us the Scriptures,
and our heart burned within us" Cleopas and another
man said to each other [{15}32]

"(the Lord) is risen indeed," said Cleopas and another man to
the eleven, and them who were with them [34]

"(the Lord) has appeared to Simon," said Cleopas and another
man to the eleven, and them who were with them [34]

Himself stood in the midst of them (the eleven and them who
were with them), but they were terrified and affrighted,
and supposed that they had seen a spirit (after His resurrection) [36-37]

showed them (the eleven and them who were with them) His
hands and feet, and while they yet believed not for joy,
and wondered, He took a piece of a boiled fish, and of an
honeycomb, and did eat before them (after His resurrection) [{36}40-43]

opened their (the eleven and them who were with them) understanding, that they might understand the Scriptures [{36}
45]

led them out as far as to Bethany, and He lifted up His hands,
and blessed them (the eleven and those who were with
them) [{36}50]

was parted from them (the eleven and those who were with
them), and carried up into heaven [{36}51]

John

"Jesus"

John 1:

was the Word [1, 14]

(the Word) was God [1, 14]

(the Word) was in the beginning with God [1-2]

(the Word) made all things [1-3]

(the Word) has life in Him [1-4]

(the Word) life was the light of men [1-4]

(the true Light) lights every man who comes into the world [1-9]

(the true Light) was in the world, and the world was made by Him, and the world knew Him not [6-10]

(the true Light) came to His own, and His own received Him not [6-11]

(the Word) was made flesh, and dwelt among us [14]

(the Word) had glory as of the only begotten of the Father [14]

(the Word) was full of grace [14]

(the Word) was full of truth [14]

Christ brought grace and truth [17]

Christ is the only begotten Son (of the Father) [17-18]

Christ is in the bosom of the Father [17-18]

Christ has declared God [17-18]

"is the Lamb of God," said John the Baptist [29]

"takes away the sins of the world," said John the Baptist [29]

"is He of whom I said, 'After me comes a man who is preferred before me: for He was before me,'" said John the Baptist [29-30]

"had the Spirit descend from heaven like a dove, and it abode on Him," said John the Baptist, baring record of Jesus' baptism [{29}32]

"is He who baptizes with the Holy Ghost," said John the Baptist, baring record of Jesus' baptism [{29}32-33]

"is the Son of God," said John the Baptist, baring record of what he saw [{29}34]

"is the Lamb of God," John the Baptist said, looking on Jesus as He walked [36]

"is the Messias, which is, being interpreted, the Christ," said Andrew to his brother, Simon [{38}40-41]

found Philip (and told him to follow Him) [43]

"of Nazareth, the son of Joseph, is Him of whom Moses in the law, and the prophets did write," said Philip to Nathanael [45]

"Rabbi, You are the Son of God," Nathanael said [48-49]

"Rabbi, You are the King of Israel," Nathanael said [48-49]

John 2:

changed water to wine at a wedding in Cana [1-10]

manifested forth His glory by this beginning of miracles (by turning the water into wine) [11]

went up to Jerusalem at the Jew's Passover [13]

drove those who sold oxen and sheep and doves, and the changers of money from the temple [13-15]

"was zealous for God's house," the disciples remembered (Psalm 69:9) [{13}17]

"what sign show You to us, seeing that You do these things (driving the sellers and the money changers from the temple)," answered the Jews [{13}18]

was in Jerusalem at the Passover, and in the feast day, many believed in His name, when they saw the miracles which He did [{13}23]

did not commit Himself to them, because He knew all men, and needed not that any should testify of man: for He knew what was in man [23-24]

John 3:

and His disciples came into the land of Judea; and there He tarried with them, and baptized [22]

"must increase, but I must decrease," answered John the Baptist [22-30]

"(the Son) is loved by the Father," answered John the Baptist [35]

"(the Son) has been given all things into His hand by the Father" (John the Baptist) [35]

John 4:

Himself baptized not [2]

was wearied from His journey [6]

"Sir, I perceive that You are a prophet," the woman (at the well) said to Him [{17}19]

disciples marveled that He talked with the woman (the woman at the well) [{26}27] "told me all things that ever I did: is not this the Christ?," said the woman at the well to the men of Samaria [{26}29]

was believed on by many of the Samaritans of that city, because of the saying of the woman (at the well), and many more believed because of His own word [{26}39-41]

"is indeed the Christ" (the people of Samaria) [{34}42]

"is indeed the Savior of the world" (the people of Samaria) [{34} 42]

Himself testified, that a prophet has no honor in his own country [44]

was received by the Galileans, having seen all the things He did at Jerusalem at the feast [{44}45]

healed a nobleman's child who had a fever [46-54]

John 5:

healed a man at the pool of Bethesda on the Sabbath, who had an infirmity thirty and eight years [1-16]

was persecuted by the Jews, and they sought to slay Him, because He had done these things (healed a man who had an infirmity) on the Sabbath [16]

was sought by the Jews the more to kill Him, because He not only had broken the Sabbath, but said also that God was His Father, making Himself equal with God [17-18]

John 6:

was followed by a great multitude, because they saw His miracles which He did on those who were diseased [1-2]

fed about 5,000 men with five loaves and two fish [1-14]

took the loaves, and when He had given thanks, He distributed them to the disciples: and likewise of the fish [11]

"is of a truth that Prophet who should (would) come into the world," said those men (His disciples), when they had seen the miracle (feeding the 5,000) that Jesus did [14]

perceived that they would come and take Him by force, to make Him king, so He departed again to a mountain Himself alone [15]

walked on the sea [15-21]

was murmured at by the Jews, because He said, I am the bread which came down from heaven [{35}41]

"is the son of Joseph, whose father and mother we know. How is it then that He says, 'I came down from heaven'?" (the Jews) [42]

knew in Himself that His disciples murmured at it, saying "This is an hard saying; who can hear it (people must eat His flesh and drink His blood to live forever)" [53-61]

taught in the synagogue in Capernaum [{53}59]

knew from the beginning who they were who believed not, and who should (would) betray Him [64]

"(Lord) to whom shall we go? You have the words of eternal life," was Peter's answer to Jesus' question, "Will you also go away?" [67-68]

"we believe and are sure that you are that Christ, the Son of the living God," Peter answered Him [67-69]

should (would) be betrayed by Judas Iscariot, one of the twelve [70-71]

John 7:

walked in Galilee: for He would not walk in Jewry, because the Jews sought to kill Him [1]

"depart hence, and go into Judea (for the Jews' Feast of Tabernacles), that Your disciples also may see the works that You do, for there is no man that does any thing in secret, and he himself seeks to be known openly. If You do these things, show Yourself to the world," said Jesus' brothers to Him, for neither did His brethren believe in Him [1-5]

when His brethren were gone up, then went He also up to the feast (the Jews' Feast of Tabernacles), not openly, but as it were in secret [{6}10]

"is a good man," some said: others said, "No, but He deceives the people" [{6}12]

was not spoken openly of by any man for fear of the Jews [{1}13]

went up into the temple and taught [14]

marvelled the Jews, and they said, "How does this Man know letters, having never learned?" [14-15]

"You have a devil. Who goes about to kill You?," some of them said [{16}20]

"is He whom they seek to kill, but lo, He speaks boldly, and they say nothing to Him. Do the rulers know indeed that this is the very Christ? Howbeit we know this Man whence He is (where He is from): but when Christ comes, no one knows whence He is (where He is from)," said some of them of (from) Jerusalem [{21}25-27]

cried out, as He taught in the temple [28]

hour was not yet come, so, although they sought to take Him, no man laid hands on Him [{28}30]

was believed on by many of the people who said, "When Christ comes, will He do more miracles than these which this Man has done?" [{28}31]

was sent officers by the Pharisees and the chief priests to take Him [{28}32]

spake concerning the Spirit, whom those who believe on Him should (would) receive: for the Holy Ghost was not yet given; because Jesus was not yet glorified [39]

brought division among the people, many of them saying, "Of a truth this is the Prophet," and others saying, "This is the Christ," but some were saying, "shall Christ come out of Galilee? Has not the scripture said, that Christ comes of the seed of David, and out of the town of Bethlehem, where David was?" [{39}40-43]

was laid hands on by no man, though some of them would have taken Him [{39}44]

"speaks like no other man," the officers answered the chief priests and Pharisees who asked them, "Why have you not brought Him (Jesus)?" [{39}45-46]

"is not believed on by any of the rulers or of the Pharisees. This people who know not the law are cursed," the Pharisees answered the officers [{39}47-48]

"should not be judged by our law, before it hear him, and knows what He does," Nicodemus said to the Pharisees [{39}49-51]

John 8:

taught in the temple [1-2]

was brought, by the scribes and Pharisees, a woman taken adultery; and they said to Him, "Master, this woman was caught in adultery, in the very act. Now Moses, in the law commanded us, that such should be stoned: but what say You?," to tempt Him, that they might have (something) to accuse Him [{1}3-5]

as though He heard them not, stooped down, and with His finger wrote on the ground (when being tempted by the scribes and Pharisees about the woman taken in adultery), and He lifted Himself up when they continued asking Him, and He told them that the one without sin should cast the first stone, and again He stooped down, and wrote on the ground [6-8]

was left alone, and the woman (the woman taken in adultery) standing in the midst, after those who heard His response to their question, being convicted by their own conscience, went out one by one, beginning at the eldest even to the last [9]

"You bear record of Yourself: Your record is not true," the Pharisees said to Him, after He said that He is the light of the world [12-13]

taught in the temple [20]

was laid hands on by no man; for His hour was not yet come [20]

was believed on by many, as He spake these words (that the Father had sent Him and that He spoke what His Father taught Him) [{28}30]

"do we not say well that You are a Samaritan, and have a devil?," the Jews answered (after Jesus told them that they were not of God) [{42}48]

"now we know that You have a devil," said the Jews to Him (after Jesus said to them that a man who keeps His saying shall never taste of death) [{49}52]

"You are not yet fifty years old, and have You seen Abraham?," the Jews said to Him [{54}57]

hid himself, and went out of the temple, going through the midst of them, and so passed by, as they (the Jews) took up stones to throw at Him [59]

John 9:

healed on a Sabbath a man who was blind from birth [1-41]

was asked by His disciples, "Master, who did sin, this man, or his parents, that he was born blind?" [2-3]

"made clay, and anointed mine eyes, and said to me, 'Go to the pool of Siloam, and wash:' and I went and washed, and I received sight," said the man blind from birth to the neighbors and those who before had seen him that he was blind [11-15]

"is not from God, because He keeps not the Sabbath day," some of the Pharisees said, and others said, "How can a man who is a sinner do such miracles?," and there was a division among them [{14}16]

"is a prophet," said the man blind from birth [{14}17]

"is a sinner," said the Jews to the man that was blind [{14}24]

"has opened my eyes, yet you know not from whence (where) He is, herein is a marvelous thing. Now we know that

God hears not sinners: but if any man be a worshipper of God, and does His will, him He hears. Since the world began was it not heard that any man opened the eyes of one that was born blind. If this man were not of (from) God, He could do nothing," said the man who was blind from his birth to the Jews [{14}30-33]

"Lord, I believe (You are the Son of God)," he (the man blind from birth) said, and he worshipped Him [35-38]

"are we blind also?," said some of the Pharisees to Him [39-41]

John 10:

sayings caused a division again among the Jews. Many of them said, "He has a devil, and is mad; why hear you Him?," and others said, "These are not the words of Him who has a devil. Can a devil open the eyes of the blind?" [{7}19-21]

"How long do You make us to doubt? If You be the Christ, tell us plainly," the Jews said to Him at the Feast of Dedication in Jerusalem, as Jesus walked in the temple [22-24]

"for a good work we stone You not; but for blasphemy; and because You, being a Man, make Yourself God," answered the Jews who took up stones again to stone Him (because Jesus said that He and His Father are one) [31-33]

escaped out of their hand, as they (the Jews) sought again to take Him [{34}39]

went away beyond Jordan; and there He abode, and many believed on Him there [{34}40-42]

John 11:

raised Lazarus from the dead [1-44]

loved Martha, and her sister, and Lazarus [5]

"(Lord) if you had been here, my brother had not died, but I know, that even now, whatever You will ask of God, God will give it (to) You," said Martha, Lazarus' sister [20-22]

"Lord, I believe that You are the Christ, the Son of God, who should (would) come into the world," said Martha, Lazarus' sister [25-27]

"Lord, if You had been here, my brother had not died," said Mary, Lazarus' sister [32]

groaned in the spirit, and was troubled, when He saw Mary and the Jews weeping [33]

wept [35]

again groaned in Himself [38]

was believed on by many of the Jews, who had seen the things which Jesus did [45]

"does many miracles, what do we (shall we do)? If we let Him thus alone, all men will believe on Him: and the Romans shall come and take away both our place and nation," said the chief priests and the Pharisees to a council [{46}47-48]

"should die for the nation; and not for that nation only, but that also He should gather together in one the children of God who were scattered abroad. It is expedient for us, that one man should die for the people, and that the whole nation perish not," Caiaphas the high priest prophesied, not saying this on his own authority [49-52]

therefore walked no more openly among the Jews; because they took counsel together for to put Him to death [53-54]

was to be taken by the chief priests and the Pharisees at the Jew's Passover feast, so they commanded, that, if any man knew where He was, he should shew (report) it [55-57]

John 12:

feet were anointed by Mary with a pound of very costly ointment of spiknard, and she wiped His feet with her hair [3]

should (would) be betrayed by Judas Iscariot [{3}4]

was believed on by many Jews, because that by reason of him (Lazarus having been raised from the dead by Jesus), so the chief priests consulted that they might put Lazarus also to death [{3}9-11]

was met by much people that were come to the feast, when they heard that He was coming to Jerusalem, and they took branches of palm trees, and cried, "Hosanna: blessed is the King of Israel who comes in the name of the Lord" (the Triumphal Entry) [12-13]

when He had found a young ass, sat thereon; as it is written, "Fear not, daughter of Sion: behold, your King comes, sitting on an ass's colt" (the Triumphal Entry) (Zechariah 9: 9) [14-15]

was glorified [16]

said this (that if He be (were) lifted up from the earth, He will draw all men to Him), signifying what death He should (would) die [30-33]

spake, and departed, and did hide Himself from them, but though He had done so many miracles before them, yet they believed not on Him: that the saying of Esaias the prophet might be fulfilled, which he spake, "Lord, who has believed our report? And to whom has the arm of the Lord been revealed?" (Isaiah 53:1) [36-38]

was believed on by many of the chief rulers; but because of the Pharisees they did not confess Him, lest they should be put out of the synagogue: for they loved the praise of men more than the praise of God [42-43]

John 13:

knew that His hour was come that He should depart out of this world to the father [1]

loved His own who were in the world to the end [1]

was to be betrayed by Judas Iscariot [1-2]

knew that the Father had given all things into His hands [3]

knew that he was come from God [3]

knew that he went (was going) to God [3]

rose from supper, and laid aside His garments; and took a towel, and girded Himself; after that He poured water into a basin, and began to wash the disciples' feet, and to wipe them with the towel werewith He was girded [3-5]

"(Lord), do You wash my feet?," Peter said to Him, and continued, after Jesus said he would know (why) hereafter (later), "You shall never wash my feet," and then said, after Jesus told him that if He washed him not, he had no part with Him, "Lord, not my feet only, but also my hands and my head" [6-10]

knew who should (would) betray Him [10-11]

was troubled in spirit (because one of His disciples would betray Him) [21]

"(Lord), who is it (who will betray you)?," said one of His disciples, whom Jesus loved; and Jesus, after He had dipped the sop (piece of bread) and said that it would be the one to whom He gave it, gave it to Judas Iscariot [23-26]

John 16:

"now are we sure that you know all things, and need not that any man should ask you: by this we believe that you came forth from God," His disciples said to Him [{19}30]

John 18:
> knew all things that should (would) come upon Him [4]
> was taken, and bound, and led away to Annas first; for he was father in law to Caiaphas, who was the high priest that same year [12-13]
> was denied by Peter when he said, "I am not," when the damsel who kept the door said to him, "Are not you also one of this Man's disciples?" [{15}17]
> was struck with the palm of his hand by an officer [22]
> was sent bound by Annas to Caiaphas the high priest [{23} 24]
> was denied by Peter when he said, "I am not," when they said to him, "Are not you also one of His disciples?" [{23}25]
> was denied again by Peter, when a kinsman of the man whose ear Peter cut off, said, "Did not I see you in the garden with Him?" {{23}26-27]
> was led from Caiaphas to the hall of judgment [28]
> "is a malefactor, so we delivered Him up to you (Pilate)," they answered [{28}30]
> "should be taken by you and judged according to your law," Pilate said to them [{28}31]
> had spoken a saying signifying what death He should (would) die [32]
> "are You the King of the Jews?," Pilate said to Him [33]
> "Your own nation and the chief priests have delivered You to me: what have You done?," Pilate answered Jesus [34-35]
> "are You a king then?," Pilate therefore said to Him [36-37]
> "I find no fault in at all," Pilate said to the Jews [{37}38]

John 19:
> was scourged (beaten) by Pilate (Isaiah 50:6) [1]
> had a crown of thorns put on His head by the soldiers, and they put on Him a purple robe, and said, "Hail, king of the Jews!," and they smote (struck) Him with their hands [{1}2-3]
> "I bring forth to you, that you may know that I find no fault in Him," said Pilate to them [{1}4]
> came forth then, wearing the crown of thorns, and the purple robe, and Pilate said, "Behold the Man!". When the chief priests therefore and officers saw Him, they cried out, saying, "Crucify Him, crucify Him." Pilate said to them, "You take Him, and crucify Him: for I find no fault in Him" [5-6]

"by our law ought to die, because He made Himself the Son of God," the Jews answered Pilate [5-7]

"whence (where) are You (from)?," Pilate said to Him, but Jesus gave him no answer (Isaiah 53:7) [9]

"speak You not to me? Know You not that I have power to crucify You, and have power to release You?," Pilate then said to Jesus [10-11]

was brought forth, and sat (set) down in the judgment seat, in a place that is called the Pavement, and it was the preparation of the Passover, and about the sixth hour: and Pilate said to the Jews, "Behold your King!" [13-14]

then was delivered therefore by Pilate to them to be crucified, and they took Jesus, and led Him away [15-16]

bore His cross to a place called the Place of a Skull, which is called in Hebrew Golgotha: where they crucified Him, and two others with Him [17-18]

"OF NAZARETH THE KING OF THE JEWS" was written as a title, and put on the cross by Pilate [18-19]

garments were given to each of four soldiers, and they cast lots for His coat that the Scripture might be fulfilled, which says, "They parted my raiment among them, and for my vesture (clothing) they did cast lots" (Psalm 22:18) [23-24]

saw His mother, and His mother's sister, Mary the wife of Cleophas, and Mary Magdalene standing by the cross, and said to His mother, "Woman, behold your son!" and then said to the disciple whom He loved, "Behold your mother!", and from that hour that disciple took her into his own home [25-26]

knowing that all things were now accomplished, that the Scripture might be fulfilled, said, "I thirst" [28]

said, "It is finished:" and bowed His head, and gave up the ghost (died) [30]

was already dead [33]

legs were not broken. This was done that the Scripture should be fulfilled, "A bone of Him shall not be broken" (Psalm 34: 20) [33-36]

side was pierced with a spear, and forthwith came there out blood and water. This was done, that again another Scripture should be fulfilled which says, "They shall look on Him whom they pierced" (Zechariah 12:10) [33-37]

body was given by Pilate to Joseph of Arimathea, a disciple of Jesus, but secretly for fear of the Jews, who with Nicodemus took the body of Jesus, and wound it in linen clothes with the spices, as the manner of the Jews is to bury, and, because of the Jews' Preparation Day, laid it in a new sepulchre, that was nigh at hand, wherein was never man yet laid [38-42]

John 20:

"(the Lord) has been taken away out of the sepulchre, and we know not where they have laid Him," said Mary Magdalene to Simon Peter and the other disciple, whom Jesus loved [1-2]

"(my Lord) they have taken away, and I know not where they have laid Him," she (Mary Magdalene) said to the two angels in white sitting, the one at the head, and the other at the feet, where the body of Jesus had lain, after they said to her, "Why weep you?" [11-13]

was standing (there), and she, (Mary Magdalene) knew not that it was Jesus [14]

came and stood in the (their) midst that same day at evening, being the first day of the week, when the doors were shut where the disciples were assembled for fear of the Jews [19]

shewed them His hands and His side (after His resurrection). Then were the disciples glad, when they saw the Lord [{19}20]

breathed on them (to receive the Holy Spirit) [{21}22]

after eight days came, the doors being shut, and stood in the midst (of His disciples) [{24}26]

"You are my Lord," said Thomas (after he had touched Jesus' hands and side) [26-28]

"You are my God," said Thomas (after he had touched Jesus' hands and side) [26-28]

truly did many other signs in the presence of His disciples, which are not written in this book [30]

is the Christ, the Son of God [31]

John 21:

after these things, showed Himself again to His disciples the third time, after that He was risen from the dead [1-14]

"(Lord) You know that I love You," said Simon Peter, after Jesus said to him, "Simon, son of Jonas, love you me more than these?" [15]

"(Lord); You know that I love You," said Simon Peter, after Jesus said to him again the second time, "Simon, son of Jonas, love you me? [{15}16]

"(Lord), You know all things; You know that I love You," said Simon, after Jesus said to him the third time, "Simon son of Jonas, love you me?" [17]

spake this, signifying by what death he (Simon Peter) should (would) glorify God [{17}19]

said not to him (Peter), "He (the disciple whom Jesus had loved, who also leaned on His breast at supper) shall not die" [20-23]

did many other things [25]

Acts

"Jesus"

Acts 1:

began to do [1]

began to teach [1]

was taken up [1-2]

had given commandments through the Holy Ghost to the apostles whom He had chosen [1-2]

shewed Himself alive after His passion by many infallible proofs to the apostles whom He had chosen [1-3]

was seen of (by) them (the apostles whom He had chosen) forty days, after His passion (death) [1-3]

spoke of the things pertaining to the Kingdom of God, after His passion (death) [1-3]

being assembled together with them (the apostles whom He had chosen), commanded them that they should not depart from Jerusalem, but wait for the promise of the Father (the Holy Spirit), which, said He, "You have heard of (from) me" [{1}4]

when He had spoken these things, while they (the apostles whom He had chosen) beheld, was taken up; and a cloud received Him out of their sight [{1}9]

"was taken up from you into heaven," said two men in white apparel to the apostles whom He had chosen [10-11]

"shall so come in like manner as you have seen Him go into heaven," said two men in white apparel to the apostles whom He had chosen [10-11]

"was taken up from us," said Peter to the disciples [{21}22]

Acts 2 (Peter's explanation at Pentecost):
"of Nazareth, a Man approved of (by) God among you by miracles and wonders and signs, which God did by Him in
the midst of you, as you yourselves also know" [22]
"of Nazareth was delivered (to death) by the determinate counsel and foreknowledge of God" [22-23]
"of Nazareth you have taken, and by wicked hands have crucified and slain" [22-23]
"of Nazareth God has raised up, having loosed the pains of
death: because it was not possible that He should be holden
(held) of (by) it" [22-24]
"of Nazareth's soul was not to be left in Hell" (Psalm 16:10) [{22}
27-31]
"of Nazareth's flesh did not see corruption" (Psalm 16:10) [{22}
27-31]
"was raised up by God, whereof we all are witnesses" [32]
"was by (to) the right hand of God exalted" [32-33]
"having received of (from) the Father the promise of the Holy
Ghost, shed forth this, which you now see and hear" [32-
33]
"was crucified by you" [36]
"was made both Lord and Christ by God" [36]

Acts 3 (Peter's response to the people at the temple):
"is God's Son [13]
"God's Son, was glorified by God" [13]
"God's Son, you (men of Israel) delivered up (to Pilate)" [13]
"God's Son, was denied by you (Men of Israel) in the presence
of Pilate, when he was determined to let Him go" [13]
"God's Son, is the Holy One" [13-14]
"God's Son, is the Just" [13-14]
"God's Son, is the Prince of Life" [13-15]
"God's Son, was killed by you (Men of Israel)" [13-15]
"God's Son, was raised from the dead by God; whereof we are
witnesses" [13-15]
"has fulfilled those things, which God had shewed by the mouth
of all His prophets, that the Christ should (would) suffer"
[{13}18]
"Christ was preached to you before" [20]
"Christ must be received by heaven until the times of resti-
tution of all things" [20-21]
"is God's Son" [26]
"God's Son, was raised up by God" [26]

"God's Son, was sent by God to bless you" [26]

Acts 4: (Peter speaking to the rulers of the people and elders of Israel and the prayer of Peter and John and their companions):

was preached (by Peter and John) regarding the resurrection from the dead [1-2]

"Christ of Nazareth, whom you crucified" (Peter) [10]

"Christ of Nazareth was raised from the dead by God" (Peter) [10]

"Christ of Nazareth, who was set at nought (deemed to be of no value) of (by) you builders, is become the head of the corner (cornerstone)" (Peter) (Psalm 118:22) [10-11]

"Christ of Nazareth is the only one with salvation, for there is none other name under heaven given among men, whereby we must (can) be saved" (Peter) [10-12]

"must not be spoken or taught about," they (the council) commanded them (Peter and John) [13-18]

"is Your holy child who was anointed by You" (prayer of Peter and John and their companions) [27]

the Lord's resurrection was given witness to with great power by the apostles [33]

Acts 5 (the words of Peter and the other apostles to the council):

"was raised up by the God of our fathers" [30]

"you slew by hanging on a tree" [30]

"has been exalted by God to His right hand" [30-31]

"has been exalted by God to be a Prince" [30-31]

"has been exalted by God to be a Savior" [30-31]

"gives repentance to Israel" [30-31]

"gives forgiveness of sins" [30-31]

"should not be spoken about," they (the council) commanded them (Peter and the other apostles) [40]

Christ was taught and preached by the apostles [40-42]

Acts 6:

"of Nazareth shall destroy this place, and change the customs which Moses delivered to us," said the Synagogue of the Libertines (and others) to the council about what Stephen allegedly said [9-14]

Acts 7 (Stephen's speech to the council):

"(the Just One) you have been now the betrayers and murderers of," Stephen said to the council [52]

"the Son of Man, is standing at the right hand of God," said
Stephen describing what he saw at his martyrdom [55-
56]

"Lord, receive my spirit," called out Stephen as he was stoned to death [59-60]

Acts 8:

Christ's name was preached by Philip to those in the city of
Samaria [5-12]

the Lord was the name in which people in Samaria were baptized [16]

was preached by Philip to a man of Ethiopia [26-35]

"Christ is the Son of God," Philip was answered by a man of
Ethiopia [37]

Acts 9:

appeared to Saul on the road to Damascus [1-19]

was being persecuted by Saul [4-5]

(Christ) was straightway preached that He is the Son of God
by Saul in the synagogues [20]

is very Christ was proved by Saul to the Jews who dwelt at
Damascus, and this confounded them [22]

"Christ makes you whole: arise and make your bed," said Peter
to Aeneas [34]

Acts 10 (Peter's speaking to Cornelius' household):

"Christ is Lord of all" [36]

"of Nazareth was anointed by God with the Holy Ghost" [38]

"of Nazareth was anointed by God with power" [38]

"of Nazareth went about doing good" [38]

"of Nazareth healed all who were oppressed of (by) the devil"
[38]

"of Nazareth had God with Him" [38]

"of Nazareth they slew and hanged on a tree" [38-39]

"of Nazareth was raised by God on the third day" [{38}40]

"of Nazareth was showed openly, after he rose from the dead,
to witnesses chosen before by God" [{38}40-41]

"of Nazareth ate and drank with witnesses chosen before by
God, after He rose from the dead" [{38}41]

"of Nazareth commanded us to preach to the people, and to testify that it is He who was ordained of (by) God to be the Judge of (the) quick (those alive) and (the) dead" [{38} 42]

"of Nazareth brings remission of sins to whosoever believes in Him" [{38}43]

Acts 11:

the Lord was preached to the Grecians by some men of (from) Cyprus and Cyrene [20]

Acts 13 (Paul speaking in the Antioch synagogue):

"is a Savior to Israel raised by God according to His promise" [23]

"was condemned by they who dwell at Jerusalem, and their rulers, because they knew Him not, nor yet the voices of the prophets which are read every Sabbath day, they have fulfilled them in condemning Him, and though they found no cause of (for) death in Him, yet desired they Pilate that He should be slain" [{23}27-28]

"was taken down from the tree (cross), when they (those who dwell at Jerusalem, and their rulers) had fulfilled all that was written of (about) Him" [{23}29]

"was laid in a sepulchre" [{23}29]

"was raised from the dead by God" [{23}30]

"was seen many days of (by) them who came up with Him from Galilee to Jerusalem, who are His witnesses to the people" [{23}31]

"was raised up by God again; as it is also written in the second Psalm, 'You are My Son, this day have I begotten You'" (Psalm 2:7) [33]

"was raised from the dead, now no more to return to corruption" (Psalm 16:10) [33-35]

"whom God raised again, saw no corruption" [{33}37]

"justifies all who believe from all things, from which you could not be justified by the law of Moses" [{33}39]

Acts 16:

"Christ the Lord, if believed on, shall save you and your house," said Paul and Silas to the keeper of the prison [25-31]

Acts 17:

Christ must needs have suffered, as reasoned out of the Scriptures by Paul to the Jews in the synagogue at Thessalonica [1-3]

Christ must needs have risen again from the dead, as reasoned out of the Scriptures by Paul to the Jews in the synagogue at Thessalonica [1-3]

"whom I preach to you, is the Christ" (as opened and alleged out of the scriptures by Paul to the Jews in the synagogue at Thessalonica) (Paul) [3]

"is another king, said Jason and some brethren," cried the Jews to the rulers of Thessalonica [6-7]

and the resurrection was preached by Paul to the philosophers of the Epicureans and the Stoicks [18]

"(that Man), whom God has ordained, will judge the world in righteousness," said Paul on Mar's Hill [31]

"(that Man) was raised by God from the dead, giving assurance to all men that Jesus will judge the world in righteousness," said Paul on Mar's Hill [31]

Acts 18:

was Christ (Paul's testimony to the Jews in Corinth) [5]

was Christ (Apollos showed this by the Scriptures, mightily convincing the Jews in Achaia of this, and that publicly) [28]

Acts 19:

the Lord's word, was heard by all who dwelt in Asia, both Jews and Greeks [10]

"I know, and Paul I know; but who are You?," said an evil spirit to certain of the vagabond Jews, exorcists who called on the name of the Lord Jesus over those who had evil spirits, saying, "We adjure you by Jesus whom Paul preaches" [13-15]

the Lord's name was magnified to all Jews and Greeks dwelling at Ephesus, and fear fell on them all [17]

Acts 22:

of Nazareth was being persecuted by Saul [5-8]

Acts 26 (Paul answered King Agrippa, citing Moses and the prophets):

was being persecuted by (me) Saul [12-15]

"(Christ) should (would) suffer" [{15}23]

"(Christ) should (would) be the first that should (would) rise
from the dead" [{15}23]

"(Christ) should (would) show light to the people and to the
Gentiles" [{15}23]

Romans

"Jesus"

Romans 1:

Christ our Lord is God's son [1-3]

Christ our Lord was made (born) of the seed of David according to the flesh [3]

Christ our Lord was declared to be the Son of God with power,
according to the spirit of holiness, by the resurrection from
the dead [3-4]

(Christ's) gospel is the power of God to salvation to everyone
who believes; to the Jew first, and also to the Greek [16]

Romans 2:

Christ shall be the one by whom God will judge the secrets of
men [16]

Romans 3:

Christ has redemption [24]

Christ has been set forth by God to be a propitiation (make
amends/atone), through faith in His blood [24-25]

Romans 4:

our Lord was raised up from the dead [24]

our Lord was delivered for our offenses (Isaiah 53:5-6) [24-
25]

our Lord was raised again for our justification [24-25]

Romans 5:

Christ our Lord brings us peace with God [1]

Christ our Lord gives us access by faith into this grace wherein we stand [1-2]

(Christ) died for the ungodly [6]

(Christ) died for us while we were yet sinners [8]

(Christ) justified us by His blood [8-9]

(Christ) saves us from wrath [8-9]

(Christ), God's Son, by His death reconciled us to God [8-10]

(Christ), God's Son, saves us by His life [8-10]

Christ our Lord gives us the atonement (reconciliation with God) [9-11]

Christ's free gift (reconciliation with God) abounded to many [9-15]

Christ's free gift is of (from) many offences to justification [15-16]

Christ the One Man shall make many righteous by His obedience [17-19]

Romans 6:

(Christ) was raised up from the dead by the glory of the Father [4]

(Christ), being raised from the dead dies no more; death has no more dominion over Him [9]

(Christ) died to sin once [9-10]

(Christ), since He lives, He lives to God [9-10]

Romans 8:

Christ, God's own Son, was sent by God in the likeness of sinful flesh, for (because of) sin [2-3]

Christ, God's own Son, condemned sin in the flesh [2-3]

(Christ) was raised from the dead [11]

(Christ) and we, God's children, are joint heirs of God: if so be that we suffer with Jesus, that we may be glorified together [16-17]

(God's own Son) was not spared by God but delivered up by Him for us all [32]

(Christ) died [34]

(Christ) is risen again [34]

(Christ) is even at the right hand of God [34]

(Christ) also makes intercession for us [34]

Christ loves us [35-39]

Christ our Lord has God's love in Him [39]

Romans 9:

(Christ) came, concerning the flesh, from the fathers (Israelites) [5]

(Christ) is over all [5]

(Christ) is God blessed for ever [5]

Romans 10:
   (Christ) is the end of the law for righteousness to everyone
      who believes [4]

Romans 14:
   (Christ) died [9]
   (Christ) rose, and revived [9]
   (Christ) is Lord of the dead [9]
   (Christ) is Lord of the living [9]
   (Christ) has the judgment seat [10]
   (Christ) died [15]

Romans 15:
   (Christ) pleased not Himself [3]
   Christ our Lord's Father is God [6]
   (Christ) also received us [7]
   Christ was a minister of (to) the circumcision for the truth of
      God, to confirm the promises made to the fathers [8]

1 Corinthians

"Jesus"

1 Corinthians 1:
   Christ is our Lord [2]
   Christ gives you the grace of God [4]
   Christ enriches you in everything, in utterance, and in all
      knowledge [4-5]
   Christ our Lord is coming [7]
   Christ our Lord has a day in which we may be blameless [8]
   Christ our Lord is God's son [9]
   Christ is our Lord [9]
   (Christ) did not send me (Paul) to baptize, but to preach the
      gospel [17]
   (Christ) has a cross [17]
   (Christ) crucified is a stumbling block to the Jews [23]
   (Christ) crucified is foolishness to the Greeks [23]
   (Christ) is the power of God [24]
   (Christ) is the wisdom of God [24]
   Christ is made to us wisdom from God [30]
   Christ is made to us righteousness from God (Jeremiah 23:6)
      [30]

Christ is made to us sanctification from God [30]
Christ is made to us redemption from God [30]

1 Corinthians 2:
Christ was crucified [2]
(the Lord of glory), would not have been crucified by the princes
of this world, if they had known the hidden wisdom of God
[7-8]
(Christ) mind is ours [16]

1 Corinthians 3:
Christ is the foundation which is laid; (any) other foundation
can no man lay [11]
(Christ) is God's [23]

1 Corinthians 5:
Christ our Lord has power [4]
the Lord has a day [5]
(Christ) is our Passover [7]
(Christ) is sacrificed for us [7]

1 Corinthians 8:
Christ is the one Lord by whom are all things [6]
Christ is the one Lord by whom we are [6]
(Christ) died [11]
(Christ) is sinned against when we wound a brother's weak
conscience [11-12]

1 Corinthians 9:
Christ our Lord I (Paul) have seen [1]

1 Corinthians 10:
(Christ) was the spiritual Rock that followed them (Israel during the Exodus) [4]

1 Corinthians 11:
(Christ) is the head of every man [3]
(Christ) head is God [3]
the Lord, the same night in which He was betrayed, took
bread: and when He had given thanks, he brake it, and
said, "Take eat: this is My body, which is broken for you:
this do in remembrance of Me" [23-24]

the Lord, when He had supped, took the cup, saying, "This cup is the new testament in My blood: this do you, as oft as you drink it, in remembrance of Me" [23-25]

(the Lord) died [26]

(the Lord) will come [26]

1 Corinthians 12:

(Christ) is one body [12]

(Christ) body is made up of you (us) [27]

1 Corinthians 15:

(Christ) died for our sins according to the Scriptures (Isaiah 53:12) [3]

(Christ) was buried [3-4]

(Christ) rose again the third day according to the Scriptures [3-4]

(Christ) was seen of (by) Cephas, then of (by) the twelve: after that, He was seen of (by) above 500 brethren at once; after that, He was seen of (by) James; then of (by) all the apostles, and last of all He was seen of (by) me also (Paul after Jesus' resurrection) [3-8]

(Christ) is risen, so there is resurrection of the dead [13]

(Christ) is risen, so our preaching is not vain and your faith is also not vain [14]

(Christ) was raised up by God, as we have testified [15]

(Christ) is risen, so the dead rise [16]

(Christ) is risen, so your faith is not vain; you are not yet in your sins [17]

(Christ) is risen from the dead [20]

(Christ) has become the firstfruits of those who slept (died) [20]

(Christ) shall make all alive [22]

(Christ), the firstfruits, will come [23]

(Christ) will deliver up the kingdom to God, even the Father (at the end) [23-24]

(Christ) will put down all rule and all authority and power [23-24]

(Christ) must reign, till He has put all enemies under His feet [{23}25]

(Christ) will destroy death, as the last enemy [{23}26]

(the Son) Himself shall be subject to Him (God) who put all things under Him (Jesus), that God may be all in all [28]

Christ our Lord is the One through whom God, gives us the victory [57]

2 Corinthians

"Jesus"

2 Corinthians 1:
    Christ our Lord's Father is God [3]
    (Christ) sufferings abound in us [5]
    (Christ) consolation abounds in us [5]
    the Lord has a day [14]
    Christ, the Son of God, was preached among you by us [19]

2 Corinthians 4:
    (Christ) is the image of God [4]
    life may be manifested in our mortal flesh [11]
    the Lord was raised up [14]

2 Corinthians 5:
    (Christ) has the judgment seat [10]
    (Christ) love constrains us [14]
    (Christ) the One died for all [14-15]
    (Christ) died for them and rose again [14-15]
    (Christ) we have known after the flesh [16]
    Christ, with God, reconciles us to God [18-19]
    (Christ) knew no sin [20-21]
    (Christ) was made to be sin for us by God; that we might be made the righteousness of God in Jesus [20-21]

2 Corinthians 6:
    (Christ) has no concord with Belial (lawlessness, Satan?) [15]

2 Corinthians 8:
    Christ our Lord was rich (while in heaven) [9]
    Christ our Lord became poor (by becoming a man and entering this world) for your sakes [9]

2 Corinthians 10:
    (Christ) was meek [1]
    (Christ) was gentle [1]

2 Corinthians 11:
    Christ our Lord's Father is God [31]

2 Corinthians 13:
   (Christ) was crucified through weakness [3-4]
   (Christ) lives by the power of God [3-4]

Galatians

"Jesus"

Galatians 1:
   Christ was raised from the dead by God [1]
   Christ our Lord gave Himself for our sins (Isaiah 53:12) [3-4]
   Christ our Lord delivers us from the present evil world [3-4]
   Christ revealed the gospel to Paul [11-12]

Galatians 2 (Paul to Peter and the others):
   "(Christ) is not the minister of sin" [17]
   "(Christ) has been crucified" [20]
   "(Christ) lives in me" [20]
   "(Christ) is the Son of God" [20]
   "(Christ) loved me" [20]
   "(Christ) gave Himself for me" [20]
   "(Christ) died in vain, if righteousness comes through the law"
      [21]

Galatians 3:
   Christ has been evidently set forth among you, (as) crucified
      [1]
   (Christ) has redeemed us from the curse of the law [13]
   (Christ) was made a curse for us: for it is written, "Cursed is
      everyone who hangs on a tree" (Deuteronomy 21:23) [13]
   Christ gives the Gentiles the blessing of Abraham [14]
   (Christ) "is the seed of Abraham" [16]
   (Christ) was put on by as many of you as have been baptized
      into Christ [27]

Galatians 4:
   (God's Son), when the fullness of time had come, was sent
      forth by God [4]
   (God's Son) was made (born) of a woman [4]
   (God's Son) was made (born) under the law [4]

(God's Son) redeems those who were under the law, that we
   might receive adoption of (as) sons [4-5]
(Christ) has made you an heir of God [7]

Galatians 5:
(Christ) has made us free [1]
(Christ) will profit you nothing, if you become circumcised, for
   I testify again to every man that is circumcised, that he is
   a debtor to do the whole law [2-3]

Galatians 6:
Christ our Lord has a cross [14]

Ephesians

"Jesus"

Ephesians 1:
Christ our Lord's Father is God [3]
Christ, the Beloved, brings us redemption through His blood
   [5-7]
Christ, the Beloved, brings us forgiveness of sins [5-7]
Christ the Lord's God is the Father of glory [17]
(Christ) was raised from the dead by God [20]
(Christ) was set at His own right hand by God [20]
(Christ) is far above all principality, and power, and might, and
   dominion, and every name that is named [20-21]
(Christ) has all things put under His feet by God [20-22]
(Christ) is the head over all things to the church, His body
   [20-23]

Ephesians 2:
Christ's blood brings us nigh [13]
Christ is our peace [13-14]
Christ has made both (Jews and Gentiles) one, and has brok-
   en down the middle wall of partition between us; having
   abolished in His flesh the enmity, even the law of commandments contained in ordinances; for to make in Himself
   of two one new man, so making peace [13-15]
Christ reconciles both (Jews and Gentiles) to God in one body
   by the cross [{13}16]

Christ preached peace to you who were far off, and to those who were nigh [{13}17]

Christ gives us access by one Spirit to the father [{13}18]

Christ Himself is the chief cornerstone [20]

Ephesians 3:

(Christ) mystery has now been revealed by the Spirit to His holy apostles and prophets; that the gentiles should be fellowheirs (with the Jews), and of the same body, and partakers of His promise in Christ by (in) the gospel [3-6]

(Christ) riches are unsearchable [8]

Christ is the One by whom God created all things [9]

Christ our Lord completed God's eternal purpose of showing His manifold wisdom by (through) the church to the principalities and powers in heavenly places [10-11]

(Christ) love passes knowledge [19]

Ephesians 4:

(Christ) "ascended on high" (Psalm 68:18) [7-8]

(Christ) "led captivity captive" (Psalm 68:18) [7-8]

(Christ) "gave gifts to men" (Psalm 68:18) [7-8]

(Christ) descended first into the lower parts of the earth [7-9]

(Christ) is also the One who ascended up far above all heavens [7-10]

(Christ) fills all things [7-10]

(Christ) gave some, apostles; some, prophets; some, evangelists; and some, pastors and teachers [{7}11]

(Christ) is the head of the body [15-16]

has the truth in Him [21]

Ephesians 5:

(Christ) also has loved us [2]

(Christ) gave Himself for us an offering and a sacrifice to God for a sweetsmelling savor [2]

"(Christ) shall give you light" [14]

(Christ) is head of the church [23]

(Christ) is the Savior of the body [23]

(Christ) also loved the church [25]

(Christ) gave Himself for it (the church) [25]

(Christ) sanctified and cleansed the church [25-26]

(Christ) will present it (the church) to Himself a glorious church, not having spot, or wrinkle, or any such thing; but that it should be holy and without blemish [25-27]

Philippians

"Jesus"

Philippians 1:
(Christ) has a day until which we are to be sincere and without offense [10]
(Christ) is preached by some even of (from) envy and strife; of (from) contention, not sincerely [15-16]
(Christ) is preached by some also of (from) good will, of (from) love [15-17]

Philippians 2:
Christ had the form of God [5-6]
Christ was equal with God [5-6]
Christ made Himself of (to have) no reputation [5-7]
Christ took the form of a servant [5-7]
Christ was made in the likeness of men [5-7]
Christ was found in fashion as a man [{5}8]
Christ humbled Himself [{5}8]
Christ became obedient to death, even the death of the cross [{5}8]
Christ has been highly exalted by God [{5}9]
Christ has been given, by God, a name which is above every name [{5}9]
shall have every knee bow to His name [10]
Christ shall have every tongue confess that He is Lord (Isaiah 45:23) [11]
(Christ) has a day that I (Paul) want to be able to rejoice in, having not run in vain, neither labored in vain, because you shine as lights in the world; holding forth the word of life [15-16]

Philippians 3:
(Christ) resurrection has power [9-10]
(Christ) suffered [9-10]
(Christ) died [9-10]
Christ the Lord is the Savior [20]
Christ the Lord shall change our vile body, that it may be fashioned like His glorious body [20-21]
Christ the Lord is able even to subdue all things to Himself [20-21]

Philippians 4:
   (Christ) strengthens me, so I can do all things (Paul) [13]

Colossians

"Jesus"

Colossians 1:
   (God's Son) is dear to God [13]
   (God's Son) has a kingdom [13]
   (God's Son) brings us redemption through His blood [13-14]
   (God's Son) brings us forgiveness of sins [13-14]
   (God's Son) is the image of the invisible God [{13}15]
   (God's Son) is the firstborn of every creature [{13}15]
   (God's Son) created all things [{13}16]
   (God's Son) is before all things [{13}17]
   (God's Son) is the One in whom all things consist [{13}17]
   (God's Son) is the head of the body, the church [{13}18]
   (God's Son) is the beginning [{13}18]
   (God's Son) is the firstborn from the dead [{13}18]
   (God's Son) has the preeminence in all things [{13}18]
   (God's Son) has all the fullness dwelling in Him [{13}19]
   (God's Son) made peace through the blood of His cross [{13}
      20]
   (God's Son) reconciles all things to Himself [{13}20-21]
   (God's Son) in the body of His flesh through death, presents
      you holy and unblameable and unreproveable in His sight
      [{13}22]
   (Christ) in you, the hope of glory, is the mystery made known
      among the Gentiles [27]

Colossians 2:
   (Christ) and His Father have all the treasures of wisdom hid-
      den in them [2-3]
   (Christ) and His Father have all the treasures of knowledge
      hidden in them [2-3]
   (Christ) has dwelling in Him all the fullness of the Godhead
      bodily [8-9]
   (Christ) is the head of all principality and power [8-10]
   (Christ) circumcision puts off the body of the sins of the flesh
      [11]
   (Christ) was raised from the dead by God [11-12]

(Christ) has forgiven you all trespasses [{11}13]
(Christ) is the body (reality?) [17]

Colossians 3:

(Christ) is above, sitting on the right hand of God [1]
(Christ) shall appear [4]
(Christ) forgave you [13]

1 Thessalonians

"Jesus"

1 Thessalonians 1:

is God's son [9-10]
was raised from the dead by God [9-10]
is coming from heaven [10]
delivers us from the wrath to come [10]

1 Thessalonians 2:

the Lord was killed by the Jews [15]
Christ our Lord with you in His presence at His coming is our
    joy [19]

1 Thessalonians 3:

Christ our Lord is coming with all His saints [13]

1 Thessalonians 4:

died and rose again, even so those also who sleep in Jesus
    will God bring with Him [14]
(the Lord) Himself shall descend from heaven [16]
(the Lord) Himself shall descend with a shout [16]
(the Lord) Himself shall descend with the voice of the archan-
    gel [16]
(the Lord) Himself shall descend with the trump of God [16]

1 Thessalonians 5:

(the Lord) day so comes as a thief in the night [2]
Christ our Lord obtains salvation for us [9]
Christ our Lord died for us [9-10]
Christ our Lord is coming [23]

2 Thessalonians

"Jesus"

2 Thessalonians 1:
the Lord shall be revealed from heaven with His mighty angels [7]
the Lord shall be revealed in flaming fire taking vengeance on those who know not God [7-8]
the Lord shall be revealed in flaming fire taking vengeance on those who obey not the gospel of our Lord Jesus Christ [7-8]
the Lord, in the day when He comes, shall be glorified in His saints [{7}10]
the Lord, in the day when He comes, shall be admired in (by) all those who believe [{7}10]

2 Thessalonians 2:
Christ our Lord is coming, and we will be gathered together to Him [1]
(Christ) day shall not come, except (until) there come a falling away first, and that man of sin be revealed, the son of perdition; who opposes and exalts himself above all that is called God, or that is worshipped; so that he as God sits in the temple of God, showing himself that he is God [2-3]
(the Lord) shall consume that Wicked (one), who shall be revealed, with the spirit of His mouth, and shall destroy with the brightness of His coming [8]
Christ our Lord Himself, and God, even our Father, who has loved us, and has given us everlasting consolation and good hope through grace, will comfort your hearts and establish you in every good word and work [16-17]

1 Timothy

"Jesus"

1 Timothy 1:
Christ our Lord is our hope [1]
Christ is our Lord [2]
Christ is our Lord [12]
Christ came into the world to save sinners [15]

1 Timothy 2:
> Christ is the Man [5]
> Christ is the one Mediator between God and men [5]
> Christ gave Himself a ransom for all, to be testified in due time [5-6]

1 Timothy 6:
> Christ, before (in front of) Pontius Pilate, witnessed (made) a good confession (that He came to be a king) (Matthew 27: 11; John 18:37) [13]
> Christ our Lord will appear, shown by God in His times (when He is ready) [14-15]

2 Timothy

"Jesus"

2 Timothy 1:
> Christ has in Himself the promise of life [1]
> Christ is our Savior [10]
> Christ has now appeared [10]
> Christ has abolished death [10]
> Christ has brought life to light through the gospel [10]
> Christ has brought immortality to light through the gospel [10]

2 Timothy 2:
> Christ is of the seed of David [8]
> Christ was raised from the dead [8]
> Christ has in Himself salvation [10]

2 Timothy 4:
> Christ the Lord shall judge the quick (living) and the dead at His appearing and His kingdom [1]

Titus

"Jesus"

Titus 1:
Christ the Lord is our Savior [4]

Titus 2:
Christ will appear [13]
Christ is our great God [13]
Christ is our Savior [13]
Christ gave Himself for us [13-14]
Christ redeems us from every lawless deed [13-14]
Christ purifies to Himself a peculiar people, zealous of (to do) good works [13-14]

Titus 3:
Christ is our Savior [6]

Hebrews

"Jesus"

Hebrews 1 (God speaks through His Son):
(God's Son) is God's spokesman in these last days [1-2]
(God's Son) was appointed heir of all things by God [1-2]
(God's Son) is the One through whom God made the worlds [1-2]
(God's Son) is the brightness of God's glory [{2}3]
(God's Son) is the express image of God's person [{2}3]
(God's Son) upholds all things by the word of His power [{2}3]
(God's Son) by Himself purged our sins [{2}3]
(God's Son) sat down at the right hand of the Majesty on high [{2}3]
(God's Son) was made so much better than the angels [{2}4]
(God's Son) has by inheritance obtained a more excellent name than they (the angels) [{2}4]
(God's Son), "You are My Son" (Psalm 2:7) [{2}5]
(God's Son), "This day have I begotten You" (Psalm 2:7) [{2}5]
(God's Son) "will be to Me a Son" [{2}5]
(God's Son) is the firstbegotten [{2}6]
(God's Son) "is to be worshipped by all the angels of God" [{2}6]

(the Son) "Your throne, O God, is forever and ever" (Psalm 45: 6) [8]

(the Son) is God [8]

(the Son) "has a scepter of righteousness as the scepter of His kingdom" (Psalm 45:6) [8]

(God's Son), "You loved righteousness" (Psalm 45:7) [9]

(God's Son), "You hated iniquity" (Psalm 45:7) [9]

(God's Son), "God, even Your God, has anointed You with the oil of gladness above Your fellows" [9]

(the Son), "You, Lord, in the beginning have laid the foundation of the earth" (Psalm 102:25) [{8}10]

(the Son), "the heavens are the works of Your hands" (Psalm 102:25) [{8}10]

(the Son), "You remain" (Psalm 102:26) [{8}11]

(the Son), "sit at My right hand" (Psalm 110:1) [{8}13]

(the Son), "I will make Your enemies Your footstool" (Psalm 110:1) [{8}13]

Hebrews 2:

was made a little lower than the angels [9]

was crowned with glory and honor [9]

tasted death for every man [9]

is the captain of their (our) salvation [{9}10]

was made perfect through sufferings [{9}10]

took part of the same (flesh and blood) [{9}14]

destroyed him who had the power of death, that is, the devil [{9}14]

delivered those who through fear of death were all their lifetime subject to bondage [{9}15]

had to be made like His brethren in all things [{9}17]

is a merciful and faithful High Priest in things pertaining to God [{9}17]

made reconciliation (with God) for the sins of the people [{9}17]

Himself has suffered [{9}18]

Himself was tempted [{9}18]

is able to succor (help) those who are tempted [{9}18]

Hebrews 3:

Christ is the Apostle and High Priest of our confession [1]

Christ was faithful to Him who appointed Him [1-2]

Christ, this Man was counted worthy of more glory than Moses, inasmuch as He who has built the house has more honor than the house [{1}3]

(Christ) is a Son over His own house; whose house we are [6]

Hebrews 4:
is the Son of God [14]

the Son of God is our great High priest [14]

the Son of God, our great High Priest, has passed into the heavens [14]

the Son of God, our High Priest, can be touched with the feeling of our infirmities [14-15]

the Son of God, our High Priest, was in all points tempted as we are [14-15]

the Son of God, our High Priest, was without sin [14-15]

Hebrews 5:
(Christ) glorified not himself to be made an High Priest [5]

(Christ), "You are My Son" (Psalm 2:7) [5]

(Christ), "Today I have begotten You" (Psalm 2:7) [5]

(Christ), "You are a priest forever after the order of Melchisedec" (Psalm 110:4) [5-6]

(Christ) in the days of His flesh, when He had offered up prayers and supplications with strong crying and tears to Him who was able to save Him from death, and was heard in that (because) He feared [{5}7]

(Christ) was a Son [{5}8]

(Christ) learned obedience by the things which He suffered [{5}8]

(Christ) was made perfect [{5}9]

(Christ) became the author of eternal salvation to all those who obey Him [{5}9]

(Christ) "was called by God a High Priest after the order of Melchisedec" (Psalm 110:4) [{5}10]

Hebrews 6:
(the Son of God) is crucified afresh and put to an open shame by those who were once enlightened, and have tasted of the heavenly gift, and were made partakers of the Holy Ghost, and have tasted the good word of God, and the powers of the age to come, if they shall fall away [4-6]

the forerunner, has entered within the veil [19-20]

was made a high priest for ever after the order of Melchisedec [20]

Hebrews 7:

(our Lord) sprang out of Judah [14]

was made a surety (the guarantee) of a better testament [22]

continues ever [{22}24]

has an unchangeable priesthood [{22}24]

is able also to save those to the uttermost who come to God by (through) Him [{22}25]

ever lives to make intercession for those who come to God by (through) Him [{22}25]

is a High Priest [{22}26]

is holy [{22}26]

is harmless [{22}26]

is undefiled [{22}26]

is separate from sinners [{22}26]

was made higher than the heavens [{22}26]

needs not daily, as those high priests, to offer up sacrifice, first for His own sins, and then for the people's, for this He did once, when he offered up Himself [{22}27]

the Son, is consecrated forevermore [28]

Hebrews 8:

(our High Priest) is set on the right hand of the throne of the Majesty in the heavens [1]

(our High Priest) has obtained a more excellent ministry, by how much also He is the Mediator of a better covenant [{1}6]

Hebrews 9:

(Christ) has (be)come an High Priest of good things to come, by a greater and more perfect tabernacle, not made with hands, that is to say, not of this building [11]

(Christ) by (with) His own blood entered in once into the Holy Place, having obtained eternal redemption for us [11-12]

(Christ), through the eternal Spirit, offered Himself without spot to God [14]

(Christ) blood shall purge your conscience from dead works to serve the Living God [14]

(Christ) is the mediator of the new testament, that by means of death, for the redemption of the transgressions that were under the first testament [14-15]

(Christ) is not entered into the holy places made with hands, which are the figures of the true; but into heaven itself [24]

(Christ) appears in the presence of God for us [24]

(Christ) now once in the end of the world has appeared to put away sin by the sacrifice of Himself [{24}26]

(Christ) was once offered to bear the sins of many [28]

(Christ) shall appear the second time without sin unto salvation, to those who look for Him [28]

Hebrews 10:

Christ has sanctified us, once for all, through the offering of His body [10]

Christ, this Man, offered one sacrifice for sins forever [{10}12]

Christ, this Man, sat down on the right hand of God [{10}12]

Christ's enemies will be made His footstool [{10}13]

Christ by one offering has perfected forever those who are sanctified [{10}14]

consecrated, by His flesh and blood, a new and living way for us to enter the Holiest [19-20]

Hebrews 12:

is the author of our faith [2]

is the finisher of our faith [2]

for the joy that was set before Him endured the cross [2]

despised the shame (of the cross) [2]

is set down at the right hand of the throne of God [2]

endured such contradiction of sinners against Himself (Isaiah 53:3) [2-3]

is the Mediator of the new covenant [24]

Hebrews 13:

Christ is the same yesterday [8]

Christ is the same today [8]

Christ is the same forever [8]

sanctified the people with His own blood [12]

suffered without (outside of) the gate [12]

our Lord was brought again from the dead by the God of peace [20]

our Lord is that great Shepherd of the sheep, through the blood of the everlasting covenant [20]

James

"Jesus"

James 2:
Christ our Lord is the Lord of glory [1]

1 Peter

"Jesus"

1 Peter 1:
Christ our Lord's Father is God [3]
Christ was resurrected from the dead [3]
Christ will appear [7]
Christ's Spirit was in the prophets [10-11]
(Christ) suffered [11]
Christ will be revealed [13]
(Christ) precious blood redeems us [18-19]
(Christ) was as a lamb without blemish and without spot [19]
(Christ) was foreordained before the foundation of the world
    [19-20]
(Christ) was manifested in these last times for you [19-20]
(Christ) was raised up from the dead by God [{19}21]
(Christ) was given glory by God [{19}21]

1 Peter 2:
(Christ) also suffered for us [21]
(Christ) left us an example (of suffering) [21]
(Christ) "did no sin" (Isaiah 53:9) [21-22]
(Christ) "had no guile in His mouth" (Isaiah 53:9) [21-22]
(Christ) was reviled [{21}23]
(Christ) reviled not again [{21}23]
(Christ) suffered [{21}23]
(Christ) threatened not [{21}23]
(Christ) committed Himself to Him who judges righteously [{21}
    23]
(Christ) bore our sins in His own body on the tree [{21}24]
(Christ) healed us by His stripes (wounds) (Isaiah 53:5) [{21}
    24]

1 Peter 3:

    (Christ) also has once suffered for sins [18]

    (Christ) is just [18]

    (Christ) was put to death in the flesh [18]

    (Christ) was quickened (raised from the dead) by the Spirit [18]

    (Christ) went and preached to the spirits in prison [18-19]

    Christ was resurrected [21]

    Christ is gone into heaven [21-22]

    Christ is on the right hand of God [21-22]

    Christ has angels and authorities and powers made subject
        to Him [21-22]

1 Peter 4:

    (Christ) has suffered for us in the flesh [1]

    Christ glorifies God [11]

    (Christ) suffered [13]

    (Christ) glory shall be revealed [13]

    (Christ) is evil spoken of on their part (those who reproach
        others for the name of Christ) [14]

1 Peter 5:

    (Christ) suffered [1]

    Christ was used by God to call us to His eternal glory [10]

2 Peter

"Jesus"

2 Peter 1:

    Christ is our God [1]

    Christ is our Savior [1]

    is our Lord [2]

    has divine power [2-3]

    has given to us all things that pertain to life and godliness [2-
        3]

    Christ has an everlasting kingdom [11]

    Christ is our Lord [11]

    Christ is our Savior [11]

    Christ is our Lord [16]

    Christ our Lord has power [16]

    Christ our Lord is coming [16]

    Christ our Lord is majestic [16]

Christ our Lord received from God the Father honor and glory
[16-17]
Christ "is My beloved Son, in whom I am well pleased" (voice
from the Excellent Glory) [16-17]

2 Peter 2:

Christ is our Lord [20]
Christ is our Savior [20]

2 Peter 3:

Christ is our Lord [18]
Christ is our Savior [18]

1 John

"Jesus"

1 John 1:

Christ is the Father's Son [3]
Christ is God's Son [7]
Christ's blood cleanses us from all sin [7]

1 John 2:

Christ is our Advocate with the Father [1]
Christ is the righteous [1]
Christ is the propitiation (make amends/atone) for our sins:
and not for ours only, but also for the sins of the whole world
[1-2]
is the Christ (denial of this makes one a liar and antichrist) [22]
(the Son) denial by a person means that person has not the
Father [23]
(the Son) acknowledgment by a person means that person has
the Father [23]
(the Son) has promised us, even eternal life [24-25]
(the Son) has anointed you [{24}27]
(the Son) will appear [{24}28]
(the Son) will come [{24}28]
(the Son) is righteous [{24}29]

1 John 3:

(the Son of God) was manifested, that He might destroy the
works of the devil [8]

Christ is God's Son [21-23]

1 John 4:

Christ is confessed as having come in the flesh by every
   spirit that is of God [2]

Christ, as having come in the flesh, is confessed not by every
   spirit that is not of God, and this is the spirit of antichrist [3]

(God's only begotten Son) was sent by God into the world, manifesting His love toward us, that we might live through Him
   (Jesus) [9]

(God's Son) was sent by God to be the propitiation (make
   amends/atone) for our sins [10]

(the Son) was sent by the Father to be the Savior of the world
   [14]

is the Son of God (whoever shall confess this has God dwelling in him, and he in God) [15]

1 John 5:

is the Christ (whoever believes this is born of God) [1]

is begotten of God [1]

is the Son of God (he who believes this overcomes the world)
   [5]

Christ came by water and blood [6]

(God's Son) has eternal life in Him [11]

(the Son of God) hears us, if we ask anything according to His
   will [13-14]

(the Son of God) gives us whatever we ask, if we ask anything
   according to His will [13-15]

(the Son of God) is come [20]

(the Son of God) has given us an understanding, that we may
   know Him who is true [20]

(the Son of God) is true [20]

Christ is God's Son [20]

Christ is the true God [20]

Christ is eternal life [20]

2 John

"Jesus"

2 John:
Christ the Lord is the Son of God the Father [3]
Christ, is come in the flesh, is confessed not by many deceivers who are entered into the world; this is an antichrist [7]

Jude

"Jesus"

Jude:
Christ the Lord has mercy [21]

Revelation

"Jesus"

Revelation 1:
Christ has the revelation (is the one who reveals) which God gave to Him to show to His servants things which must shortly come to pass [1]
Christ is the faithful witness [5]
Christ is the first begotten from the dead [5]
Christ is the prince of the kings of the earth [5]
Christ loved us [5]
Christ washed us from our sins in His own blood [5]
Christ has made us kings and priests to God and His Father [5-6]
Christ comes with clouds; and every eye shall see Him, and they also who pierced Him: and all kindreds (people) of the earth shall wail because of Him [5-7]
(One like the Son of Man) was clothed with a garment down to the foot, and girt about the paps (chest) with a golden girdle [13]
(One like the Son of Man) head and His hairs were white like wool, as white as snow [13-14]
(One like the Son of Man) eyes were as a flame of fire [13-14]
(One like the Son of Man) feet were like fine brass [13-15]

(One like the Son of Man) voice was as the sound of many waters [13-15]

(One like the Son of Man) had in His right hand seven stars [13-16]

(One like the Son of Man) had a sharp two-edged sword that went out of His mouth [13-16]

(One like the Son of Man) countenance was as the sun shining in its strength [13-16]

Revelation 5:

(the Lamb), "is the Lion of the tribe of Judah," an elder said to John [5-9]

(the Lamb), "is the root of David," an elder said to John [5-9]

(the Lamb), "has prevailed to open the book, and to loose the seven seals thereof," an elder said to John [5-9]

(the Lamb), "You are worthy to take the book, and to open the seals thereof," sung by four beasts and four and twenty elders who fell down before the Lamb [8-9]

(the Lamb), "You were slain," sung by four beasts and four and twenty elders who fell down before the Lamb [8-9]

(the Lamb), "You have redeemed us to God by Your blood out of every kindred, and tongue, and people, and nation," sung by four beasts and four and twenty elders who fell down before the Lamb [8-9]

(the Lamb), "You have made us to our God kings and priests: and we shall reign on the earth," sung by four beasts and four and twenty elders who fell down before the Lamb [8-10]

"(the Lamb) was slain," said with a loud voice by many angels, the beasts and the elders: the number of them was ten thousand times ten thousand, and thousands of thousands [11-12]

"(the Lamb) is worthy to receive power, and riches, and wisdom, and strength, and honor, and glory, and blessing," said with a loud voice by many angels, the beasts and the elders: the number of them was ten thousand times ten thousand [11-12]

"(the Lamb) is to have blessing, and honor, and glory, and power forever and ever," said every creature which is in heaven, and on the earth, and under the earth, and such as are in the sea [13]

Revelation 6:

"(the Lamb) great day of wrath has come, and who is able to
stand? Fall on us (mountains and rocks) and hide us
from the face of Him who sits on the throne and from the
wrath of the Lamb!," said the kings of the earth, and the
great men, and the rich men, and the chief captains, and
the mighty men, and every bondman, and every free man;
all of them had hidden themselves in the dens and in the
rocks of the mountains [15-17]

Revelation 7:

"(the Lamb) is in the midst of the throne," an elder said to
John [17]

"(the Lamb) shall feed them and shall lead them to living fountains of waters," an elder said to John [17]

Revelation 11:

"(our Lord's Christ) the kingdoms of this world are become
the kingdoms of our Lord and of You, His Christ" (great
voices in heaven) [15]

"(our Lord's Christ) shall reign forever and ever" (great voices
in heaven) [15]

Revelation 12:

"(God's Christ) power has come" (a loud voice in heaven) [10]

Revelation 13:

(the Lamb) was slain from the foundation of the world [8]

Revelation 14:

(One like the Son of Man, sitting on a cloud) had on His head
a golden crown, and in His hand a sharp sickle [14]

(One like the Son of Man, sitting on a cloud) thrust in His
sickle on the earth; and the earth was reaped [14-16]

Revelation 17:

"(the Lamb) will overcome them (the beast and the ten Kings),"
an angel said to John [12-14]

"(the Lamb) is Lord of lords and King of kings," an angel said
to John [14]

Revelation 19 (King on white horse with Jesus' characteristics 11-16):

"(the Lamb) will be married" (voice of a great multitude) [7-9]

testimony is the spirit of prophecy [10]

(the king on a white horse) was called faithful [11-16]

(the king on a white horse) was called true [11-16]

(the king on a white horse) in righteousness judges and makes war [11-16]

(the king on a white horse) eyes were as a flame of fire [11-16]

(the king on a white horse) has many crowns on His head [11-16]

(the king on a white horse) had a name written, that no man knew, but He Himself [11-16]

(the king on a white horse) was clothed with a vesture (garment) dipped in blood [11-16]

(the king on a white horse) name is called The Word of God [11-16]

(the king on a white horse) has a sharp sword that goes out of His mouth, that with it He should smite the nations [11-16]

(the king on a white horse) shall rule the nations with a rod of iron [11-16]

(the king on a white horse) treads the winepress of the fierceness and wrath of Almighty God [11-16]

(the king on a white horse) has on His vesture (garment) and on His thigh a name written: KING OF KINGS AND LORD OF LORDS [11-16]

Revelation 20:

(Christ) will reign for a thousand years [4]

(Christ) will reign for a thousand years [6]

Revelation 21:

"(the Lamb) has a bride, a wife," an angel (one of the seven angels who had the seven vials full of the seven last plagues) said to John [9]

(the Lamb) and the Lord God Almighty are the temple of it (the New Jerusalem) [22]

(the Lamb) is its (the New Jerusalem) light [23]

(the Lamb) has the Book of Life [27]

Revelation 22:
  (the Lamb) and God's throne has a pure river of water of life,
    clear as crystal, proceeding from it [1]
  (the Lamb) and God's throne shall be in it (the New Jerusalem)
    [3]
  (the Lamb) servants shall serve Him, see His face, and His
    name shall be in their foreheads [3-4]

APPENDIX B
The Good News

Below is my version of the good news. It is, of course, considerably less than the totality of the gospel, but is sufficient for a basic understanding and gives enough information for one to be 'born again'.

The God of heaven and earth has revealed to us the purpose of creation, what is expected of us and what His plan is for the future. This is indeed good news, because it gives us purpose, hope and a glorious future to live for. The outline of His plan, events and actions follow (man is used generically for male and female).

1. **God exists, has always existed and will always exist. He is totally separate (holy) from everything else in creation (including man) and is totally righteous.**

2. **God, through His son Jesus, created everything we can see and cannot see. It was perfect when He created it. He sustains it with His power {Colossians 1:16-17, Genesis 1:31, Job 38:4-7}.**

3. **God cares deeply about His creation and especially about man whom He created in His image: perfect and with intelligence, emotions and free will {Genesis 1:26}.**

4. **Man, using his free will, disobeyed God {Genesis 3:1-24}. This disobedience, called sin, separated the now unrighteous man from the righteous God with the consequence that all of creation now is subject to decay and destruction and man has to live by the sweat of his brow, existing with pain and sorrow and finally dying physically. Each man in turn also disobeys (rebels against) God, so is responsible for his own death and sorrow. {Romans 3:23, Galatians 3:22, 1 John 1:8}**

5. **There is nothing man can do to make himself good enough to escape God's wrath against sin. {Romans 3: 10, Isaiah 64:6}**

6. God has taken action to redeem this situation of man and of creation by reconciling man to Himself, forgiving him of his disobedience. He did this by sending His son, Jesus (which means Savior), into the world as a human being born of a virgin, who lived on earth without sinning (though tempted to as we are) {Hebrews 4:15, 2 Corinthians 5:21}, who even now is despised and rejected by us {Isaiah 53}, whose blood was shed on a cross, who died and was in the grave three days, who was raised from the dead by God and who is now seated at God's right hand interceding for us. {I Corinthians 15:1-4, Acts 1:9, Romans 8:34, Hebrews 7:25}

7. We can now be reconciled to God because of what Jesus did and is doing. This reconciliation includes being forgiven the sins we have committed (particularly our rebellion against God and His ways), freed from sin's power over us, adopted into God's family, given God's assistance to live a satisfying life and given His promise of living forever with Him in a perfect, new creation. {2 Corinthians 5:18-21, 1 John 1:9-10, Ephesians 1:3-23}

8. Jesus will come again as our Lord and King to judge, to set everything right, to build a new creation and to live with us. {Acts 1:11, 1 Thessalonians 4:16-17, 2 Peter 3:10-13, Revelation 21:1-4}

9. So, what must I do to be reconciled to God, to obtain all of His promises? I must have the attitudes and beliefs below, tell them to God and to man:
   • agree that God exists and cares
   • admit that I am a sinner and I have rebelled against God
   • be sorry for my sin and rebellion, desiring to change
   • acknowledge Jesus as my savior, agreeing with God that Jesus has paid the price for my sin and rebellion and accepting that
   • acknowledge Jesus as my lord (Master), desiring to do what He wants me to do and doing it through the power of His Holy Spirit.

To order additional copies of

Jesus is God, Savior, Lord and Master,

complete the information below.

Ship to (please print):

Name:_____

Address:_____

City, State, Zip Code:_____

Phone:_____

_____copies of **Jesus is God, Savior, Lord
and Master** @ $8.00 each $ _____

Postage and handling @ $2.00 each $ _____

Total enclosed $ _____

Make checks payable to: **Douglas Keasling**

Send to: **Douglas Keasling
217 Orilla Del Lago
Fort Collins, CO 80524**